The Declining Significance
of Homophobia

Sexuality, Identity, and Society Series

Series Editors
Phillip L. Hammack and Bertram J. Cohler

The purpose of this series is to foster creative scholarship on sexuality, identity, and society that integrates an appreciation for the historical grounding of sexuality research, seeks to transcend or integrate the boundaries constructed by disciplinary approaches, and takes theoretical and methodological risks to move the field forward. As such, the books presented here identify with a new kind of inquiry in sexuality research—one that moves us beyond questions of "origins" and "categories" toward the *meaning* of desire, experience, and identity in particular contexts. They are designed to be useful in both teaching and research.

BOOKS IN THE SERIES

The Story of Sexual Identity:
Narrative Perspectives on the Gay and Lesbian Life Course
Phillip L. Hammack and Bertram J. Cohler

The Monogamy Gap:
Men, Love, and the Reality of Cheating
Eric Anderson

The Declining Significance of Homophobia:
How Teenage Boys are Redefining Masculinity and Heterosexuality
Mark McCormack

The Declining Significance
of Homophobia

How Teenage Boys are Redefining
Masculinity and Heterosexuality

MARK McCORMACK

OXFORD
UNIVERSITY PRESS

OXFORD
UNIVERSITY PRESS

Oxford University Press, Inc., publishes works that further Oxford University's objective of excellence in research, scholarship, and education.

Oxford   New York
Auckland   Cape Town   Dar es Salaam   Hong Kong   Karachi
Kuala Lumpur   Madrid   Melbourne   Mexico City   Nairobi
New Delhi   Shanghai   Taipei   Toronto

With offices in
Argentina   Austria   Brazil   Chile   Czech Republic   France   Greece
Guatemala   Hungary   Italy   Japan   Poland   Portugal   Singapore
South Korea   Switzerland   Thailand   Turkey   Ukraine   Vietnam

Published by Oxford University Press, Inc.
198 Madison Avenue, New York, New York 10016

www.oup.com

Oxford is a registered trademark of Oxford University Press, Inc.

Library of Congress Cataloging-in-Publication Data

McCormack, Mark, 1984-
  The declining significance of homophobia : how teenage boys are redefining
masculinity and heterosexuality / Mark McCormack.
    p. cm. — (Sexuality, identity, and society series)
  Includes bibliographical references and index.
    ISBN 978-0-19-977824-9 (hbk. : alk. paper) 1. Homophobia—Great Britain. 2. Homophobia in high schools—Great Britain—Case studies. 3. Teenage boys—Great Britain—Attitudes—Case studies.
4. High school students—Great Britain—Attitudes—Case studies. 5. Gay teenagers—Great Britain—Case studies. 6. Masculinity—Great Britain—Case studies. I. Title.
    HQ76.45.G7M33 2012
    306.76'6083510941—dc23   2011027583

Printed in the United States of America
on acid-free paper

To my parents,

For their love, encouragement and support

In 2005, leading scholar of gay youth Ritch C. Savin-Williams declared the dawn of a "new gay teenager"—one for whom "being labeled as gay or even being gay matters little" (p. 1). His radical reinterpretation of the context of sexual identity development in the twenty-first century sparked a flurry of debate among social scientists. After all, there is plenty of evidence that same-sex attracted youth continue to identify with the gay and lesbian community (e.g., Russell, Clarke, & Cary, 2009). And there is evidence that plenty of same-sex attracted youth continue to experience harassment, victimization, and sometimes outright violence in contexts that remain committed to a rigid conception of heteronormativity (e.g., Rivers, 2011). The string of gay suicides in the United States in the fall of 2010, which received widespread media attention, certainly suggest that some "new gay teenagers" continue to face "old gay teenager" problems.

Savin-Williams might have signaled the death of gay adolescence prematurely, but he was on to something. In his critique of what had become the mainstream social science discourse on same-sex attracted youth—the master narrative of profound psychological struggle and success through coming out as gay or lesbian—Savin-Williams was capturing a lived reality for many same-sex attracted youth today. Part of this lived reality clearly involves challenging the taxonomy of gender and sexuality of a previous generation. Mark McCormack's *The Declining Significance of Homophobia: How Teenage Boys are Redefining Masculinity and Heterosexuality* directly interrogates this lived reality through a compelling ethnography of three high schools in England.

The early twenty-first century—the historical context of McCormack's ethnography—is a time in which the social movement for the recognition and legitimacy of same-sex attraction has achieved remarkable success. Half a century after the birth of the movement, same-sex attracted people now find a plethora of models in the media, and more in politics and other spheres of public life every day. Resources such as the Internet have, within a single generation, completely altered the possibilities for connection and support for same-sex attracted youth. It is now possible, with a simple click of the mouse, to discover that one is not alone.

   With the now-rapid exchange of information about all facets of human behavior and experience that is available, an era of invisibility for same-sex desire has certainly declined. Many governments attempt to regulate access to such information by blocking particular websites, but the arc of history appears to be on the side of increasing awareness and recognition that same-sex attraction is a normative and pervasive feature of human life, and that the organization of such desire through communities of self-identified gay men, lesbians, and bisexuals has legitimacy. This increasing recognition and legitimacy has been on display in the political developments of many nations in the past decade, many of which have now legalized same-sex marriage.

   In our view, these social and political changes, which have occurred in many (though certainly not all) reaches of the globe, have most certainly created a new context for the development of sexual identity among youth. In this respect, we agree with Savin-Williams. However, we have argued in a number of our writings in the past few years that youth do not simply engage with a narrative of "emancipation," as we called it in our 2007 article in the *Journal of Youth and Adolescence*, from sexual identity labels. Rather, the narrative of emancipation is simply one of several discourses or master narratives about the meaning of sexual desire to which contemporary youth have access. We have argued, and demonstrated in our research (e.g., Hammack & Cohler, 2009, in press; Hammack, Thompson, & Pilecki, 2009), that youth remain exposed to classic narratives of same-sex attraction as a "sickness" and to the redemptive narrative of gay or lesbian identity development. In other words, same-sex attracted youth certainly continue to struggle, even as they inhabit a context in which their desires are increasingly viewed as legitimate and normative—part of the "natural" spectrum of human experience. But many youth do indeed interrogate the received taxonomy of gender and sexual identity, in ways that have remained insufficiently examined among social scientists. Simply put, the empirical work of the social sciences has lagged behind the lived experience of contemporary youth, and McCormack's book offers a vital corrective to this trend. This book gets us to engage directly with the voices of youth, so that we might get beyond the question of *whether* same-sex attracted youth continue to struggle and address the question of their actual, everyday lived experience—a question that is well addressed by McCormack's ethnographic method.

   The point to this important dialogue among social scientists who study same-sex attraction among today's youth is not whether youth generally have it easier than or equally as hard as previous generations. We challenge the assumption of historical linearity in this framing of the issue. Rather, we think the task is to carefully and rigorously document the particular settings in which contemporary youth engage with the sometimes conflicting rhetoric about sexual desire and identity. By interrogating particular contexts and the actual experience of same-sex attracted youth within them, we come to a "thick description" (Geertz, 1973) of the phenomenon that is more concerned with the documentation of human development at a particular time and place, with insights for our theories and our understanding of the life course, than with making sweeping generalizations about "gay adolescence" or "gay identity."

Mark McCormack's timely ethnography seeks precisely to generate the type of knowledge we believe is critical for sexual science in the twenty-first century. As with all ethnographies, McCormack is careful to acknowledge that his study is limited in analysis to a particular time and place, but his findings will captivate the reader who seeks to understand how the larger social, cultural, and political shifts we have witnessed since the dawn of the gay and lesbian civil rights movement have affected today's adolescents. He focuses on the way in which discourses related to masculinity, same-sex desire, and homophobia are being radically reshaped by today's youth in England. As he notes, the three schools examined here are not located in identical liberal communities in a cosmopolitan area such as London. Rather, they are diverse in terms of the communities from which they draw, yet they are remarkably similar in the storyline they present about gender, sex, and sexual identity.

The Oxford Series on Sexuality, Identity, and Society is a space for interdisciplinary scholarship on sexuality that challenges the balkanization of ideas into disciplinary silos. In the case of McCormack's pathbreaking work, the author masterfully fuses ideas from the sociology of sex and gender with developmental and educational psychology, grounding his argument about the "declining significance of homophobia" in rigorous empirical work in the schools. We are pleased to introduce this important work to the continued dialogue among social scientists, policy makers, practitioners, and the general public interested in the development and well-being of same-sex attracted youth. McCormack's book offers a fresh and compelling analysis of the lived experience of sexuality and gender in a particular setting, with profound implications for how we think about adolescent masculinity and same-sex desire in the twenty-first century.

Phillip L. Hammack
Santa Cruz, California, USA

Bertram J. Cohler
Chicago, Illinois, USA
August 2011

REFERENCES

Cohler, B. J., & Hammack, P. L. (2007). The psychological world of the gay teenager: Social change, narrative, and "normality." *Journal of Youth and Adolescence, 36,* 47–59.

Geertz, C. (1973). *The interpretation of cultures.* New York: Basic Books.

Hammack, P. L., & Cohler, B. J. (2009). Narrative engagement and sexual identity: An interdisciplinary approach to the study of sexual lives. In P. L. Hammack & B. J. Cohler (Eds.), *The story of sexual identity: Narrative perspectives on the gay and lesbian life course* (pp. 3–22). New York: Oxford University Press.

Hammack, P. L., & Cohler, B. J. (in press). Narrative, identity, and the politics of exclusion: Social change and the gay and lesbian life course. *Sexuality Research and Social Policy.*

Hammack, P. L., Thompson, E. M., & Pilecki, A. (2009). Configurations of identity among sexual minority youth: Context, desire, and narrative. *Journal of Youth and Adolescence, 38,* 867–883.

Rivers, I. (2011). *Homophobic bullying: Research and theoretical perspectives.* New York: Oxford University Press.

Russell, S. T., Clarke, T. J., & Clary, J. (2009). Are teens "post-gay"? Contemporary adolescents' sexual identity labels. *Journal of Youth and Adolescence, 38,* 884–890.

Savin-Williams, R. C. (2005). *The new gay teenager.* Cambridge, MA: Harvard University Press.

Every so often, a new piece of research pushes a discipline's paradigmatic assumptions. In the field of youth and masculinities, Connell (1987, 1995) helped us understand the hierarchical ordering of masculinities and the way in which boys who occupied the dominant position maintained their status. Pollack (1998) helped us understand the extensive psychological damage that adherence to orthodox notions of masculinity bore upon male youth. And Thorne (1993) helped us understand that despite considerable pressure to enact particular gender roles, youth were not totally complicit in their adoption of gendered behaviors. With the work of West and Zimmerman (1987), we grew to understand that we all have agency to contest oppressive power structures. Now, with the publication of *The Declining Significance of Homophobia*, Dr. Mark McCormack provides the next paradigmatic challenge to those concerned with the relationship between male youth and their gender.

In his research on three very different high schools in England, Dr. McCormack shows us that the relationship between male youth and masculinities is changing. Whereas research from the 1980s and 1990s showed us that teenage boys were particularly susceptible to adopting the homophobia of their peers, he documents that at the end of the first decade of the new millennium, matters have changed substantially for young people: *it is no longer fashionable to be homophobic.*

In this extremely well-written and accessible book, Dr. McCormack shows us that for boys attending the three high schools he studied, pro-gay attitudes are esteemed and gay peers are valued. Thus, *The Declining Significance of Homophobia* is vital to the field of sexualities, gender, and educational research because the findings present a game-changer for the field: *it is no longer valid to assume homophobia among young men.*

This perhaps should not be overly surprising. Large-scale quantitative research has suggested that cultural homophobia is dropping at a dramatically rapid rate. As any sociologist, or even any casual observer of our changing culture, will know, this is particularly true among youth. Most will have seen the increased representation of sexual minorities in the media; any user of Facebook or MySpace will have noticed that it is now acceptable to list one's sexuality alongside other basic demographic variables, and anybody who works with kids will know that apart from using homophobic language, youth today are simply not as bothered by homosexuality as they were two decades ago, when the majority of gender scholarship was produced. With this in mind, McCormack first documents these pro-gay attitudes, showing that youth view overt homophobia in the same unacceptable light as racism. Some of the young men he interviewed were even shocked that people ever thought in such hateful ways. In fact, these young men are so in tune with social inclusion that they critically identify certain acts that privilege heterosexuality and call them homophobic.

Documenting these attitudes is important and interesting. Yet unique to this project, Dr. McCormack also analyzes what occurs *within* these cultures of decreasing or nonexistent homophobia. This is where *The Declining Significance of Homophobia* really pushes us to consider new ways of thinking about youth and sexuality. From understanding how popularity is maintained to examining the increased tactility of these boys, this book provides an exciting, captivating picture of how young men interact once freed from the shackles of homophobia.

This is good sociology because rather than simply passively observing young people's interactions the way some researchers have recently done, McCormack makes it his mission to gain entry into their lives and to understand their gendered world from *their* perspective. He conducts interviews and participant observation with high school boys from various social groups at three schools (including jocks, artists, and those more focused on their studies). It is quite evident that he was successful in this venture. Although his participants knew he was older, they readily shared with him their world. Thus, rather than looking at youth through a top-down model, McCormack delivers an exposé of youthful practices from *their* perspective. This produces a very different, much more valid type of work than remaining socially distant from the boys one studies.

In his ethnographies of a religious high school, a high school that represents the median of England's race and class background, and a high school for troubled youth, McCormack shows us that although heterosexual boys relate to one another in different ways, the lack of homophobia has permitted them to engage in relationships with their same-sex peers in ways previously unaccounted for in the sociological or educational literature. McCormack shows us that when boys no longer stigmatize gay males, they cease to fear being thought gay themselves. This has a very powerful effect on their attitudes and behaviors: instead of trying to act tough and macho in order to distance themselves from the thought of being gay, or suppressing emotions of fear, weakness, or homosocial intimacy, or out-grouping those who fail to meet the most stringent standard of masculinity, these boys do things differently.

McCormack navigates a world in which gay students are accepted and integrated into peer groups alongside their heterosexual brethren. This is a world in which being gay is celebrated, where openly gay 16-year-old boys are elected school president by their peers. But the pinnacle of this research is not in its documenting the multiple and varied ways in which gay youth no longer have troubled experiences in these high schools; rather, it is its description of how this culture of antipathy for homophobia promotes the social relationships of heterosexual youth.

Dr. McCormack shows that the influence of a homophobia-free youth culture is evident the moment one steps foot into these youth's social spaces. Using vivid and memorable examples, he shows us how these boys act toward one another—tenderly stroking each other, hugging, and even grooming their male friends. This is an existence in which boys positively comment on each other's bodies, clothing, and hair. Better than this, the heterosexual youth McCormack researches in this sophisticated book are emotionally supportive of one another. Encouragement is expected among peer groups, and bullying is unacceptable.

Some will find this shocking. Many will doubt that this exists. I was one of those people. As was the case for most gay youth who grew up in the 1980s (graduating from high school during the apex of cultural homophobia), my high school experience was horrific. Homophobia was expected and omnipresent; nobody even admitted to masturbating because it was associated with homosexuality. Accordingly, in high school, boys were emotionally and physically distant from one another. It was not acceptable to touch another boy, to hold his hand, to lay your head upon his shoulder, to massage him, or even to simply tell him whether his new clothes looked good or not. It was also unacceptable to admit to fear or weakness, or (worse) to admit to loving a male friend.

Informed by my research on openly gay male athletes (Anderson, 2005a), I knew that things were changing among university youth. Accordingly, I developed inclusive masculinity theory (Anderson, 2009) in order to theorize and better understand this change. As part of that theory, I predicted that when one lives within a culture of diminished homophobia, the rules of masculinity change—that boys are able to present softer, more inclusive forms of masculinity. Even so, when I walked through the doors of what McCormack calls "Standard High" in order to co-verify and validate his findings, I too was shocked. This was something entirely different. The tactility, emotional support, and softness of these boys was that much more frequent and normalized than even I was expecting, particularly because this was entirely opposite to what leading scholars in the field were saying (and what some continue to say) about masculinities and schooling.

For several years now, I have been showing that undergraduate male team-sport athletes are not as homophobic as commonly thought. In fact, through my multiple ethnographic investigations of soccer players in the United States and United Kingdom, rugby players in the United Kingdom, and male cheerleaders in the United States (men who were once high school football players), alongside my surveys of athletes from multiple sports in both countries, I show that men are exhibiting inclusive masculinity. This is crucial, for if it can be shown that team-sport athletes have shed the baggage of homophobia, one would expect that non-team-sport athletes will have done the same. After all, it is team-sport athletes who are *supposed* to be the most conservative, the most homophobic, of men.

In addition to finding better attitudes and homosocial relations among heterosexual male team-sport athletes, in my extensive studies of the experiences of openly gay male high school and university athletes, I have shown that when they come out of the closet, they overwhelmingly play equally alongside their heterosexual teammates. Now, this is not to suggest that any athlete could come out in the institution of sport; those who came out evaluated their local cultures first. Nonetheless, this still indicates that something radically different is happening among youth in contemporary culture.

Dr. McCormack adds to my research in useful and important ways. First, he extends the research into a younger demographic of heterosexual men than I have studied (16- to 18-year-olds), in another socially conservative institution—the British high school. But more important, he uses grounded theory to add to my theory of inclusive masculinity. McCormack fleshes out and conceptualizes how this is done in great detail. For example, my research does not explain how boys will become popular in this type of setting. Literature from two decades ago showed that the most popular boys in high school settings where those who were the best at sports—particularly football in America and football (soccer) in England. But McCormack shows this not to be true in these school settings. Popularity is no longer based on athleticism.

This is not to say that jocks can't be popular (it seems that they still are), but rather to suggest that athleticism is no longer a requirement for popularity. Instead, McCormack shows that boys in British high schools are popular if they are charismatic and authentic—in possession of a genuine personality that is engaging and entertaining. And instead of boys' being required to "stick to their own kind" lest they be thought traitors for socializing with those outside their clique, McCormack shows that these young man value the ability to mingle with boys of all different types. His conceptual developments—including "heterosexual recuperation" and his definitive "model of homosexually themed language"—mean that the reader will be emotionally captivated by the data and intellectually stimulated by the analysis.

Collectively, this means that *The Declining Significance of Homophobia* is of great significance for a variety of reasons. First, it provides an important counternarrative to the assumption that male youth are homophobic. This is particularly important for members of the gay and lesbian community to understand. We are all too good at reading one headline about one incident (or even a rash of incidents) and generalizing homophobia onto all youth. We are very good at remembering one incident of homophobia and ignoring or being blind to the acceptance that many, perhaps most, experience in their daily lives. McCormack's work forces us to remember that, in the face of teenage suicides and in a day in which one incident of homophobia is broadcast internationally (striking fear into us all), the average student in the average high school is no longer culturally compelled to espouse homophobia; an individual student may maintain personal homophobia or be incredibly gay friendly, but I suggest that the "average" student's opinion is more inclusive than we might think.

Dr. McCormack also helps us to realize the centrality of homophobia in gendered behaviors. Whether we have traditionally thought of homophobia as an aspect of masculinity or central to masculinity, there has been a general view in the academic community that young men are *necessarily* or *inevitably* homophobic—and that this leads to stunted emotions, the oppression of peers, and aggressive, macho young men. Yet McCormack shows us that the absence of homophobia is as significant to gendered behaviors as high levels of homophobia are. That is, in a culture of acceptance toward homosexuality, these masculine attributes disappear and are replaced by much more positive behaviors. This shows us that the ugliness of masculinity is not something that boys "just do." Rather, the findings presented here empirically validate the notion that gender is socially constructed, and they highlight the fact that homophobia is equally as damaging to heterosexuals as it is to homosexuals.

Finally, *The Declining Significance of Homophobia* should serve as a wakeup call in response to the intolerance of the American Christian Right, and it should serve as a call to arms for school teachers and administrators to battle those who thwart progress in developing gay-friendly high schools, forming Gay–Straight Alliances, and permitting positive discussions of homosexuality in school settings. When we read about how loving young men *can* be toward one another when they don't care whether their friends are gay, it should inspire us all to learn from the boys that McCormack gives voice to in this important, timely, and long-overdue book.

Professor Eric Anderson
University of Winchester, England

ACKNOWLEDGMENTS

My thanks must first go to Professor Eric Anderson at the University of Winchester for his mentorship. I owe him a great debt for his academic critiques, his vision, and his enduring friendship. His innovative scholarship and exciting theoretical developments have paved the way for this research, and I consider it a privilege and honor that he has written a foreword for this book. I would also like to thank Professor Debbie Epstein at the University of Cardiff for her pioneering work in the field, as well as for her encouragement, insight, and support on this and other projects. I would also like to thank Professor Ian Rivers at Brunel University, London, for his guidance and support, as well as his expertise in the psychological effects of homophobia in schools that has helped raise the importance and visibility of this topic.

I have been fortunate to have a number of other senior scholars contribute to my research. I am very grateful to Professor Judy Treas at the University of California, Irvine for alerting me to the call for this book series, and to Professor Stephen T. Russell at the University of Arizona for his support in career development. Professor Robert Barratt at Bath Spa University was a source of support throughout the writing of this book and the work that led up to it. I am also grateful to Dr. Elizabeth Atkinson at the University of Sunderland for the invitations to the seminars where I first met some of the young people whose voices are heard in this book.

I would also like to thank the Education, Identities and Social Inclusion Research Group at Brunel University and the Sexualities and Gender Research Group at Cardiff University, which provided intellectual spaces in which my ideas could flourish.

Much of the reality of this book is due to those who helped with the tasks of proofreading and providing input on the manuscript itself, including Professor Eric Anderson, Dr. Grant Tyler Peterson, Dr. Ady Evans, Max Morris, Dr. Dawn Leslie, Adi Adams, Ben Rockett, Dr. Shaun Filiault, Matt Ripley, and Robin Pitts. I would also like to thank the series editors, Dr. Phil Hammack and Professor Bert Cohler, for their support, as well my editor at Oxford University Press, Abby Gross. I am also grateful to the Rutlish Foundation and the Teacher Development Agency for their financial assistance throughout my doctoral studies. Finally, I would like to thank my family and friends for their support, friendship, and stress relief throughout this process.

CONTENTS

In the month of September 2010, 11 gay youth committed suicide in the United States. They had all experienced such devastating harassment because of their sexuality that they felt the only option was to end their lives. In the same period, the news media reported homophobic attacks in New York City that were notable for their extreme violence, while right-wing politicians stirred anti-gay hatred and the Obama administration appealed federal court rulings that would have overturned the homophobic Defense of Marriage Act and the Don't Ask, Don't Tell policy affecting the United States military.

Yet in 2004 antisodomy laws were ruled unconstitutional, and by the fall of 2010 several U.S. states had legalized gay marriage. Gay rights are now seen as human rights, and the visibility of gay and lesbian identities in wider culture is high: lesbians and gay men are now commonplace on television shows, and they are well represented in the broader media. And even though the leading organization campaigning for equality of sexuality in American schools, the Gay, Lesbian and Straight Education Network, released a report in 2009 that documented continued homophobia in the U.S. school system, increasing numbers of school students are coming out of the closet, supported by gay-friendly administrators. Gay–Straight Alliances (GSAs) are also commonplace across many parts of the United States, providing safe spaces for and institutional recognition of lesbian, gay, bisexual, and transgender (LGBT) youth (Miceli, 2005). Indeed, in 2011, an openly gay high school student, Craig Cassey, Jr., was made prom king at Penncrest High School in Pennsylvania (Forman, 2011).

On the other side of the Atlantic, the situation is much better for LGBT students. In my ethnographic study of three high schools in the United Kingdom, homophobia is condemned and openly gay students have happy and productive school lives. Even though these schools continue to reproduce heteronormativity through the presumption of heterosexuality and other mechanisms (see Epstein & Johnson, 1994), this does not translate into homophobic attitudes or the marginalization of LGBT youth. Indeed, one gay student, Max, was elected by his peers as the student president of his high school, and Harry, a bisexual student, often came to school wearing makeup or women's accessories, including belts and scarves. No LGBT student experienced any overt homophobia at these high schools, and their heterosexual peers argued that homophobia was equivalent to racism.

Of course, the political context in the United Kingdom is different from that of the United States. During the British general election in 2010, leaders of the three main political parties condemned homophobia, supported civil partnerships (not quite gay marriage, but getting there), and spoke of the importance of developing school cultures free from homophobia. Furthermore, in the fall of 2010, a new Single Equalities Act made discrimination on the grounds of sexuality illegal in the workplace, and schools were legally compelled to promote inclusivity of sexual minorities. The right-wing coalition government has recently revealed plans for gay marriage as well. Progress has occurred in the United Kingdom without the acrimony found in the United States.

This book, then, is situated within the British context—in a country and a culture that is not mired in the culture wars found still raging in the United States. There are, however, two fundamental reasons why this book speaks across the Atlantic divide—why this book has resonance and maintains important implications for American schools. First, the United States is a country of polarities, of contradictions and extremes. Although there are horror stories of homophobic abuse, there are also high schools in the United States that mirror those in this book—just like Penncrest High School, where Craig Cassey Jr. was made prom king. Indeed, on a recent research trip to Southern California, I spoke with students at what would generally be deemed a socially conservative school. Even there, there were openly gay students—several of them—and they had started their own GSA. Although I did not conduct formal research with these youth, my impression was that they had not been assaulted because of their sexuality and that they generally seemed to have positive school experiences.

The second reason why this book is of importance to an international readership is that the United Kingdom has not always had such benevolent attitudes toward homosexuality. By examining the transition from homophobic to gay-friendly high schools, and by exploring what a gay-friendly high school looks like, important implications for inclusive educational practice can be acknowledged and applied by educators and academics on both sides of the Atlantic.

It is important to recognize that gay men have been subject to a great deal of homophobia in Britain. For example, gay sex was legalized only in 1967. This homophobia extended to the educational system as well. In the 1980s and 1990s, homophobia in British schools was pervasive. Anti-gay insults were used daily as boys bullied their peers and jockeyed for popularity (Epstein, 1997). Fights were frequent, and any boy who behaved in a feminine manner was considered gay and harassed accordingly. Schools were not safe spaces for gay youth (Rivers, 2001).

Discrimination against gay and lesbian youth was also institutionalized in the education system. This was best exemplified by Section 28, legislation that "banned the promotion of homosexuality" in schools. Introduced in the 1980s to prevent left-wing councils (local government that had control over many educational issues) from using books that promoted equality (see Atkinson & DePalma, 2008), it left many progressive teachers fearful of combating homophobic bullying.

This law was repealed only in 2003, and while in effect it helped support a homophobic school environment (Epstein & Johnson, 1998; Nixon & Givens, 2007).

Having been a closeted student in the late 1990s and early 2000s and having personally experienced the homophobia of the British school system, I was nervous the first day I collected data for this book. It had been six years since I had left school as a shy, geeky, closeted teenager—not the best recipe if you wanted to be popular or attend parties. For that, one needed to be hypermacho, homophobic, misogynistic, and aggressive. Returning to do fieldwork just these few years later, I was worried that what was required in order to be popular had not changed.

However, even as I first entered the common room where students socialized in their free time, the difference from my experience was palpable. In that large open space, full of young men and women eating lunch and passing the time, I was immediately struck by the physical affection of the male students. These young men weren't only close to each other, they were touching—and they were gently touching their friends with care and affection.

I walked over to a group of students I had seen earlier in physical education. These young men, congregated in the center of the common room, were different from the high school students of my day. They were fashion conscious, wearing tight, low-slung jeans and designer underwear that showed above their belts. Not only did they style their hair, they used moisturizer and even tanning products. But the difference was not only about looks; they also interacted and spoke differently. These boys hugged each other hello and goodbye, sat on each other's laps, and gave their friends back rubs. Back when I was a student in school, similar behaviors would have coded boys as gay, and they would have been bullied for it. Yet at these schools, these behaviors made them some of the most popular male students. What was going on? This book provides the answer to that question.

Although this change is the result of many different social forces, the transformation is primarily the result of a shift in attitudes toward homosexuality in the United Kingdom. In recent history (effectively from 1870 to the 1960s), homosexuality was deemed a perversion, and gay men were thought to be sick or depraved (Weeks, 1990). Homophobia was based on revulsion toward same-sex sex that was part and parcel of Victorian antisex sentiment. However, in recent decades, homophobia transitioned from physical and intellectual disgust about gay sex to a mechanism for policing other boys' behaviors (Plummer, 1999). This meant that in order to maintain the image of a "lad" or "jock," boys espoused homophobic attitudes even if they did not really believe what they were saying.

This regulation of a boy's behaviors, rather than of his sexuality, was something I experienced as a student at school. I saw students I perceived as heterosexual being subjected to homophobic abuse, yet I escaped homophobic censure myself by staying in the closet. I realized that many of the boys were enacting a charade of competitive homophobia in order to avoid bullying themselves. At that young age, I recognized that homophobia was more than simply antipathy toward same-sex attraction; it was a way of stratifying students. It was the "best" insult, and one that could be refuted only through the labeling of another boy as gay.

Yet with growing theoretical, political, and cultural awareness about the effects of homophobia (Rivers, 2011), increased gay visibility in the public sphere (Walters, 2001), and more inclusive attitudes concerning gay men (Anderson, 2009), the acceptability of expressing homophobia has decreased. Attitudes toward homosexuality have improved in the United Kingdom to such an extent that the expression of homophobia has become stigmatized. It has moved from being the "best" insult to being an unacceptable one. As is now the case with racism, people can no longer be openly homophobic without (at least some) censure (see McCormack & Anderson, 2010). The declining significance of homophobia has meant that young British men do not fear being socially perceived as gay, and this has expanded the range of behaviors that they can enact without social regulation. An example that epitomizes this change comes from Max, an openly gay student at one of the three schools I studied.

While I was writing this book, Max sent me a Facebook message telling me about a protest he was organizing at his high school. It was just after the election of a socially conservative government in the United Kingdom, and Max wanted me to know that the Students Union, of which he was the elected president, was hosting a "kiss-in" to protest the appointment of Theresa May as Minister for Equalities. Theresa May, a Conservative MP, had voted for Section 28 and voted against an equal age of consent for gay sex in 2000. The kiss-in was a spontaneous symbolic protest of her appointment. Max wanted to know whether I could come and observe it.

At the kiss-in, which occurred in the social area of the school, the gay students received a lot of support. Several students (not all of whom identified as LGBT) kissed another person of the same sex, and there were cheers when they did so. When this finished, Max and his friends went from table to table, handing out leaflets, discussing an International Day of Protest against Homophobia (known as IDAHO), and talking to straight students about heterosexual privilege.

Of the hundreds of onlookers, there were only a few kids at one table who opposed the kiss-in and the political discussion surrounding it. Larissa said, "Leave it, Max, I don't care." Max responded, "You don't care about homophobia, about gays getting discriminated against?" Larissa tersely replied, "No," and her boyfriend added, "Why should we care? It's their choice, they should face the music." In response to this, a group of sporty boys at the next table called Max over. Isaac shouted, "Max, leave them. Show us your leaflets." Max walked over and sat next to Barry. Barry and his friends listened attentively as Max explained about the homophobia of Theresa May, the Minister for Equalities.

The kiss-in was an important event in my research, not because it documented a particularly gay-friendly episode, but because it represented the only homophobia[1] I encountered during my four months in that school. Whereas previous research has documented high numbers of homophobic incidents in school

---

1. I use the term "homophobia" to refer to anti-gay attitudes or behaviors.

settings (Epstein, 1997; Mac an Ghaill, 1994), particularly when considering homophobic language (Ellis & High, 2004; Thurlow, 2001), I found that the expression of homophobia was stigmatized.

This episode is also noteworthy because it encapsulates what is going on at the three high schools where I collected data. In these places, openly gay students have positive school experiences and are supported by the overwhelming majority of their heterosexual peers. Of course, some students continue to maintain personal homophobia, but they are reprimanded by other students if they express it. In these schools and wider British society, gay rights have become human rights, and young LGBT people are increasingly out, happy, and proud (Weeks, 2007).

These actions, and the responses of those viewing them, might sound somewhat implausible to many readers. After all, the traditional story of gay students in schools is one of marginalization and fear (Epstein, 1994), and the general story about boys is that if they aren't failing, they are being expelled for behaving badly (Salisbury & Jackson, 1996). These stories are not without merit; they powerfully capture what was occurring in the 1990s, and they accurately describe my own school experiences. However, they do not describe what is going on with young people in Britain today, nor do they represent the *only* story to be told in schools in the United States, Australia, or Canada.

This book is an attempt to describe what is happening in schools in the United Kingdom, explaining the multifaceted reasons why these schools have become gay friendly. I provide a counternarrative to the dominant discourse that argues that gay students are victims in schools and that young heterosexual men are violent, homophobic, and emotionally stunted. Furthermore, I trace how the intersection of masculinity, sexuality, homophobia, and education has dramatically shifted in school cultures, and I explore the impact that this has on the gendered behaviors and school experiences of both LGBT students and heterosexual boys.

Drawing on rich ethnographic data collected in three schools over a year and using innovative social theories, I explicate the ways in which the stratification and estimation of masculinities has changed. I also refine and develop existing theory by looking at the social dynamics of boys in inclusive settings: I examine how boys' friendships are more open and emotional, I theorize how to understand homosexually-themed language in the absence of overt homophobia, and I discuss the emergence of what I call the gay-friendly high school. Using Anderson's (2009) inclusive masculinity theory to frame my results, I develop and refine this theory by fleshing out how boys engage with issues of sexuality and gender in inclusive school settings.

Although unusual for sociological work on sexuality and gender, this is a good-news story—a story of increasing equality for LGBT students, and a story of increasing inclusivity among straight students. Although I examine the continued presence of heterosexual privilege and provide a new conceptual apparatus with which to understand its endurance, the main focus of this book is an examination of the sociopositive shifts that have occurred for young men in British schools today.

I hope one important aspect of this book is the way it situates the findings in their proper social, historical, and cultural context and builds on a strong feminist tradition of accessible, insightful sociology. Part 2 provides a review of this academic work in order to enable the reader to understand the dramatic change that has occurred among young men. This is important because it is my hope that when academics, politicians, and journalists start to recognize how pro-gay today's students are, particularly in comparison to those of the 1980s and 1990s, we can have more intelligent and open discussions about sex, sexuality, and relationships in school.

Of course, not every school will be as progressive as those that I describe here. Gay rights have become entangled in the culture wars that continue to rage in the United States, and pockets of homophobia remain in the United Kingdom, too. It is a sad fact that homophobia continues to blight some students' lives. The terrible stories of teen suicides in the United States are all too powerful reminders of the damage that homophobic bullying inflicts. Indeed, as a British observer of the American battles over sexuality, I find the hostility expressed by many toward the progressive social changes that have occurred in the United States disheartening. Even so, we need to look beyond the worst-case examples to see what is happening in the majority of schools. We do no-one any favors if we only fight prejudice that is, for some, yesterday's battle. We simply must examine every avenue for gaining equality of sexualities. For those readers who do not see their own local culture described in this book, it is my hope that you nonetheless find it a source of encouragement and hope, and that you see these schools as a destination at which we can all arrive.

ORGANIZATION OF THE BOOK

In this book, I use ethnographies of three high schools in the United Kingdom to examine the contemporary dynamics of sexuality and masculinity among 16- to 18-year-old boys. The book is divided into three sections. The first section provides both an introduction to the book and the context of my research. In Chapter 1, I provide a brief overview of the ethnographic tradition of studying sexuality and gender in schools and discuss issues including researcher effect and reflexivity. I also explicate my epistemological framework and explain my reasons for writing in my chosen style. In Chapter 2, I give contextual information regarding the three research sites, as well as details about the methodological procedures I employ. In that chapter, I talk about some of the strategies I used to collect data and minimize my social distance from participants, and I critically reflect on the data collection process.

In Part 2, I provide a comprehensive review of the sociological study of masculinities. Given the change that has occurred with respect to boys' behaviors in schools, it is necessary to discuss this previous research in order to understand both the continuities and the differences between my research and the older literature. This section should provide readers who are new to this topic with an accessible and detailed introduction to the issues.

In Chapter 3, I provide a historical discussion of the scholarship of sexuality and gender and explore how this research influenced cultural understandings of masculinities, focusing on the centrality of homophobia in modern-day constructions of masculinity. I also explicate my use of hegemony theory to understand the operations of power in society, as well as how this theory is particularly appropriate for studying sexuality and gender.

In Chapter 4, I examine contemporary theorizing of the stratification and regulation of masculinities. Here, I discuss the utility of hegemonic masculinity theory, but I also situate it in its appropriate historical and cultural context. Highlighting the serious and substantive differences between hegemony and hegemonic masculinity (theories that are all too commonly conflated), I argue that inclusive masculinity theory is best placed to clarify the changing stratification and estimation of masculinities that I find in this research.

In Chapter 5, I situate our knowledge of teenage masculinities in the context of schooling. Research on masculinities is important in a wide range of settings, from sports (Messner, 1992) to global politics (Connell, 2008a), and it is necessary to consider masculinities in school in their own specific educational context. This is particularly important given the homophobia that once pervaded high school, a view that still holds cultural traction among many activists and campaigners.

A driving principle of my work is that attitudes toward masculinity and sexuality are markedly changing in Western cultures. Accordingly, in Chapter 6, I explore the issue of this changing social zeitgeist in depth. First highlighting that homophobia reached an apex in the late 1980s, I then document how attitudes toward homosexuality have dramatically improved over the past two decades and discuss why these changes have occurred.

In the third section of the book, I present the findings from my research. In Chapter 7, I document how, in an era in which boys no longer fear being socially perceived as gay, heterosexual male students intellectualize and espouse pro-gay attitudes, esteeming the social inclusion of gay students. In addition to condemning overt forms of homophobia, heterosexual male students intellectualize the support of gay rights, and they are inclusive of their openly gay peers.

The attitudinal positions taken by heterosexual students are corroborated by the experiences of openly gay students. The LGBT students thrive at school, and none have been bullied at these high schools. Highlighting this, at a high school with a religious affiliation, an openly gay student was elected student president, and a transsexual student who changed his public gender identity to male was not bullied or harassed for doing so. Furthermore, homophobic language is absent from these settings, and LGBT students report maintaining good friendships with their heterosexual peers.

I also demonstrate an expanded range of socially esteemed behaviors available to heterosexual boys, attributing this to the fact that these students no longer fear being homosexualized. Boys at these schools no longer feel the need to be emotionally or physically distant from one another in order to prove their heterosexuality the way they once were shown to (Pollack, 1998). Instead, homosocial tactility is a regular part of daily interaction at all three high schools. These behaviors range from drawing on each other's hands to prolonged periods of sitting on each other's laps. This tactile bonding is complemented by expressions of emotional support, which are esteemed by heterosexual male students.

This is not to say that heterosexual boys in these schools do not desire to project an image of heterosexuality. Instead, these boys do not wish to project an image of *homophobic* heterosexuality. Accordingly, in Chapter 8, I document the ways in which these boys consolidate their identities as heterosexual by conceptualizing *heterosexual recuperation* as a set of mechanisms that boys use to reproduce their heterosexuality *without* invoking homophobia. These boys maintain their straight personas by talking about their (hetero)sexual potency and by ironically proclaiming same-sex desire. However, what is notable is the infrequency with which such processes are employed: these boys do little identity work in order to be socially perceived as heterosexual the majority of the time.

Having documented the gay-friendly nature of these schools, I then explore the social dynamics of these inclusive settings by examining the way boys are stratified according to popularity. In Chapter 9, I show that boys do not maintain their popularity at the expense of their peers, and that popularity is not used to exclude or marginalize boys who do not rank highly in this stratification. Boys ascribing to different masculine archetypes can each maintain high social status. However, a social stratification of boys nonetheless exists. I conceptualize four variables that impact the level of popularity one maintains: charisma, authenticity, support, and social fluidity.

This book also advances the understanding of homosexually themed language. In Chapter 10, rather than categorizing all use of the word "gay" as homophobic, I highlight the social context of language, arguing for a more nuanced approach to understanding its varied usage. In examining the political, intentional, and inadvertent effects of these boys' use of language, I define and discuss the notion of gay discourse as a form of heteronormativity that is distinct from the well-established use of homophobic language. I also discuss the pro-gay language that is used by gay students as a mechanism to bond with their heterosexual peers. Furthermore, I present a new model for understanding homosexually themed language, arguing that the cultural context is of primary importance in understanding its social effect.

In Chapter 11, I discuss what these findings mean in a broader social and academic context. I theoretically situate these empirical findings by using Eric Anderson's (2009) inclusive masculinity theory. This theory incorporates Connell's (1987, 1995) hegemonic masculinity theory by recognizing that masculinities are sometimes stratified by discursive marginalization (such as name calling and ridicule) as well as physical assault. However, inclusive masculinity theory historically situates this, arguing that Connell's theory is accurate only in highly homohysteric settings in which boys fear the stigma associated with being homosexualized and alter their behaviors in attempt to avoid being thought gay. Anderson theorizes that the gendered behaviors of boys and men will be radically different in settings where overt homophobia is absent, and he argues that this will lead to multiple archetypes of masculinity being esteemed in an inclusive setting.

Inclusive masculinity theory therefore provides a framework for understanding the gendered dynamics of spaces where overt homophobia has diminished—something Connell's work fails to address. However, by examining the social dynamics of these inclusive settings, my research also theoretically develops inclusive masculinity theory, as well as applying it to a new social and institutional demographic.

Because it documents the low levels of homophobia in high schools, this is in many ways an encouraging book. My findings show that we need to recognize that levels of homophobia in school settings are geographically and historically situated, and that young heterosexual men are not uniformly homophobic. Although heterosexuality is still esteemed, the experiences of LGBT students, and the attitudes and behaviors of their heterosexual male peers, demonstrate that the discourses of sexuality and gender in these high schools are markedly different from what the academic literature has traditionally shown.

I also discuss the implications of these findings more broadly. I argue that the transition to gay-friendly high schools is ultimately the result of broader social changes regarding sexuality and gender, particularly among young people. Although institutional directives have helped provide safer spaces for LGBT youth, the remarkable transformation in young men's attitudes and behaviors is not the result of these initiatives. I also discuss the applicability of my findings to other English-speaking countries, and I highlight the impact that this has with regard to combating homophobia.

Finally, the positive findings I document in this book could be read as a critique of the feminist sociology of gender and education—as a statement that I reject the work that identified the deleterious effects of orthodox gender norms. Such an interpretation would be a profound error. I do present results that often conflict with the existing literature on the topic, but this is not because I do not accept or agree with the tenets of feminist research or the findings presented in studies on the topic. I am firmly located within feminist ideals and politics. Rather, I suggest that we need to recognize social change when it occurs, and I argue that feminist research on sexuality, gender, and schooling needs to be historically situated and contextualized with respect to the social demographics of the participants, their geographical location, and the broader cultural context.

Setting the Scene

Researching Gender and Sexuality in Schools

Research examining the hierarchies, stratifications, and dynamics of gender and sexuality in school settings overwhelmingly employs qualitative methodologies. Here, the investigator situates himself or herself within the school and collects rich data about the topic under examination by interviewing, observing, and socializing with students (Pascoe, 2007; Renold, 2005). Although some quantitative (statistical) research examines the intersections of sexuality, gender, and schooling (Ellis & High, 2004; Wilkinson & Pearson, 2009), the most theoretically illuminating research has come from the use of ethnographic methods (Ferguson, 2000; Mac an Ghaill, 1994; Thorne, 1993), where one situates oneself in the school for months on end. Ethnographic inquiry is particularly suited to the examination of sexuality and gender because it emphasizes an understanding of the meanings and context of social action (Denzin & Lincoln, 2005).

Ethnography developed as a heuristic tool for understanding the social dynamics and local meanings of social interaction in particular cultural contexts. It privileges the experience of engaging in a social setting as a way of understanding its social dynamics (Davies, 1999; Willis & Trondman, 2002). As Chang (2005) summarizes, ethnography is "the study of people in naturally occurring settings or fields, using methods of data collection which capture the social meanings of ordinary activities" (p. 179).

With its historical roots in the anthropological scholarship of foreign cultures (see Malinowski, 1922), ethnography applies the methods used to understand other societies to the study of subcultures within its own. Accordingly, ethnography has often been described as the process of the researcher moving from being an outsider, or stranger, to someone who is accustomed to the social conventions and lived experiences of those under study (Agar, 1980). Even when scholars are acquainted with the culture being studied, they normally experience familiar settings in new and unaccustomed ways (Coffey, 1999). It is the lengthy process of familiarization from which an understanding of the meanings and conventions of a culture is wrought in ethnographic study (Geertz, 1973).

FORMAL AND INFORMAL ETHNOGRAPHIES

There are two main approaches to negotiating the relationship between the participants and the researcher in school-based ethnographies. In one, ethnographers retain an adult, expert role (Pascoe, 2007). In the other, researchers actively place themselves into the students' world (Ferguson, 2000). I refer to these two ethnographic forms as *formal* and *informal*, with the names characterizing the interactions and relationships that the researcher maintains with participants.

With the formal method, the ethnographer seeks to understand the local culture from the perspective of the participants while maintaining social distance from them. Students are encouraged to interact with the ethnographer without getting *too* personal (Swain, 2006a). With the informal method, the ethnographer works to minimize his or her social distance from the participants. Here, the ethnographer maintains distance from figures of authority within the school, and even colludes in rule-breaking behaviors with participants. The informal method rests on the belief that the richness of the data collected is of greater importance than the possible threat of researcher effect (Hodkinson, 2005).

The predominant style of ethnography in school settings has traditionally been that of the formal model (Mac an Ghaill, 1994; Swain, 2006a; Thorne, 1993). In that model, participants who ask personal questions, particularly about the researcher's sexuality, are told that such questioning is inappropriate, as the researcher keeps his or her "private life" private. Discussing this approach to ethnography, Pascoe (2007) describes how she sought to define herself as "an outsider, albeit a privileged one, an expert, someone who knew more about the boys than they knew themselves" (p. 180). For others, there have been reasons that mandated this form of ethnography. Mac an Ghaill (1994), for example, was a teacher in the school in which he conducted much of his research. This undoubtedly enabled him to develop a level of trust and intimacy with some students, but it also meant that he had to present himself in particular adult and institutionally-condoned ways.

Although formal ethnographies minimize the likelihood of "going native," whereby a researcher identifies too closely with participants and loses the ability to critique the negative aspects of a culture (Delamont, 2002), this ethnographic style has serious implications with regard to the richness of the data collected. Emerson, Fretz, and Shaw (1995) suggest that the distance from participants in formal ethnographies can (although it does not necessarily) lead to the researcher being detached from the research setting. As LeCompte and Goetz (1982) argue, "Detachment can destroy rapport and cause participants to infer indifference or even hostility on the part of the researcher" (p. 46).

In contrast to the formal ethnography, the informal approach requires that the social distance between the researcher and the participant be minimized (Adler & Adler, 1987; Hoffman, 2007). Perhaps the best example of informal ethnography in the educational literature is Ferguson's (2000) study of the intersection of race, gender, and schooling. In that work, Ferguson discusses how she started off expecting to conduct (what I call) a formal ethnography. However, she soon realized that this would not allow her to understand how her participants experienced school life. Ferguson writes about how her experience in the field caused her to question her relationship with her participants:

> I assumed at the start that I would learn about kids; but it was not long before I was obliged to question this premise and begin to learn from children. This enabled me to tell their story from a fresh viewpoint. (p. 11)

With this recognition, Ferguson spent more time with her participants, both in and out of school. She broke rules with them, visited their homes, and became their friends. Adopting such a style provided Ferguson with a breadth and depth of rich ethnographic data that made her study groundbreaking.

Ferguson's research represents one end of a spectrum of ethnographic research. The boundaries between informal and formal ethnographies are blurred, and I argue that an influential factor in determining which type is used is the deportment of the researcher and the manner in which he or she interacts with the participants. For example, Pascoe's (2007) formal style impacts the way in which she answers questions about herself. Pascoe comments that when she was asked questions about her personal life, she would try to "respond as neutrally as possible while encouraging boys to continue to talk about their feelings" (p. 185). This is markedly different from Blackman (2007) and Anderson (2009), who both describe socializing, drinking, and discussing personal issues in a relaxed and friendly manner. Regardless of which style is used, it is necessary for all researchers to critically analyze how their position in the field affects the collection of data. The process through which this is primarily done is known as reflexivity.

REFLEXIVITY

Reflexivity is an important component of rigorous and credible qualitative research. The strength of reflexivity, as Willis (1978) argues, is in the ability of the researcher to "analyse the intersection of his own social paradigms with those of the people he wishes to understand" (p. 197). It is through the continual questioning of a researcher's experience of data collection, and through the corresponding impact of personal history on data analysis, that rigor is achieved. Although reflexivity has become a key component of ethnographic research, the extent to which it should be employed is a matter of considerable debate (Roberts & Sanders, 2005).

I argue that too intent a focus on the methods and impact of the researcher can be troubling, and that too much reflexivity can impede the production of high-quality research. Patai (1994) suggests that the "preoccupation with method becomes an occasion for both a claim to and a display of power" (p. 71). Robertson (2002) develops this argument, suggesting that an over-focus on reflexivity actually serves to reinforce the authority of the researcher, with the potential for the research to become egocentric. Instead of a focus on the personal history of the researcher, Robertson argues that rigor is maintained through "the assiduous fieldwork and archival research necessary to generate historically resonant, thick descriptions and subtly evocative interpretations of people's lives in all their messy complexity" (p. 786). This is not to disregard methodological rigor or critique methodological discussion; nor is it to suggest that autobiographical discussions in research cannot be empirically or theoretically enlightening. It is, rather, to argue that methods should be seen primarily as a heuristic tool for understanding the social world. The refinement and improvement of these tools is necessary and important work, but it should not be undertaken at the expense of empirical findings and theoretical discussion. For this reason, I follow Delamont's (2002) suggestion of critically reflecting on my role in the field.

CHOOSING AN APPROPRIATE THEORETICAL FRAMEWORK

Academic debates about theories of knowledge (that is, how we know what we know) require that gender scholars situate their research within a particular theoretical framework. Although a substantial body of work examines gender from a social constructionist perspective, there has been a recent poststructural "turn" in the sociological theorizing of gender (Denzin & Lincoln, 2005). The aim of poststructuralism is to deconstruct and subvert dominant conceptions of sexuality and gender, with a particular focus on the heterosexual/homosexual binary, whereby people are viewed as either gay or straight (Epstein, 1994; Sedgwick, 1990). Poststructuralists also highlight that studying homosexuality without also examining heterosexuality consolidates social categorizations that exclude a wide range of people, not least bisexuals (Firestein, 1996; Gamson, 2000).

Poststructuralism and social constructionism both recognize that current conceptions of gender and sexuality are socially constructed and historically situated (Foucault, 1984; Weeks, 1985). This means that although one's own sexual orientation is biologically determined (LeVay, 2010), the way society understands forms of sexuality is determined by the politics and people of the time, and this will vary across cultures. Both frameworks are anti-essentialist, meaning that they reject the conceptualization of people and institutions as "having fixed identities which deterministically produce fixed, uniform outcomes" (Sayer, 1997, p. 454). Despite these similarities, debates rage about the precise nature of these frameworks and their appropriateness for the sociological study of gender (see Benhabib, 1995; Brickell, 2006; Butler, 1990; Green, 2007).

One of the main debates is about the utility of identity categories in understanding sexuality and gender. Poststructuralists maintain that identity categories are "regulatory regimes" that necessarily reinscribe the oppressive normalizing structures of social life (Butler, 1990, 1991), essentially forcing people to behave in a particular, socially acceptable manner. Accordingly, because these categories can never escape a binary of domination/subordination, their continued use is problematic. The "deconstructive impulse" (Green, 2007, p. 32) of poststructuralism seeks to dissolve identity categories, seeing categorization as problematic and damaging in and of itself (Butler, 1990; Jagose, 1996).

Indeed, Stein and Plummer (1996) argue that a hallmark of queer theory (the application of poststructuralist theory to the study of sexuality) is the "rejection of civil-rights strategies in favour of a politics of carnival, transgression, and parody which leads to deconstruction . . . and an anti-assimilationist politics" (p. 134). Poststructuralists maintain that it is through anti-assimilationist politics that homophobic and sexist societal norms are contested (Butler, 1991; Rasmussen, 2006). This is a contentious issue.

Social constructionists argue that political action organized around identity has proven to be the most effective way of contesting oppression, particularly concerning race, gender, and sexuality (Anderson & McCormack, 2010a; Bernstein, 2005; hooks, 1992). It seems both counterintuitive and counterproductive to reject the political model that has brought about more inclusive discourses of sexuality and gender (Anderson, 2009; Epstein, 1993; Weeks, 2007). Furthermore, accepting that identity categories are always in some way fictions does not contradict the point that people live in these identities as if they are real (Cohler & Hammack, 2007; Hammack & Cohler, 2009). Similarly, regardless of how gender and sexuality are constructed, discrimination and oppression exist in social reality and are experienced in people's lives (Crawley, Foley, & Shehan, 2008; MacKinnon, 1999).

Indeed, social constructionist theorizing maintains that recognizing group differences as socially constructed does not preclude organizing politically around these identities (Taylor, 1989). The histories of oppression that these groups share justify—even necessitate—collective forms of action based on these social categorizations (Anderson & McCormack, 2010b; Bernstein, 2005). This is because poststructural scholarship, being wedded to transgression and subversion, cannot theoretically legitimate *particular* forms of anti-assimilation; it must valorize all or none. That is, poststructuralism does not have the conceptual tools to distinguish ("bad") sexist and homophobic norms from ("good") normative ideals such as antidiscrimination and law-abidance (Nussbaum, 1999a).

This problem is exacerbated when one considers that the political effectiveness of anti-assimilationist politics is highly contested. As Walters (1996) argues, rejecting identity categories does not neutralize the social construction of social reality—it does not overcome the inequalities of class, race, gender, etc. Instead, this rejection dispels the possibility of politically organizing against oppression. Kirsch (2000) argues that by ignoring the structural elements of inequality, poststructuralist theory disables the possibility of the construction of a platform for social change. Thus, anti-assimilationist subversion becomes ineffective liberal individualism (Blasius, 1998).

I therefore argue that until sexuality and gender cease to be discourses that stigmatize desires and identities, subordinated groups must continue to contest and challenge these norms through identity politics. If minorities concede their identity labels, they are at risk of the exclusion that dominant groups historically, repeatedly, and even contemporarily levy against them (Collins, 2000; LeVay, 1996; Rubin, 1984). Indeed, as Lorde (1984) states, "It is axiomatic that if we do not define ourselves for ourselves, we will be defined by others—for their use and to our detriment" (p. 45). Accordingly, as Anderson (2009) argues, the rejection of categorical labels must first come from those who maintain power.

It should also be noted that social constructionists do not use categories uncritically. Various social constructionist scholars have called for the nuancing of categories, and intersectionality has been one way of theorizing this (Crenshaw, 1991). For example, McCall (2005) argues for an intercategorical approach to studying oppression, suggesting that scholars "provisionally adopt existing analytical categories to document relationships of inequality among social groups and changing configurations of inequality along multiple and conflicting dimensions" (p. 1773). Here, categories serve as a tool for recognizing and resisting discrimination and oppression.

Of course, the boundaries between frameworks are always blurred. For example, although much excellent poststructural scholarship exists (see, for example, Davies, 1993; Pascoe, 2007; Renold, 2005), I question the extent to which it really is "poststructuralist." That is, I doubt that there are any substantive theoretical differences as compared to existing social constructionist theories. For example, I have read several articles that use Butler's theory of performativity (so abstract and "poetically" written that the precise meaning is impossible to determine), when they could just as easily use West and Zimmerman's (1987) seminal and *accessible* concept of "doing gender." Indeed, in a heated discussion about this issue, I once asked a poststructuralist academic to explain the benefit of performativity over West and Zimmerman's framework. All she could offer as an answer was that Butler asserted that "there is no doer behind the deed." Well, quite—but try telling that to kids who are being bullied by homophobic thugs.

To be fair, some poststructuralists argue that categories still maintain analytic utility. For example, while supporting Butler's theorizing, Hey (2006, p. 442) argues that deconstruction is "largely a more self-conscious and stringent application of the conventional academic device . . . that has always supported students and scholars in their quest to get on some sort of terms with ideas." As Hey suggests, deconstruction in this form is nothing new. Indeed, Seidman (1996, p. 9) comments that queer theories are "often impossible to differentiate from constructionist texts." This is a distinction, but not a difference. The question then becomes, what does poststructuralism add to feminist social constructionist theorizing in its many forms (see MacKinnon, 1999)?

ACCESSIBILITY AND WRITING STYLE

This "soft" version of poststructuralism that maintains a great similarity to social constructionist theory perhaps bypasses the political problems outlined above. However, it necessitates the consideration of the presentational style of each theoretical framework. There exists a strong tradition in the sociological study of gender that argues for clear and concise writing that can influence people beyond the walls of the academy (Burawoy, 2004; Sprague, 2008). This tradition has been adopted by social constructionist scholars of masculinities as well

(Anderson, 2009; Kimmel, 2008; Mac an Ghaill, 1994), and I hope this book is another addition to this form of "public sociology."

I have nothing against a soft form of poststructuralist scholarship that is accessibly written (see, for example, Davies, 1993; Hey, 1993; Renold, 2005), although I might question why it is based in poststructural theory. However, and unfortunately, the writing style of many poststructuralist theorists is so dense and obscure that it is understandable to only a subgroup of academics (Butler, 1990). And they only imagine that they read clarity in the writing.

Trenchant criticism of this style comes from a broad range of scholars (Anderson, 2009; MacKinnon, 1999; Walters, 1996). In a searing and accurate critique, leading feminist philosopher Martha Nussbaum (1999a) argues that this writing is a willful attempt to "bully" readers into docility, and Anderson (2009) calls it a "violent, shameful act of academic exclusion" (p. 33). Even poststructural scholars recognize the impediment to coherency that this style poses (Hey, 2006).

This issue is brought into stark relief by considering Collins's (2000) discussion of the former slave Sojourner Truth. Truth could not read or write, yet she deconstructed the category "woman" in her famous speech, "Ain't I a Woman?" Long before poststructuralism, Truth highlighted the exclusions and oppressions that can stem from identity categories. In a striking and accessible manner, she highlighted the inequalities of class, race, and gender that existed at the time. When one considers that Butler's impenetrable *Gender Trouble* (1990) effectively asks the same questions, the utility of such ponderous and elitist writing is further called into question.

I feel, though, that I need to add a clarification at this point. I have encountered an argument against this position—one in which it is (or, rather, I am) labeled "anti-intellectual." I find the accusation of anti-intellectualism particularly troubling because I am not sure that it even is an argument. It seems to me rather more like an ad hominem attack—an accusation that it is my fault that I do not understand what Butler (or whoever) is saying. To me, this seems antithetical to the feminist commitment to public intellectualism, accessible sociology, and the dissemination of research ideas (Burawoy, 2005; Sprague, 2008), concerns that are particularly important in a political and economic world in which the social sciences must demonstrate their impact and pay their way.

Given these problems, I politically and theoretically locate myself in the social constructionist tradition and critique many aspects of poststructuralist thought. However, recognizing the utility in some of its scholarship, I seek to incorporate poststructuralist insight when relevant, as Brickell (2006, p. 89) writes, "privileging sociology's traditions but, where appropriate, bringing in poststructuralist ideas for consideration along the way." As Anderson (2009) argues, theory should be a tool used to interpret and conceptualize social life, rather than a rigid abstraction to which data must fit.

I recognize that the position outlined above could be termed a "hard" form of social constructionism (just as poststructuralism has been labeled "hard" and "soft"), and I would not object to this characterization. It is because I passionately believe that social constructionist thinking offers the best way of understanding society—for theoretical, political, and feminist reasons—that I provide such a robust defense (see also Jackson & Scott, 2010). Social constructionism is still the best theoretical perspective from which to investigate sexuality, gender, and issues of social justice.

The Study

Data for this research come from the ethnographic study of three high schools in the south of England: "Religious High," "Standard High," and "Fallback High." The schools are located in "Standard Town," where the majority of students live. However, the schools also draw students from rural areas and residents of the nearby major city, and Religious High has the widest geographic intake. All schools take students from the south of England, and more precise locations are not given in order to preserve the anonymity of the institutions.

RELIGIOUS HIGH

Religious High is the largest of the high schools, with approximately 1,000 students between the ages of 16 and 18. The school is situated just outside Standard Town, and students come from the town, the nearby major city, and the surrounding rural area. Accordingly, there is a broad range of students, with a spectrum of class and racial groups. Students there are granted more social freedoms than students at the other sites. For example, there is a smoking area for students, no uniform policy is prescribed, and students are allowed off campus when they are not in lessons. However, Religious High has a religious affiliation, and it is therefore guided by a Christian ethos that might be expected to uphold socially conservative views concerning gender and sexuality. The Christian denomination of the school is kept secret here in order to preserve the anonymity of the high school.

STANDARD HIGH

Standard High is situated on the north side of Standard Town, near a local park. Middle-class families live in the surrounding area, and Standard High is the school of choice for most of these households. A former grammar school,[1] Standard High maintains a reputation for good behavior and high grades, and its results are rated

1. Grammar schools select students according to their ability. Students who wish to attend a grammar school have to pass a test that they take at the age of 11. This academic history often means that former grammar schools have a good reputation.

as "good" (rather than "excellent" or "satisfactory") by the school inspectorate. There is no school uniform for the 16- to 18-year-olds, but other rules about smoking, piercings, and behavioral codes still apply.

Standard High maintains demographic similarity to the population of the United Kingdom—its students reflect the race and class profile of the country as a whole. Students come from working- to upper-middle-class families. Ninety percent of the students are white British, and the remaining ten percent comprise a variety of other racial and ethnic groups. There are approximately 200 students aged 16–18 in the high school, almost all of whom attended Standard School from the age of 11.

FALLBACK HIGH

Fallback High is situated 1.5 miles from Standard High. It is found south of the river in Standard Town, and the nearby houses are smaller and more dilapidated than those near Standard High. Fallback High has a poor reputation in the area compared to the other schools, but it is rated by the school inspectorate as good (the same as Standard High). Although the high school is affiliated with Fallback School, few students move on to the high school. This is attributable to the fact that Fallback High functions primarily to provide educational opportunities to troubled students who have previously struggled academically and/or behaviorally. With only 18 male students in total, the school's focus is on giving students the opportunity to achieve a range of key skills that will equip them with entry-level qualifications required for the workplace. All students are white and working class. However, because of their troubled social and educational lives, these students are not representative of working-class youth more generally.

All three high schools are located approximately two miles from each other in Standard Town. There are no other schools for residents this age nearby, so there is no selection bias with these research sites. Data collection occurred between March 2008 and July 2009.

The participants are the 16- to 18-year-old male students in each school. Most of these boys self-identify as heterosexual, although there are also some openly gay and bisexual students, and one openly (female-to-male) transsexual student. I also did not ignore female students' behaviors or views when they had relevance for the research. Although the majority of students have lived nearby in recent years, three students I interviewed had moved south in the previous year. These boys did not, however, comment on a North/South divide.

THE BRITISH CONTEXT: THE SIXTH FORM VERSUS THE HIGH SCHOOL

There is an important contextual issue with regard to the schools in which I collected data. Although I call the research sites "high schools," there are in fact differences between U.S. high schools and what we in Britain call "sixth forms." One key issue is that attendance at a sixth form is not compulsory in the United Kingdom. Those youth who have not engaged at school or who desire to leave for any reason are able to find employment or training in other areas.[2] I have called my research sites high schools because they resemble high schools found in the United States and because this book is aimed at an international market. However, there are some considerations that need to be taken into account when thinking about the British sixth form and how it relates to the U.S. high school.

It is a substantive issue that sixth forms have their own discourses of gender and sexuality that might differ from those in earlier levels of schooling. The move from compulsory state education to sites where students have actively chosen to stay in education (instead of entering the labor market) is, as Redman and Mac an Ghaill (1997, p. 169) comment, a "key cultural transition that involves young people in new social relations . . . and requires new forms of identity to handle them." They argue that the sixth form is a space where forms of masculinity that are more dependent on intellectual capability than on displays of physical strength or sexual prowess are available. Archer and Yamashita (2003) document that when working-class boys consider staying on in postcompulsory education, they experience a tension between holding onto their "authentic" masculinities, which are linked with educational failure, and staying on in education and "leaving" these identities (p. 127).

Drawing on the issue of class, Kehily and Pattman (2006) argue that sixth form students negotiate their middle-class identities as a mechanism to distance themselves from younger school students. This seemingly draws on Aggleton's (1987) study of sixth form students at a private school, where privileged students seek to portray themselves as autonomous and authentic individuals. However, although the issue of postcompulsory education is likely important, it is hard to distinguish the impact of this from that of the age of the students and, with Aggleton's study, the fact that data was collected at a private school[3].

Pertaining to the age of students, the 16- to 18-year-old age bracket appears to be the point at which young people start seriously defining themselves *against* institutional norms (Anderson, 2009), and they are less likely to passively adopt the rules that society dictates to them. This means that 16 to 18-year-old boys are perhaps better labeled as emerging adults (see Arnett, 2004). In short, researching male youth in sixth forms—or, indeed, in high schools—means that one is investigating people with a well-developed sense of *agency*, in an age range that is characterized by the attempt to develop an individual identity and sense of purpose (Arnett, 2004; Csikszentmihalyi & Larson, 1984).

None of this is to suggest, however, that sixth forms are ideal sites in which students can float free of social structures. In many ways they are very similar to

2. Young people in the UK now have to stay in education or training until the age of 18, but this change occurred after data collection.

3. Private schools make up a small percentage of schools in the United Kingdom, with approximately 7% of students attending them.

high schools, particularly with respect to the discourses of sexuality and gender that circulate within them. Redman and Mac an Ghaill (1997) argue that sixth form students adopt an "intellectual muscularity" in place of physical displays of dominance. They posit, however, that this is merely a new style of the same type of orthodox masculinity. That is, boys do not adopt pro-gay attitudes and esteem feminine behaviors in the process of entering sixth form settings. Instead, they recontextualize once-feminized activities (namely, academic success) as consistent with orthodox forms of masculinity. Redman and Mac an Ghaill argue that "muscular intellectualness did not transform heterosexual masculinity's disavowal of the 'feminine' and the homosexual, it merely reproduced them in a new form" (p. 171).

Accordingly, although it is necessary to recognize that the sixth form is a unique educational site, one must be cautious about how much change this space provides. Given what the relatively sparse literature on masculinities in sixth form education shows with regard to heteromasculinity (see in particular Redman and Mac an Ghaill, 1997), as well as the research from other countries (see Pascoe, 2007), it would be wrongheaded to argue that sixth forms have traditionally been cultural sites where more progressive attitudes proliferate.

DATA COLLECTION AT THE HIGH SCHOOLS

I first collected data at Standard High for a period of six months, a duration that LeCompte and Goetz (1982) suggest is suitable for a school-based ethnography. By the sixth month in this setting, the continued collection of data was not adding conceptually to my emerging theoretical framework. Instead, examples confirmed and supported the classification system I had devised (Goetz & LeCompte, 1981). Rather than continue to collect data at Standard High, I decided to expand my research to two other high schools. This was to guard against the argument that Standard High was an anomaly—that even though students at Standard High represent the demographic make-up of most of the British population (primarily white and middle class), Standard High was for some reason more gay-friendly than most high schools in Britain. Accordingly, I selected two high schools where elevated levels of homophobia might be expected to be found; if these sites were also gay-friendly, it would suggest that what was occurring was the result of a broad cultural shift and not of institutional factors.

I undertook research at Fallback High because it was a site where high levels of homophobia might prevail. As a school that exists for disaffected, socio-economically disadvantaged students who are seeking to gain basic qualifications for manual labor and other low-paid work, it might be expected that students here would maintain higher levels of homophobia (Froyum, 2007; Redman & Mac an Ghaill, 1997). Second, the site was chosen because of its geographical proximity to Standard High. Geographical proximity helps one to limit geographical location as a factor while recognizing the unique local culture of each site.

I carried out the same methodological procedure, which I detail below, as I did at Standard High. One difference, however, is that I planned to spend less time at this site. This is because I had already developed the main analytic themes from Standard High. The reason for collecting data at Fallback High was to investigate the extent to which the findings (of low homophobia and high physical tactility) might be a unique phenomenon of Standard High. Accordingly, I sought to compare findings between the two sites.

After spending three months at Fallback High, I expanded my research to a third high school. Having found lower rates of homophobia than expected, I selected Religious High because of its religious affiliation. This was strategic because religious schools are sites that are likely to maintain elevated rates of homophobia (Hillier & Harrison, 2004). Its proximity to the other research settings held geographical location as constant as possible in this research.

It is also worth noting that Standard Town is not known as a metropolitan or liberal town. Its main employer is a large factory, and it does not have high street fashion outlets in its shopping mall. In other words, there is no obvious reason for Standard Town to be particularly socially liberal. Furthermore, selecting schools that are expected to have higher-than-average levels of homophobia adds to the credibility of my findings, as well as to claims of generalizability. Flyvbjerg (2006) calls this the "most likely" case, in that these were sites where homophobia was more likely to be found. By finding the opposite of what is expected to occur, the rigor of the findings is improved.

CONDUCTING THE STUDY

Data was collected with as diverse a set of students as possible at all these sites. This was facilitated by undertaking initial observations of a wide variety of lessons (including art, music, physical education, math, and english). This enabled me to socialize with a broad range of students. I also came into contact with students in their social areas, and I attended various clubs and group meetings. Although I undertook measures to ensure that a diverse sample of students was accounted for, it is possible that a small selection bias occurred, as homophobic students might have distanced themselves from me—however, there is no evidence that this was the case.

The most illuminating data was collected away from teacher supervision—in the common rooms, on playing fields, and off site during break times and lunch. I maximized the time I spent socializing with students in these environments, and I adopted an informal ethnographic approach. I sought to minimize social markers of difference between myself and the participants, styling my hair and dressing as was fashionable in each setting. This was made easier by my age (24). I also adopted many of the male students' colloquialisms. However, it is important to note that I did not try to present myself *as* a student. As Wax (1971, p. 49) comments, such attempts can look "silly, phony, and mendacious." Wax further argues that participants can view assurances that the researcher is one of them as "rude, presumptuous, insulting, or threatening." Accordingly, I presented myself as sympathetic to students' views, eager to get to know them better, and appreciative of their engagement with me.

In order to gain students' trust, and consistent with this type of informal ethnography, I participated in minor rule-breaking behaviors. Examples of this varied across the different settings. For example, at Standard High this included playing sporting games in the common room, accompanying students off campus for lunch (not allowed at that school), and not commenting when I witnessed students copying homework. At Fallback High, students would loiter around the main gates of the school, which was prohibited by the administration. I would socialize with the students here. When students were reprimanded for doing this, I was treated as if I were one of them. This was prearranged with the school administration and seemed to strengthen my rapport with these students. At Religious High, there was less opportunity to engage in such activities because of the more lenient rules. The main ways in which I broke rules there were by occasionally helping students with homework and not commenting on other work being copied in my presence.

My own identity also influenced my social interaction with students in other ways. Many students asked about my relatively recent experiences at university. They wanted to know what it was like living away from home, attending lectures, and experiencing university life. Although I was clearly older than the students, my similar ethnicity and class status relative to the majority of students meant that I was familiar with many of their cultural references. For example, I shopped in the same clothes shops as many participants (*River Island* and *Topman*), watched the same television shows that they enjoyed (including *Skins* and *Family Guy*), and listened to the same radio stations (*Kiss* and *Radio 1*). These similarities enabled me to join in the informal discussions that pervade daily life.

In order to reduce the visibility of the research process, the taking of notes was left to immediate recall (Spradley, 1970). Often notes were recorded using immediate recall after leaving the presence of participants, but on other occasions I was able to use my mobile phone to text message notes to myself. This was frequently possible given the prevalence of texting in the common room. If, as happened on occasion, I was asked whom I was texting (a question I interpreted as a mechanism for starting a conversation), I would respond by giving a short answer such as, "Just sorting my plans for tonight," and then I would chat with the student.

In order to follow a controlled method of recording, managing, and interpreting field notes, annotations were recorded as quickly and in as much detail as possible after the event. After taking notes in the field, I systematically spent an hour or two writing them up and making initial interpretations (Barnard, 2002). Furthermore, time was taken to reflect upon earlier steps, using a method of making notes upon notes (Holt & Sparkes, 2001). I also discussed my findings with colleagues, who would often interrogate some of my early interpretations. All of this contributes to what I perceive to be a cyclical rather than linear method of ethnographic interpretation and analysis (Delamont, 2004).

In-depth interviews complement the participant observations by providing rich data about participants' attitudes. In addition to hundreds of informal conversations, I conducted 22 semistructured, in-depth interviews at Religious High, 10 at Fallback High, and 12 at Standard High, strategically selecting boys from a representative sample of subcultures within these settings. Each interview covered issues of friendship, bullying, attitudes toward homosexuality, perceptions of masculinity and popularity among peers, and understandings of homophobia and homosexually-themed language. The interviews were semistructured, meaning that although an interview code was prepared beforehand, it was used only for reference. I worked to ensure that interviews were as relaxed and informal as possible. That being said, in order to ensure the confidentiality of the interviews, they occurred in a private room with the door shut. Permission for interview was obtained from the head teacher (principal), the student, and a guardian of each student being interviewed. No student or guardian refused, and several students volunteered to be interviewed.

Being a Gay Researcher

Given the impact of sexuality on the research process (Coffey, 1999) and the positive outcomes of discussing one's sexuality freely (Kong, Mahoney, & Plummer, 2002), I deemed it necessary to be open about being gay. I came out in the third week of data collection at each site, initially examining levels of homophobia when students did not know of my sexual orientation. I detected no change in levels of homophobic language as a result of my being open about my sexuality. I also believe, as Anderson (2009) suggests, that my openness about my sexuality enabled me to undertake an informal ethnography and facilitated the further reciprocal disclosure of personal information with students. For example, some students asked what it was like to attend gay clubs and pubs, what it was like coming out, and how it affected my school experience. This enabled me to examine participants' attitudes toward homosexuality in a natural and free-flowing way. Talking about my sexuality made me closer to several key informants, and it certainly helped develop my relationships with lesbian, gay, bisexual, and transgender (LGBT) students.

Being open about my sexual identity was also important ethically. First, it promoted a positive attitude toward gay visibility, potentially providing a role model for LGBT youth. Furthermore, it meant that I treated participants with respect for their role in the research process. As Chang (2005, p. 192) writes, "[I]f a researcher can choose to hide his or her sexual orientation for certain reasons, then why do participants need to be honest in telling their own stories without any struggle?" The obvious point is that in the absence of extreme and overt homophobia, the disclosure of personal information regarding one's sexuality is likely to encourage mutual respect and reciprocity.

It is also possible that knowledge of my sexuality influenced some students to avoid contact with me. Some students might have exaggerated their support of gay rights or tempered their use of homophobic language because they knew of my sexuality. There is, however, evidence to suggest that this was not the case: Students did not change how they acted after I came out. Although I do not believe that being openly gay caused me to miss aspects of homophobia, it must be pointed out that if that were the case, this would be unique data in and of itself because it would indicate that homophobia has been driven underground. This is notably different from a time when students were homosexualized for associating with gay people (Mac an Ghaill, 1994).

With regard to my own reflexivity, I employed several procedures to ensure critical reflection. Following Mauthner and Doucet (2003), I explicitly examined my personal, emotional, and theoretical influences that are implicated in any analysis of data. I allocated specific times and places to reflect on my data collection, maintaining a reflexive and critical position throughout the data analysis. I also had other scholars cross-code parts of my data. Recognizing the ways in which my own feelings and emotions affect the collection of data, it is also important to be aware of the trepidation I felt initially entering the field. Having a school experience that I feel is accurately described by Mac an Ghaill's (1994) and Epstein's (1997) work, I had worried about entering an educational setting that I had experienced as homophobic in my youth. However, questions of how I would deal with observing social marginalization and homophobia ultimately were not important; I never witnessed these behaviors or attitudes. These students did not bully each other, marginalize less popular students, or deploy overt homophobia.

Being surprised by how these findings contrasted with my own experiences, I analyzed my data. Maybe I was exhibiting a form of reverse relative deprivation; Anderson (2005a) documents this with the openly gay athletes he researches, who did not recognize the homophobia they encountered because they were expecting it to be worse than it turned out to be. Also, I wondered whether my acceptance into their social groups meant that I did not recognize their faults. Had I grown too close to my participants? Had I "gone native?" I believe I guarded against these issues on several counts.

First, I used inter-rater reliability. Accordingly, another experienced ethnographer observed lessons and collected data with students in the common room at Standard High. He spent four months in the setting and collected data both independently and with me. This strengthened the reliability and validity of my findings, enabling interrogation of the ways in which my own personality influenced my data (May & Pattillo-McCoy, 2000). It also provided the opportunity to further improve my data collection techniques. And when this openly gay researcher collected data in the field, he did not find homophobia either.

Second, I am conscious of the seriousness of implicit forms of homophobia (and heteronormativity) and critically interrogated my own analysis and observations. I looked for other interpretations of events, examined the links between the interview and observational data, and considered the different views of a wide range of students. Put simply, I do not want to write away a form of social oppression, so I took steps to guard against this. Finally, as my time in the field progressed, I recalibrated my frames of analysis to look for more implicit forms of homophobia and heteronormativity. It is based on this analysis that I discuss the way many participants are still implicated in the privileging of heterosexuality, and I develop the concepts of "heterosexual recuperation" and "gay discourse" in order to understand the mechanisms by which this occurs.

Third, I investigated the extent to which participants acted differently when I was present, as students can have hidden motives for their engagement with adults. Willis (1977), for example, documents the ways in which school-aged boys actively "wind up" teachers, knowingly altering their self-presentation. With this in mind, I checked on the extent to which participants might have intentionally misrepresented the levels of homophobic language I found in the schools. I spoke with two key participants about my findings in each setting (Carspecken, 1996). I even strategically presented some untrue findings regarding homophobia in order to check whether these students were willing to contest me. All but one of the six students disagreed with the false findings, and the other deferred to me as the expert. Furthermore, I spoke to members of the staff who spent time with students but maintained little authority over them. This group comprised women who worked in the common lunch areas, as well as cleaners at each school. All adults said that they noticed no difference in how the students behaved when I was in the school as opposed to when I was absent.

Masculinities

3

Sex, Gender, and Power

The sociological study of masculinities is a recent addition to the field of gender studies. It differs from earlier feminist concerns with men because it holds men as the principal focus of analysis, explicitly recognizing them as gendered beings (Connell, Hearn, & Kimmel, 2005). This body of work, which Hearn (2004) calls "Critical Men's Studies," shows that a plurality of masculinities exist, and that they vary both within and between cultures (Kimmel & Messner, 2007). Furthermore, masculinities scholarship examines the gendered nature of men's power, showing that male privilege is maintained at the expense of particular groups of men as well as of women (David & Brannon, 1976; Pleck, 1981). As the discipline developed, it was established that rigorous theorizing of the gendered nature of men, substantiated by empirical research, is essential to fully understand patriarchy, the dominance of heterosexuality, and the operations of gender within society.

However, gender theory has gone through many stages in attempting to understand the manifest differences between men and women. From biological theories that posit "natural" differences that are the result of dichotomized bodies (man and woman) to Freudian notions of fixed psychological sex roles, gender relations have been the site of an ongoing and challenging debate about the distribution of male power in society. These debates are by no means settled, and I both recognize biological aspects of gender and sexuality (LeVay, 2010; Wilson & Rahman, 2005) and understand these identities to be historically and culturally situated (Fausto-Sterling, 1992; Weeks, 1985). However, it is also important to recognize that some academically discredited work (such as Freud's theory on the genesis of homo sexuality) still maintains influence on cultural understandings of masculinity today. Thus, in order to understand this legacy and appreciate the strengths and weaknesses of contemporary sociological theories of masculinities, it is necessary to examine the various theories that have maintained cultural and academic credence in the history of gender scholarship.

In this chapter I provide a historical overview of the study of sexuality and gender and discuss hegemony as a way of understanding the operation of power in society. Starting with functionalist theorizing of gender, I explore the roots of critical gender and sexuality scholarship in the psychological work of Freud. I examine how this shaped sex role theory, and how influential theorists developed and contested this dominant trend. This historical summary permits the examination of contemporary social constructionist theories of masculinities and

enables me to discuss their importance in understanding masculinities in contemporary society.

SEX DIFFERENCE RESEARCH

The most enduring cultural belief about gender is that it is the natural conse-
quence of biological sex (Fausto-Sterling, 1992). In this theory, it is argued that
men and women behave differently because they have been biologically pro-
grammed to do so. The academic work underpinning this reasoning is, however,
only a thinly veiled conservative attempt to maintain the status quo of male power
(Rose, Kamin, & Lewontin, 1984). Indeed, much of this scholarship can now be
read as a justification of the existing gender inequalities of the time. As Edley and
Wetherell (1995, p. 11) write, "[I]t can be argued that the history of sex difference
research represents one of the more politically transparent areas of scientific
investigation."

Early forms of sex difference research sought to prove that, among other differences in physical characteristics, women's skulls were on average smaller than
men's. This was thought to demonstrate that women were intrinsically less
intelligent than men. Although these claims can now be easily disregarded as
part of a misogynistic climate that sought to perpetuate gender inequality, Bem
(1993) highlights that more insidious forms of sex difference research persist. She
describes how, as moral and theological arguments supporting patriarchy became
increasingly untenable in academic debate, conservative scholars turned to
Darwin's theory of natural selection to argue that biology was responsible for sex
differences in order to foster the gendered oppression of society.

One of the principal arguments comes from Wilson's (1975) theory of sociobiology. In its original form, sociobiology provided a framework for understanding
the social behaviors of animals by examining the evolutionary benefits that these
behaviors might have. Although it was relatively uncontroversial (and also particularly useful) when applied to animals, it proved to be a contentious and divi-
sive theory when applied to human beings. The primary critique of sociobiology
applied to humans was that it evacuated all cultural and historical considerations
from gendered behaviors, focusing solely on evolutionary ideas (Rose et al., 1984).
Furthermore, as Kimmel (2004) highlights, the traditional application of sociobiology to humans was highly selective and tended to conform to preconceived
ideas of how gender "should" be. Kimmel calls these "just-so stories" of gender
because they consistently supported dominant notions of gender in society and
rarely offered new ways of thinking about a particular action or set of behaviors.

However, many progressive scholars have responded to these critiques by
developing a form of sociobiology that argues that biology is important in the
formation of gender and sexual identities without ignoring the role of the social.
For example, Bem (1993) argues that culture and biology interact in ways that
produce inventive and unexpected phenomena. Bem says that some gender and
sexual norms are the synergistic product of biology and culture, an argument that

Anderson (2011a) develops in relation to monogamy. Thus, although gender theorists agree that sex difference research is unable to explain the complex social dynamics of gendered behaviors (Connell, 1995; Fausto-Sterling, 1992), sociologists would also be amiss if they rejected any biological influences in the construction of sexuality and gender (LeVay, 2010; Wilson & Rahman, 2005).

THE PSYCHOLOGICAL ROOTS OF CRITICAL GENDER SCHOLARSHIP

An enduring cultural conception of gender is that sexual orientation can be inferred from a person's gendered displays. Put simply, male homosexuality is equated with effeminacy, and women's "acting butch" is deemed synonymous with lesbianism (Griffin, 1998; Pronger, 1990). In this framework, gender is not only a biological manifestation of sex; it is the window to one's sexuality. This fallacy was supported by the first academic scholarship that sought to understand gender as conditioned and shaped by society: the psychoanalytic theories of the late nineteenth and early twentieth century.

The conflation of sexuality and gender has its intellectual origins (at least in modern times) in the work of German sexologists Westphal, Ulrichs, and Kraft-Ebbing (see Dollimore, 1994; Weeks, 1985). Their work can be seen as the first steps in forming political action around homosexuality as an identity. For example, working in Berlin, Kraft-Ebbing theorized that homosexuality was a sexual inversion that resulted from an inborn reversal of gender traits (Spencer, 1995). From this he argued that homosexuals were deserving of some rights, and his work gained both popularity and notoriety in the academy. However, the conflation of femininity with male homosexuality gained cultural traction because of the combination of the dramatic social change of the industrial revolution and the proliferation of Freud's (1905) theories of childhood sexuality.

From the mid-1800s through to the beginning of the twentieth century, British and American societies underwent radical social change (Hartmann, 1976). In this period, known as the second industrial revolution, Anglo-American societies became increasingly industrialized, transitioning from rural populations to countries in which the majority of the population lived in cities (Cancian, 1987). It was also during this period of mass migration that men and women acquired the gender roles that we now consider as gender stereotypes. Theorized by Cancian (1987) as the separation of gendered spheres, men took on salaried factory jobs while women were domesticated. This was a marked change from rural life, in which men and women worked together (Williams, 1993). In the cities, however, women became the primary caregivers while men worked long hours away from home. As Anderson (2009) writes:

> As a result of industrialization, men learned the way they showed their love was through their labor. Being a breadwinner, regardless of the working conditions upon which one toiled, was a labor of love. . . . The antecedents of

men's stoicism and women's expressionism were born during this period. (p. 26)

However, Anderson (2009) argues that in order to recognize the full impact of this demographic change on masculinities, one must also consider the changing cultural understandings of sexuality.

The expansion of city dwelling meant that the rates of sex between men increased. This was because with the much more concentrated populations in cities, it was far easier for men with homosexual desire to meet and form social networks (Spencer, 1995). Gay men frequented "Molly Houses" (Norton, 1992), and same-sex sex was commonplace in nineteenth-century England (Miller, 1995). In this era, homosexuality became associated with dandyism and effeminacy through the fame of Oscar Wilde. Oscar Wilde maintained much recognition in English society, and his conviction for gross indecency (i.e., homosexuality) in 1895 linked homosexuality and dandyism in the cultural imagination (Anderson, 2009). Wilde, a famous playwright, declared homosexuality to be "the love that dare not speak its name" during his trial. In doing this, he made the first recorded public defense of homosexuality (Miller, 1995). Wilde became a symbol of homosexuality at the time, linking same-sex desire and effeminacy in cultural understandings of gender and sexuality—an association that found intellectual support in Freud's (1905) theory of childhood sexuality.

Freud's theorizing started from the position that sexual orientation was not innate but structured by one's upbringing. Living in Vienna, Freud witnessed this mass expansion of cities, and he simultaneously noticed an increase in sex between men. However, Freud misattributed this to the absence of men from child rearing, leading to overly feminized boys (Anderson, 2009). Freud argued that homosexuality, which he called "inversion," was a process of gendered wrongdoing, something formed in the early stages of a child's life. He wrote, "[T]he absence of a strong father in childhood not infrequently favors the occurrence of inversion" (1905, p. 146). Irrespective of the veracity of his theories, Freud's notions of sexuality and gender provided academic respectability to the cultural understanding that femininity in men was indicative of homosexuality. Although Freudian theories of homosexuality are no longer directly used in gender scholarship, his pioneering work left a lasting imprint on gender scholarship throughout the twentieth century, and his theories still hold traction in some parts of the media today. For example, fears about the feminization of education are ultimately rooted in Freudian concerns about boys not having proper male role models (see Lingard, Martino, & Mills, 2008).

THE USE OF SEX ROLE THEORY TO UNDERSTAND GENDER

Developing from Freud's groundbreaking work on sexuality, the psychological theory of sex roles offered a more nuanced understanding of the gender differences manifest in society. Sex role theory argued that there are a set of behaviors that men and women are expected to enact in order to "properly" conform to their biological sex. As Kimmel (2004, p. 95) comments, "Sex role theorists explore the ways in which individuals come to be gendered, and the ways in which they negotiate their ways toward some sense of internal consistency and coherence." Sex role theory was instrumental in gender scholarship because it provided an initial understanding of the role of the social in gender, and because it was later used by feminist scholars as a form of emancipatory research.

It is necessary to distinguish two forms of sex role scholarship. Early functionalist work thought that socialization was a necessary process that people needed to undergo in order to produce a stable society (Parsons & Bales, 1955). As Connell (1995) writes, this research argued that "internalized sex roles contribute to social stability, mental health and the performance of necessary social functions" (p. 22). In this vein, sex role theory was a conservative rationale that sought to maintain the status quo. However, feminists also used sex role theory to try and challenge gender inequality in society. Positioning the female sex roles as oppressive to women, feminist scholars used the female sex role as part of an argument for social reform.

Nancy Chodorow (1978) provided a psychoanalytic theory of gender reproduction that built on sex role theory. Developing Freudian theorizing, Chodorow examined how gender is reproduced through the process of mothering. She argued that girls learn their sex role with relative ease, because they are taught how to be appropriately feminine and heterosexual by their mothers. Girls are passive in the production of their sexual identities, as they are socialized into their sex role by copying how their mothers act. Whereas the reproduction of femininity was near-seamless for Chodorow, she argued that it is much harder for boys to successfully attain their sex role.

Chodorow theorized that it is more difficult for boys to attain the socially esteemed form of masculinity, because whereas a girl is socialized into femininity by mirroring her mother, a boy has to construct his gender *in opposition* to his mother's example. This means that masculinity is a negative identity—it is constructed by being unlike women, by *not* being the mother. Following Freud, Chodorow argued that a boy must break his primary attachment to his mother in order to realize a heterosexual and masculine identity. Chodorow argued that male femininity and homosexuality are linked, and that masculinity is predicated fundamentally on what it is not; masculinity is understood as not-femininity.

Robert Brannon (1976) identified four components to which men must conform in order to attain their gendered role. The first is that there must be "no sissy stuff." This highlights how masculinity was, at the time, predicated on distancing oneself from femininity, and how femininity in men was stigmatized. The second is that one must "be a big wheel"—masculinity was measured by power, status, wealth, and success. The third, "be a sturdy oak," documents the stoic nature of masculinity, and the imperative that boys do not cry. Brannon's final component of the male role is to "give 'em hell." To be appropriately masculine, men must take risks, demonstrate courage, and be aggressive. However, although such scholarship critically examined men's position in society, and although some of this work still maintains utility today, the value of sex role theory is limited because it lacks the sophistication to deal with the intricacies of gender relations (Connell, 1995). It also fails to address intermasculine domination.

Limitations of Sex Role Theory

Although it maintained a respected position in gender scholarship for many years, sex role theory came under fierce criticism in the 1990s (Connell, 1995). One reason for this is that feminist scholarship questioned the naturalness and supposed inevitability of the sex binary. For example, feminist biological research details the diversity in human bodies in order to disrupt the seemingly self-evident universal of dichotomized sex (Fausto-Sterling, 2000; Kessler & McKenna, 1978). Fausto-Sterling's (1992, 2000, 2005) work reconsiders the sex/gender dualism, arguing that allowing sex to stand as a biological fact already concedes too much to functionalist gender scholarship. Instead, she argues that sex and gender are mutually constitutive and reinforcing. By examining intersexed bodies that require surgery in order to "fit" the sexual binary, Fausto-Sterling (1992, 2000) shows that the production of scientific knowledge (here, of a sex binary—man and woman) is deeply situated in and influenced by cultural histories, human practices, language, and politics. She argues that sex is the rationale for gender differences and inequality, but she provides substantial empirical evidence to show that this sex binary is enforced through dominant cultural understandings of gender. The power of a sex/gender distinction is that gender differences "prove" the naturalness of the sex binary that establishes gender roles. She argues that it is the work of critical scholars of gender to disentangle this complex and circular process.

Another problem with sex role theory is that it does not sufficiently examine the structural elements of gender. As Stacey and Thorne (1985, p. 307) argue, "the notion of 'role' focuses attention more on individuals than on social structure. . . . It strips experience from its historical and political context and neglects questions of power and conflict." Sex role theory cannot account for the different roles people must aspire to in different institutions. This can be seen if one considers how men are supposed to act in church as compared with their sex role on a football pitch. Further supporting the argument that sex role theory lacks an account of structural inequalities, Connell (1995) argues that there is nothing in sex role theory that requires an analysis of power. Evidencing this, she comments that both black and gay men are consistently excluded from the theorizing of sex roles, and resistance by these groups cannot be accounted for by the sex role terminology of "norm" or "deviance."

Furthermore, this theory of gender lacks an account of agency. In the sex role framework, gender roles are attained by passively submitting to the dominant gender order. Here, a macro-level gender order is imposed upon individuals, and those who do not conform are labeled as deviant. However, feminist scholarship since the mid-1980s documents the ways in which gender is produced and regulated in social interaction (Thorne, 1993; West & Zimmerman, 1987). With its top-down understanding of power, sex role theory cannot account for this production of gender.

UNDERSTANDING GENDER AT THE INDIVIDUAL AND CULTURAL LEVEL

A holistic understanding of gender requires analysis at both the cultural (macro) and individual (micro) levels. The seminal study explicating the construction of gender at a micro-level is West and Zimmerman's (1987) "Doing Gender." In it, West and Zimmerman focus on how gender is reproduced and consolidated through social interaction. They write that gender "is not simply an aspect of what one is, but, more fundamentally, it is something that one *does*, and does recurrently, in interaction with others" (p. 140). Gender is reproduced and potentially changed by social acts (Fenstermaker & West, 2002; Lorber, 1994).

West and Zimmerman argue that the social construction of gender is more than the gender-specific meanings we attribute to our behaviors. Drawing on Kessler and McKenna (1978), they highlight that even though the essential characteristics thought to constitute our sex (such as genitalia) are hidden, we are always socially perceived as either male or female. Great emphasis is therefore placed on our gendered behaviors, as they are seen to confirm (or, alternatively, question) the "true" status of our sex. All of our gendered behaviors and the meanings attached to them are therefore framed and distilled through the aim of demonstrating our united sexed and gendered selves. West and Zimmerman argue that our continual quest to be seen as maintaining the appropriate sex and gender is how we "do" gender in social interaction (this formulation predates Butler's [1990] heterosexual matrix, a concept that has great similarities to the one outlined above).

This interactional approach to gender has been particularly effective in the study of gender dynamics in school cultures. For example, Thorne (1993) applies this framework in her ethnographic study of elementary school students, showing that children actively shape their own and others' gendered identities. Mac an Ghaill (1994) also evidences the utility of this approach by showing that social interaction between boys created the various archetypes of masculinity that were present in the school he researched.

However, although social interaction is of paramount importance in understanding gender in society, it is also necessary to examine the macro-level construction of gender in order to have a comprehensive understanding of masculinities. Sociological studies of institutions demonstrate that gender is also a form of power that pervades the social structures of society. Joan Acker (1990) explicates the ways in which organizations are gendered, where "advantage and disadvantage, exploitation and control, action and emotion, meaning and identity, are patterned through and in terms of a distinction between male and female, masculine and feminine." Her analysis presents gender as a form of power that permeates society and structures how we interpret and mediate our social lives. Acker argues that even the concept "job" is gendered, and that our understandings of masculinity and femininity are contingent upon the organizational structures of societal institutions.

Seeing institutions as gendered recognizes that gender is an organizing principle in social life (Acker, 1992). However, it is insufficient to argue solely that organizations are gendered through their structure and design; it is also necessary to examine the discourses of gender that circulate within them (Britton, 2000), viewing the reproduction of gender as a synergistic relationship between social interaction and societal structures.

Indeed, one of the main benefits of the sociological study of gender is that it fosters a multilevel analysis of masculinities and femininities. Rather than focusing on gender as solely the property of individuals, social constructionist theorizing examines the *interplay* between individuals and institutions. As Kimmel (2004, p. 102) argues,

> To say that gender is socially constructed requires that we locate individual identity within a historically and socially specific and equally gendered place and time, and that we situate the individual within the complex matrix of our lives, our bodies, and our social and cultural environments.

It might be necessary for an individual piece of scholarship to focus on just one of these concerns, but a comprehensive understanding of masculinities (and gender more broadly) must account for both levels of analysis.

THE ROLE OF FEMINISM

Feminism has been a key influence on the sociological and psychological study of gender in Western cultures. Beginning as a social and political movement, feminism paved its way into the academy, where scholars have helped activists transform debates concerning the role of women in society. Daniels (1975) writes:

> The development of a feminist perspective in sociology offers an important contribution to the sociology of knowledge. And through this contribution, we are forced to rethink the structure and organization of sociological theory in all the traditional fields of theory and empirical research. (p. 349)

Feminist scholarship was instrumental in advancing the multilevel study of gender. However, it also illuminated unseen operations of male power and the ways in which male privilege is sustained.

In her seminal essay, Adrienne Rich (1980) advances the notion of *compulsory heterosexuality* to argue that the regulation of homosexuality is a fundamental practice of patriarchy. Focusing on the censure of lesbianism, Rich contends that heterosexuality is so pervasive that it needs to be understood as a political institution. She argues that countless women have lived heterosexual married lives not through choice, but because they were culturally compelled to do so. For Rich, compulsory heterosexuality is the key mechanism in controlling women and maintaining patriarchy. Although her work presents a romantic and naturalized vision of lesbianism (Weeks, 1985), it also highlights how sexuality works to police gender and demonstrates the regulatory power of homosexuality in women's lives.

One of the key political methods of feminism is that of consciousness raising. A prime example is of the use of the male pronoun to stand for both men and women. Feminists highlight this through changing "history" to "herstory" (Cameron, 1985; Holmlund & Youngberg, 2003). Although etymologically nonsensical—the "his" in "history" has no relation to the gendered pronoun— such wordplay highlights how only a few exceptional women are ever considered in historical scholarship; in this context, herstory makes sense because it illustrates the gendered bias of so much historical writing. This is important because the obscuring of power relations makes them harder to contest. Accordingly, this has helped combat the invisibility of masculine privilege.

This is important because the elision of gender is not trivial but a fundamental mechanism through which gender inequality is perpetuated. The invisibility of masculinity—the supposed genderlessness of men—is key to understanding the continuation of gender inequality (see Kimmel, 2004). Feminism has made fundamental theoretical and political contributions to this cause, which is why many male critical masculinity scholars who employ feminist frameworks often call themselves "pro-feminist" (Whitehead, 2001).

POWER AND HEGEMONY

In order to think about gender as a dynamic social system of relations between groups, it is necessary to consider how power operates in society. The first consideration is that power is not an artifact—it is not a "thing" that people maintain (Russell, 1938). It is instead a social matrix, a set of relations between people. For example, a teacher maintains power in a school because of a complex array of social structure, social dynamics, and cultural expectations. Discipline is maintained when both teacher and student conform to the social roles expected of them. If a student deviates from these scripts, the teacher can do little to regain control. This is because power is not possessed but is instead a mediated relationship. As Arendt (1971) comments, "[P]ower is never the property of an individual; it belongs to a group and remains in existence only so long as the group keeps together" (p. 41).

It is particularly striking that in many situations in which there are disparities of power, this inequality is not contested by the majority of those who are excluded in the culture. A question that articulates this conundrum is, "Why aren't all women feminists?" Or, "Why don't all gay men support gay rights?" Rather than contest the unequal distribution of power and privilege in society, many women and gay men often support the existing system of inequality. One theoretical explanation of this comes through Antonio Gramsci's theory of power, hegemony.

Gramsci (1971) wrote his theory of power while in prison. As a Marxist thinker in Mussolini's Fascist Italy, he was incarcerated for his radical thinking because it was feared his political theories might provoke civic unrest. It is interesting to note, however, that prisons do not feature in hegemony theory. This is because Gramsci was interested in the ways in which people obey authority when they are not culturally compelled to do so. In prison, a person has no option but to obey the rules of the insulated institution in which he or she is forced to live— something Goffman (1961) called a "total institution." In such a situation, individuals are denied agency, and total power is maintained by those in positions of authority within the institution.

Instead of total institutions, Gramsci was interested in places where people maintain some level of agency—where it is possible for them to contest and challenge dominant rules. He was interested in why people collectively conform to norms and explicit rules when there is no immediate physical compulsion for them to do so. Starting from an understanding that our beliefs and moral codes are socially constructed, Gramsci (1971) provided a framework for understanding how we are conditioned into believing particular ideas and viewing events from certain standpoints. This recognizes that stratifications of society are not preordained but are constructed and reproduced through social interaction, be it with respect to sexuality (Rubin, 1984), gender (Lorber, 1994), race (Collins, 2000), or any other stratification of power (Anderson, 2010).

From this constructionist starting point, hegemony theory conceptualizes a particular form of social control, one in which force is not a fundamental component of maintaining the social order. Although force might be a characteristic of a particular hegemonic society, it is not fundamental to the continual privileging of the dominant group. As Anderson (2005a, p. 21) comments, "While there is often the threat of rules or force structuring a belief, the key element to hegemony is that force cannot be the causative factor in order to elicit complicity."

Supporting the perspective that Gramsci differentiated between force and complicity, Joseph Femia (1981) distinguishes between domination and coercion. Femia describes domination as an "external" control that induces behavior through reward and punishment, whereas coercion is a form of "internal" control that changes people's beliefs. Femia describes this internal control as hegemony, saying that hegemony "refers to an order in which a common social-moral language is spoken, in which one concept of reality is dominant, informing with its spirit all modes of thought and behavior" (1981, p. 24). Here, hegemony refers to the *acceptance* of the social order as natural and morally right—something Femia describes as individuals consenting to the dominant social order. This means that the dominant group maintains its power through the acquiescence of other members of a setting.

Hegemony theory is a substantive heuristic tool in understanding how and why people believe in ideas and notions that go against their own self-interest. Gramsci applied his theory of hegemony to class relations, examining how the bourgeoisie maintained the dominant position in society at the time. From a Marxist perspective, he was concerned with why, in opposition to what Marx predicted, capitalism was becoming increasingly entrenched in society. Gramsci wanted to understand the reasons why the proletariat was not rising up against the bourgeoisie, despite the unequal and unfair distribution of wealth and power at the time. His argument was that through discourse and ideology, the values of the ruling class become accepted by others in society—they become "common sense" notions that people see no need to question.

This lack of questioning is particularly important. This is because it is a mechanism that enables the dominant group to hide its dominance. For example, considering the marginalization of racial groups in Western cultures, one reason that whiteness maintains its hegemonic position is that unlike people of color, white people are not seen as belonging to any race (Dyer, 1997). And because race is seen to negatively affect people of color rather than Caucasians, it is white people who determine what is and is not considered racist. In this context, white culture is the benchmark for acceptable behaviors. Black people are thus praised for "acting white," and those who contest the racist system are viewed as troublemakers and are condemned accordingly (West, 1993). This process of normalizing inequality is one of the most effective ways in which groups maintain a hegemonic position in society.

However, another fundamental component of hegemony is that it is not seamless (Ransome, 1992). Hegemony describes not a static system of hierarchy but one in which different groups compete for hegemonic dominance. There are always cracks in the system, from individuals who use their agency to contest the current stratification to social discourses and ideas that counter the hegemonic modes of thought. The power of hegemony is located in the fact that maintaining hegemonic dominance is far easier than attaining it; by using the idea that one's position is natural and morally right, it is possible to discredit those men and women who argue for social change. Hegemonic relations are achieved through negotiation and consent, and they perpetually shift to accommodate challenges to their authority. Indeed, the social relations that constitute hegemony are always changing, and often incorporate (or assimilate) forces that seek to disrupt the social order.

Raymond Williams (1977, p. 112) further developed this idea by discussing a "lived hegemony." Understanding hegemony in this way recognizes that hegemony "does not just passively exist as a form of dominance, [but] has continually to be renewed, recreated, defended, and modified." Hegemonic relations are constantly shifting, always achieved through negotiation and consent, and they often retain dominance by incorporating challenges to the hegemonic norm (Bocock, 1986).

Williams (1977) developed the heuristic utility of hegemony by presenting a framework for mapping how internal groups or ideas compete for social dominance within a hegemonic system. Williams describes the "dominant," the "residual," and the "emergent" as three stages or positions that are occurring at any moment in a lived hegemony.

The dominant refers to the group that maintains hegemonic power in a society. The residual refers to practices and beliefs that were formed in the past and are recognized to be part of a "bygone age," but which nonetheless maintain relevance to the present. Epstein and Johnson (1998) describe residual ideas as those that "seem to have had their day, to be almost quaint, but have left traces and still influence our everyday experience" (p. 191). Sometimes people seek to revive the residual, and an example of this with regard to masculinity is men who participate in the mytho-poetic men's movement (Messner, 1997), in which they seek to reclaim an old, romantic view of masculinity. Finally, Williams (1977) describes the emergent as the fact that "new meanings and values, new practices, new relationships and kinds of relationships are continually being created" (p. 123). The emergent is a challenge to the dominant culture, but its success is never certain. Both the residual and the emergent can be reincorporated into the dominant, but it is the emergent that has the potential to transform social life.

THE HEGEMONY OF SEXUALITY

Alongside race, class, and gender, sexuality is one of the fundamental ordering principles of society. Hegemony theory is particularly useful in examining the sexual stratification of a society, because it helps explain how conservative sexual morality is produced and perpetuated. In a highly influential book chapter, Gayle Rubin (1984, 1993b) explicates the ways in which certain forms of sexuality are privileged within an esteemed "charmed circle," whereas other sexual practices are removed to the stigmatized "outer limits." She discusses the hierarchy of sexuality, with "marital, reproductive heterosexuals alone at the top of the erotic pyramid" (1993b, p. 14), and prostitutes, transsexuals, and pedophiles (among others) at the very bottom. Rubin goes on to describe the hegemony that keeps this sexual caste system in place:

> Individuals whose behavior stands high in this hierarchy are rewarded with certified mental health, respectability, legality, social and physical mobility, institutional support, and material benefits. As sexual behaviors or occupations fall lower on the scale, the individuals who practice them are subjected to a presumption of mental illness, disreputability, criminality, restricted social and physical mobility, loss of institutional support, and economic sanctions. (p. 15)

Rubin describes how the varying levels of stigma and privilege attached to different forms of sexual desire and expression make the hegemony of sexuality difficult to contest.

The repression of sexuality is found throughout Western law and is manifest in legal sanctions that seek to criminalize behavior that is "freely chosen and avidly sought" (Rubin 1993b p. 26). Rubin provides a genealogy of sex laws, arguing that they are both severe and expansive. They are particularly effective, however, because their occasional enforcement ensures that sexual minorities continue to live in fear of the punishments that result from their enactment.

Although Rubin shows the power of the law in the regulation of sexuality, she also shows that most of the regulation of sexuality is "extralegal." As hegemony theory suggests, the powers of cultural coercion and stigma are effective in muting challenges to laws concerning sexuality. Here, one of the fundamental mechanisms is the social censure of "deviant" sexualities, and shame is a key emotion that is invoked for all those who stray from the heterosexual, married norm. Of course, although there are important examples of the hegemony of sexuality being contested—particularly women's sexuality (Hite, 1976)—these are merely "cracks in the system" when compared to the panoply of sexual practices, desires, and identities that are stigmatized and/or repressed in Western culture (Rubin, 1984).

Another crack in the system comes from the recent gay rights political movement, which has achieved some success in gaining legal and social rights for gay men and lesbians (Weeks, 2007). Indeed, the growing acceptance of homosexuality can be viewed as a considerable challenge to the system. However, homosexuality is still a particularly pertinent example when examining the hegemony of sexuality. One can consider, for example, the depression felt by gay youth and their elevated rates of suicide as compared to heterosexual children (Morrison & L'Heureux, 2001; Remafedi 1994). As hegemony theory suggests, some gay youth internalize the cultural disgust toward homosexuality. It should be noted, however, that the suicide stories that were once a normal part of coming out stories for gay youth are increasingly rare in contemporary culture (Savin-Williams, 2005), and new research suggests that the suicide rates of lesbian, gay, bisexual, and transgender youth might now be comparable to those of urban heterosexual youth (Mustanski, Garofalo, & Emerson, 2010). Nonetheless, Plummer (2001) suggests that the myriad forms of homophobia—from verbal abuse and physical assault to intellectualized disgust and the conflation of homosexuality with HIV—combine to provide a hostile environment for gay youth, providing "reasons" for the censured position of homosexuality in society.

In his autoethnographic work on coming out as the first openly gay high school coach, Anderson (2000) provides vivid details of the ways in which homophobia operates to marginalize and attack those even associated with homosexuality. He discusses a shocking episode in which a student is violently assaulted by a fellow student for maintaining friendship with Anderson. Anderson uses hegemony theory as a lens through which to interpret this violent act: the perpetrator, who was not arrested or expelled for his actions, was fulfilling what was culturally expected of him. Anderson (2009) later wrote of the incident, "He was rewarded by his teammates, and encouraged into homophobia by his coach. Indeed, after the beating, the football player earned hero status among his teammates" (p. 3). The social privileging of homophobia and the framework of homosexual stigma resulted in a violent attack going unpunished, and even being praised.

The hegemony of heterosexuality is important in understanding masculinities at two levels. First, as sociological lenses, gender and sexuality overlap. Examining the hegemonic dominance of heterosexuality in society requires considering the effect of gender relations, and theorizing about male power cannot be adequately considered without reference to forms of sexuality. Multiple scholars do this in a number of different ways (Connell, 1995; Crawley, Foley, & Sheehan, 2007; Nussbaum, 1999b). Second, at a cultural level, heterosexuality and masculinity are conflated so that masculinity is deemed synonymous with heterosexuality. Clearly having roots in the Freudian linking of male femininity and homosexuality (Kimmel, 1994), demonstrating masculinity automatically "proves" one's hetero-sexuality. This is something Pronger (1990) conceptualizes as "heteromasculinity." Accordingly, it is necessary to consider heterosexuality when thinking about mas-culinities. The close relationship between heterosexuality and masculinity has been increasingly accounted for in masculinities' scholarship (see Connell, 1995; Mac an Ghaill, 1994; Pronger, 1990), and contemporary theorizing recognizes the centrality of homophobia in determining the sexual and gendered attitudes and behaviors of heterosexual men.

4

From Hegemonic Masculinity to Inclusive Masculinities

One of the principal aims of masculinities scholarship is to examine the diverse and unequal distribution of the privilege that men maintain because of their gender. It provides what is essentially an intersectional analysis of patriarchy, complicating the understanding of homogenous male power by discussing the importance of heterosexuality, whiteness, and other differentials concerning the privilege of individual men (Carrigan, Connell, & Lee, 1985; S. Jackson, 2006). The theory that has proven most popular among academics for studying the stratification of men in society has been Connell's (1987, 1995) theory of "hegemonic masculinity."

From a social constructionist perspective, hegemonic masculinity theory articulates the social processes by which a masculine hierarchy is created and legitimized. Connell argues that although there are multiple masculinities, one form is culturally esteemed above all the others. She argues that this archetype maintains *hegemonic* dominance. By using the concept of hegemony to theorize the process of stratifying masculinities, Connell (1995) argues that force is not the primary way in which a masculine hierarchy is inscribed. Instead, two interactional mechanisms produce this hegemony. Connell proposes that physical domination and discursive marginalization are the two key processes that reproduce hegemonic stratifications of masculinity. Domination conceptualizes the material acts that subordinate specific groups of boys and men, and marginalization represents the discursive challenging of the legitimacy of particular masculinities.

These mechanisms are of fundamental importance to hegemonic masculinity theory. In the second edition of *Masculinities*, Connell (2005) continues to stress the centrality of these social processes in her theory of gendered relations. Furthermore, Connell and Messerschmidt (2005, p. 844) maintain that "to sustain a given pattern of hegemony requires the policing of men." Indeed, they argue that "the concept of hegemonic masculinity presumes the subordination of nonhegemonic masculinities" (p. 846). It can therefore be reasonably concluded that these social processes are fundamental to the operation of hegemonic masculinity in society.

Connell (1995) describes three forms of masculinity that are the result of the hegemonic processes of marginalization and domination: complicit, subordinated, and marginalized masculinities. Complicit masculinities conceptualize men who, while not embodying the archetype of hegemonic masculinity or practicing its tenets, nonetheless gain from male privilege, something she calls the "patriarchal dividend." As Connell (1995, p. 80) writes,

> A great many men who draw the patriarchal dividend also respect their wives and mothers, are never violent towards women, do their accustomed share of the housework, bring home the family wage, and can easily convince themselves that feminists must be bra-burning extremists.

And because the hegemonic form of masculinity is often an idealized archetype that few men can embody, complicit masculinities often comprise the majority of men.

Subordinated masculinities represent men who actively suffer due to the stratification of masculinity—men who experience exclusion through tangible and substantive cultural practices. Connell (1995) identifies gay masculinity as "the most conspicuous" (p. 79) form of subordinated masculinity, with gay men "subordinated to straight men by an array of quite material practices" (p. 78). For Connell (1995), these include "political and cultural exclusion, cultural abuse . . ., legal violence . . ., street violence . . ., economic discrimination and personal boycotts" (p. 78). These abuses have been documented in many institutions, from sports (Anderson, 2002) to schools (Epstein & Johnson, 1998), and from the judiciary (Nussbaum, 1999b) to the navy (Barrett, 1996).

The final category of masculinity Connell describes is marginalized masculinities. These comprise men who are subordinated by the hegemonic form of masculinity because of their race or class. Connell (1995) separates this from the "relations internal to the gender order" (p. 80), but she does not make clear why race and class are "external" factors and sexuality is an "internal" one. Nonetheless, Connell argues that it is through marginalization and domination that men are stratified into these groups.

Connell has also sought to expand hegemonic masculinity theory beyond the local, examining how a hegemonic form of masculinity operates at both national and international levels. Although this debate is certainly interesting and may be important for theorizing on how masculinities and gendered power impact global politics and the formations of masculinity at a global scale, I share Beasley's (2008) and Howson's (2008) concern that such a focus is problematic because of its shift away from the inherently situated nature of masculinities, in terms of geography, local culture, institutional setting, and other factors. It is my belief, alongside Redman and Mac an Ghaill (1997) and others (Mac an Ghaill & Haywood, 2007; Stoudt, 2006), that hegemonic masculinity theory maintains the most utility when investigating the patterns of masculinity within a particular institutional or local context.

DOES HEGEMONIC MASCULINITY THEORY WORK?

The simple yet controversial answer to this question is, "sometimes." Hegemonic masculinity theory has certainly been a salient heuristic tool for understanding male cultures and examining the manner in which male power and privilege are reproduced (see Connell & Messerschmidt, 2005). Its take-up in the literature has been wide, and it provides a theoretical template for the critical scholarship of men across several academic disciplines. Yet in this section I argue that there is a tendency to overstate the utility and applicability of hegemonic masculinity theory.

There are a number of reasons for the popularity of hegemonic masculinity theory. Firstly, Connell's theory effectively captures the homophobic zeitgeist of the time in which it was devised (Anderson, 2009). Connell (1995) situates a hegemonic form of masculinity as necessarily heterosexual, with gay men "at the bottom of a gender hierarchy among men" (p. 78). Considerable research establishes that heterosexuality is the most fundamental characteristic of dominant masculinities in Western cultures (Kimmel, 1994; Richardson, 1996; Skelton, 2001), and the hegemonic dominance of heteromasculinity has been well established in research on masculinities and homophobia (Plummer, 1999; Pronger, 1990).

Hegemonic masculinity theory has also been particularly useful in analyzing male power in bastions of traditional masculinity, such as sport. Competitive team sports have been shown to actively instruct men to value and reproduce orthodox notions of masculinity (Anderson, 2005a; Messner, 1992; Pronger, 1990). As Connell (1995, p. 54) comments, "[M]en's greater sporting prowess has become . . . symbolic proof of superiority and right to rule." Indeed, male team-sport athletes are encouraged to sexually objectify women (Schact, 1996), and Kreager (2007) argues that the masculine cultures fostered in team sports influence men to commit violence against women. Team sports also promote the attitude that homophobia and aggression are necessary elements of masculinity (Messner, 1992). Players who do not live up to the expected orthodox scripts of masculinity are subordinated through physical dominance and discursive ridicule.

As well as maintaining heuristic utility, there are pragmatic reasons for the wide take-up of hegemonic masculinity theory. Moller (2007) argues that the theory has immediate impact because it uses familiar concepts, such as hegemony and subordination, in an accessible manner. Of greater importance, the framework sets out a way of understanding the production and regulation of the stratification of men, and it highlights the unequal distribution of power and privilege between them (Connell, 1995). As Connell and Messerschmidt (2005, p. 846) write, "the fundamental feature of the concept remains the combination of the plurality of masculinities and the hierarchy of masculinities . . . [and this] has stood up well in 20 years of research experience."

However, although Connell's theory has been a useful heuristic tool for understanding masculinities, the theory has been critiqued on a number of fronts.

Wetherell and Edley (1999) argue that hegemonic masculinity theory does not account for the complex and conflicting discursive positions that men take up in society. Men ascribe to orthodox masculinity in some respects, but they also distance themselves from it. As Wetherell and Edley (1999) comment, "recognised social ideals (such as a macho man) can act both as a source for invested identity and as an 'other' to position oneself against" (p. 351). They argue that hegemonic masculinity theory does not account for the contradictory ways in which men position themselves as both contesting and conforming to the rules of masculinity. Wetherell and Edley argue that Connell's theory is, in effect, "too neat" and does not recognize that "complicity and resistance can be mixed together" (p. 352). This critique carries some weight, highlighting the need for scholars to pay close attention to the contextual specificity of masculinity and to fully examine how men contest and comply with the norms in any given setting.

The issue of how men engage with dominant discourses of masculinity remains particularly important, given that scholars have warned that an over-reliance on Connell's theory leads to selective accounts of masculinity and diminished lines of academic inquiry (Pringle, 2005; Rowe, 1998; Sparkes, 1992). Moller (2007) makes the point that academics too readily see patterns of hegemonic masculinity when the social dynamics are in fact far more complex. He argues that solely looking for processes of marginalization and domination can "*reduce* our capacity to understand the ways in which the performance of masculinity may be productive of new socio-cultural practices, meanings, alliances and feelings" (p. 275). Accordingly, it is necessary to guard against a hegemony that sees hegemonic masculinity theory as the first (or even only) explanation for men's gendered behaviors.

This critique is particularly apt because of the level of indeterminacy of hegemonic masculinity theory. Precise definitions are relatively sparse in Connell's work, with, for example, no concise explications of subordinated, complicit, or marginalized masculinities. Instead, Connell provides sections on subordination, complicity, and marginalization, within which the archetypes of masculinity are discussed. This is most problematic for complicit masculinities, which can be understood as conceptualizing men who gain from the patriarchal dividend. Using this definition, it is hard to distinguish men who do *not* have complicit masculinities, and Connell does not offer a framework to do this empirically.

Furthermore, hegemonic masculinity is defined in different ways—as both "the masculinity that occupies the hegemonic position in a given pattern of gender relations" (Connell, 1995p. 76) and the "gender practice which embodies the currently accepted answer to the problem of the legitimacy of patriarchy" (p. 77). The definitions given, particularly of "hegemonic" and "complicity," appear to work as catch-all statements that encompass a large and diffuse range of gendered behaviors. The lack of precise definitions means that hegemonic masculinity theory is only ever fully realized when one considers both the mechanisms of hegemonic masculinity (marginalization and domination) and the archetypes of masculinity provided (complicit, marginalized, etc).

One result of this definitional indeterminacy is that the process of hegemonic masculinity is often conflated with the esteemed archetype of masculinity in a specific setting. This critique is less relevant when one archetype of masculinity maintains hegemonic dominance, as was the case in the 1990s. Research comprehensively documented that esteemed masculinities in that era were predicated in homophobia, aggression, and misogyny (Davis, 1990; Messner, 1992; Pharr, 1997; Sargent, 2001; Williams, 1989). However, the conflation of process and archetype cements the notion of a laddish (or macho) version of heteromasculinity being the only form of masculinity that can be hegemonic, and it makes it harder for changes in esteemed masculinities to be documented (see Lyng, 2009; Moller, 2007). To avoid the conflation of archetype with process, I employ Anderson's (2005b) nomenclature of "orthodox masculinity" to refer to the masculinity that has been shown to have been hegemonically esteemed in Western cultures in the 1990s. A final critique of Connell's work is with regard to how "pure" a form of hegemony is used in her theorizing. This is a substantive issue, and I address it in the next section.

DISTINGUISHING HEGEMONIC MASCULINITY THEORY FROM HEGEMONY

From the discussion of hegemony and hegemonic masculinity above, it is clear that Connell employs hegemony in her theorizations of masculinity, patriarchy, and power. In *Gender and Power*, Connell (1987) provides a short discussion on the use of hegemony, describing it as a "social ascendancy achieved in a play of social forces that extends beyond contests of brute power into the organization of private life and cultural processes" (p. 184). Connell proceeds to explicate two "common misunderstandings" about hegemony. She first highlights that hegemony does not preclude the use of force, and that force in terms of physical, economic, and legal violence is often an important part of a hegemonic system. She also points out that hegemony does not mean the obliteration of other forces, and that hegemony will always be contested by some members of the system. It is clear that hegemony is, as Howson (2006, p. 4) describes, the "foundational concept" of hegemonic masculinity theory.

However, although hegemonic masculinity theory is predicated on an understanding of hegemony, it is not at all clear that hegemonic masculinity is simply the application of hegemony to the study of men. Indeed, Connell's discussion of hegemony is quite brief in *Gender and Power*, and even shorter in *Masculinities*, in which Gramsci's scholarship is not even cited. Several scholars have highlighted that hegemonic masculinity theory is an adaptation or modification of Gramsci's (1971) hegemony theory (Beasley, 2008; Hearn, 2004; Howson, 2006). Because of the subtle and fluid nature of hegemony, it is important to explicate the relationship between hegemony and hegemonic masculinity in order to enable an evaluation of the heuristic utility of each theory in a particular setting.

Howson (2006) critiques Connell's application of hegemony in a densely argued book that examines in great detail the intricacies of hegemony theory as laid out by Gramsci (1957, 1971, 1975, 1985) and others (Femia, 1981;

Laclau & Mouffe, 1985; Mouffe, 1979). Howson (2006) argues that Connell's use of hegemony is somewhat unclear, with the descriptions of hegemony subtly changing throughout Connell's scholarship. To enable an examination of the precise conceptualization of hegemony that Connell uses, Howson (2006) develops what he calls a "tripartite model of hegemony" (pp. 26–33). This consists of "detached hegemony," "dominative hegemony," and "aspirational hegemony."

For Howson, detached hegemony refers to a period in which a ruling elite has become distant from those under its control, who have lost the ability to organize against or even critique the ruling regime. The political elite is sustained by the passivity of the ruled, which turns the groups detached from power into, as Howson (2006, p. 28) describes them, "helpless observers of their own political domination."

Dominative hegemony refers to a period or setting in which there is an organized, active group that campaigns against the ruling class. Accordingly, the ruling elite must "develop its hegemony through the mobilization of State institutional mechanisms, through which its will is enforced as the collective will" (p. 30). This is the conceptualization of hegemony that Connell employs, and it is an oppressive and dominating form of social control.

Finally, aspirational hegemony refers to a benevolent form of hegemony in which the ruling group works with the challenges to its authority to develop responses that are deemed beneficial and positive to all. Howson describes aspirational hegemony as a "programme of profound and continual critique, education and action" (p. 31), and says that it can lead to positive social change.

Howson applies this tripartite model of hegemony to Connell's scholarship in order to highlight the restricted conceptualization of hegemony that Connell employs. Howson (2006, p. 42) writes, "Not withstanding the various descriptional shifts, the theme that persists and is, in effect, threaded through the understanding of hegemony in the theory of practices is *domination*." Howson argues that Connell's work deals only with dominative hegemony, which precludes the possibility of benevolent forms of hegemonic masculinity. Howson (2006, p. 44) writes, "[T]he operation of dominative hegemony must produce domination as natural, thereby blurring the complexity of the cultural framework and negating the possibilities for challenge that can lead to a new social justice."

The idea that hegemonic masculinity is concerned only with a dominating form of social stratification is also raised by other scholars (Beasley, 2008; Demetriou, 2001). Michael Flood (2002) has critiqued hegemonic masculinity theory as being about domination *by definition*. Flood argues that it is fatalistic to assume that the most dominant form of masculinity is one that works to guarantee patriarchy, suggesting that this conceptualization does not allow for a progressive (and hegemonic) coalition of men working toward gender equality. Collier (1998) supports this by arguing that hegemonic masculinity automatically excludes the positive behaviors of men. In response, Connell and Messerschmidt (2005) suggest that this critique is based on a "rigid trait theory of personality" (p. 840) and highlight how many men complicit with hegemonic masculinity undertake actions with sociopositive effects, such as being a good father. This, however, evades the issue raised by Flood and Howson of how the hegemony of hegemonic masculinity (rather than the solitary acts of individuals) is necessarily damaging. Indeed, although Connell and Messerschmidt (2005, p. 846) reconceptualize hegemonic masculinity by rejecting "a single pattern of power, the 'global dominance' of men over women," they continue to argue that hegemonic masculinity is a solution to tensions within gender relations, "tending to stabilize patriarchal power or reconstitute it in new conditions" (p. 853).

Howson (2006) investigates the implications of this point. He argues that even though Connell recognizes the situational and temporary nature of a dominant form of masculinity, this ability for change is limited because it assumes that the project of hegemonic masculinity is primarily aimed at ensuring men's dominance over women. Howson (2006, p. 61) writes:

The imperative to ensure this focus on all things masculine as the basis of the current gender worldview means that the nature of power, which must be cultivated within the complex of gender relations, needs to emphasise a restorative and, therefore, dominative rather than revolutionary and aspirational function.

The conclusion that Howson draws is that a benevolent form of hegemonic masculinity is not possible; Howson (2006, p. 154) argues that for Connell, "hegemony and social justice are mutually exclusive socio-cultural phenomena."

Based on this critique, Howson (2006, 2008) and others (Beasley, 2008; Demetriou, 2001; Hearn, 2004) call for a more nuanced understanding of hegemony to be developed into Connell's work. They argue that this will enable the theory to move beyond understandings that see hegemonic masculinity as a necessarily oppressive form of social control. However, although Connell is open to revising hegemonic masculinity theory (Connell, 2005; Connell & Messerschmidt, 2005), there is little engagement with nuanced understandings of hegemony. Connell and Messerschmidt seem more concerned with the application of hegemonic masculinity at regional and global levels than with refining the theoretical use of hegemony within the theory (Connell & Messerschmidt, 2005; Messerschmidt, 2008).

It is important to note that Connell and Messerschmidt's resistance to changing the theoretical understanding of hegemony in hegemonic masculinity theory is based on a sound argument of empirical heuristic utility. They highlight the success of the fundamental feature of hegemonic masculinity—that central to the social organization of groups of men is "the plurality of masculinities and the hierarchy of masculinities" (Connell & Messerschmidt, 2005, p. 846)—as well as the subordination of nonhegemonic masculinities (Connell, 2005; Connell & Messerschmidt, 2005). They rightly highlight that "this basic idea has stood up well in 20 years of research experience" (Connell & Messerschmidt, 2005, p. 846).

Indeed, Demetriou (2001, p. 347) makes the point that the majority of empirical research that uses hegemonic masculinity theory subscribes to Connell's conceptualization of a dominative form of hegemony. For example, when Mac an Ghaill (1994) and Stoudt (2006) found hegemonic masculinity to be the best way of explaining the behaviors of boys in the schools they studied, this was because the dominant boys' behaviors were oppressive and masculinities were hierarchically stratified.

It is possible that hegemonic masculinity theory has maintained great heuristic utility precisely to the extent that it has employed a restricted notion of hegemony. In other words, it is unknown what the heuristic utility of hegemonic masculinity would be if the theoretical refinement that Beasley (2008), Howson (2006), and others (Hearn, 2004) suggest were implemented.

Given that there are both strong advantages and serious critiques of hegemonic masculinity as theorized by Connell, I now turn to a recent addition to theory on the social construction of masculinities by examining Anderson's (2009) "inclusive masculinity theory," which simultaneously critiques and builds on the theory of hegemonic masculinity. The strength of Anderson's theory is that it keeps the heuristic utility of Connell's scholarship while providing a new way of understanding cultures in which the social order is not maintained through an oppressive form of hegemony.

INCLUSIVE MASCULINITY THEORY

Hegemonic masculinity theory has maintained heuristic utility in understanding men's gendered behaviors in the twentieth century. However, the hegemony of heteromasculinity is not a necessary requirement of the relations between men. Anderson (2009) develops the concept of homohysteria in order to understand the power of cultural homophobia in regulating masculinities. Homohysteria is defined as the cultural fear of being homosexualized, and Anderson suggests that two key factors affect a culture's level of homohysteria: the awareness that anyone can be gay, and the level of cultural homophobia. For Anderson (2009), these factors create "the need for men to publicly align their social identities with heterosexuality in order to avoid homosexual suspicion" (p. 8). He argues that in the period since the emergence of masculinities studies, Western cultures have been highly homohysteric.

Homohysteria is a particularly useful concept here because it historically situates levels of homophobia and theorizes how changing levels of homophobia will impact upon the construction of masculinities in any given culture. For example, in periods of high homohysteria, hegemonic masculinity theory captures the social dynamics of male peer group cultures. However, Anderson (2009, 2011b) argues that this is not the case when levels of homohysteria decrease. He theorizes about the impact this has on men's gendered behaviors with inclusive masculinity theory.

Inclusive masculinity theory employs Connell's theorizing for periods of high homohysteria. Here, homophobia polices and marginalizes boys who stray from the rigid strictures of heteromasculinity. However, Anderson argues that as the level of homohysteria declines, the mandates of the hegemonic form of masculinity hold less cultural sway. For example, in a setting in which homohysteria is decreased but still present, Anderson finds two archetypes of masculinity that vie for dominance: inclusive and orthodox. In this cultural moment, orthodox masculinity remains homophobic but does not maintain cultural control over men ascribing to the more inclusive, pro-gay form of masculinity. Accordingly, neither form of masculinity maintains a hegemonic position.

Inclusive masculinity theory next argues that when a culture is no longer homohysteric, there will be a marked expansion in the range of permissible behaviors for boys and men. The regulative mechanisms of hegemonic masculinity—physical domination and discursive marginalization (Connell, 1995; Connell & Messerschmidt, 2005)—are no longer present or lose utility in such a setting. This is because boys no longer fear being homosexualized, meaning that they can act in ways once considered transgressive without the threat of homophobic policing. This means that although some boys will continue to maintain personal homophobia, the expression of this will be stigmatized in their peer group (Anderson, 2009).

In settings in which overt homophobia is absent, Anderson theorizes that many archetypes of masculinity can be equally socially esteemed. This greatly diverges from Connell's model, and it is supported by a growing body of work documenting multiple masculinities being esteemed in male youth cultures (Adams, 2011; Anderson, 2011b; Anderson & McGuire, 2010; Markula & Pringle, 2005). For example, recent research in school settings documents that decreased homophobia results in the expansion of gendered behaviors for male students (Kehler, 2007; Renold, 2004; Swain, 2006b). Inclusive masculinity theory therefore provides a framework for understanding the gendered dynamics of temporal spaces in which overt homophobia has diminished—something Connell's (1987, 1995) work fails to address.

5

Teenage Boys and Schooling

In *Masculinities*, Raewyn Connell (1995) highlights the importance of schooling in the construction of masculinity. She argues that schools have a pivotal role to play in gender politics, not only because schools provide formal learning around issues of masculinity and femininity, but also because they are sites where masculinity is constructed, often in opposition to the school and authority figures within them. More recently, Connell (2008b, p. 138) has written the following:

> The school as an institution shapes patterns of masculinity by forming a social milieu in which hundreds of children or youth are thrown together over long periods. A peer forum is created in which relations between patterns of masculinity are highlighted.

With this argument, Connell refers to the social interaction that regulates gendered identities in schools. This social reproduction of norms has been conceptualized as the "hidden curriculum." It consists of a multitude of "rules, regulations, and routines . . . students must learn if they are to make their way with minimum pain in this social institution" (Jackson, 1966, p. 353).

The hidden curriculum maintains cultural influence because of the large proportion of time that students are mandated to spend in schools. Indeed, although the school cannot be described as a total institution (Goffman, 1963), the lack of autonomy that students have while compelled to attend school means that the school can be considered what Anderson (2005a) calls a near-total institution. Accordingly, schools are highly influential institutions for male youth with regard to how they understand gender and sexuality (Epstein & Johnson, 1998; Mac an Ghaill & Haywood, 2007).

Although the hidden curriculum is of vital importance to the school experiences of boys, it is also important to recognize the structural impact of schools. Through formalized curricula, policies, and social codes, schools demarcate acceptable modes of behavior and topics of discussion within their walls. For these reasons, Allen (2007b, p. 578) describes schools as "agencies of cultural reproduction;" they do not merely passively reflect societal discourses of sexuality and gender but are active in producing the discourses that circulate within them. This can best be understood as an iterative process between school structures and school cultures that come together to esteem and privilege a charmed set of sexual and gender identities (Connell, 1992; Rubin, 1984). As Pascoe (2007) argues, both "formal and informal sexuality curricula . . . encourage students to craft normative sexual and gendered identities" (p. 27). It is the interaction of a meso- and a micro-level of the social that provides the encompassing and influential discourses of gender and sexuality.

MASCULINITIES IN SCHOOL

One of the first studies of the patterns of masculinities in schools was Paul Willis's (1977) *Learning to Labour*. Here, Willis examined the reproduction of poverty by undertaking an ethnography with a group of working class "lads." He argued that rather than being passive victims, these young men developed a culture of resistance to the institutional middle class norms of the school. Accordingly, their academic failure and social exclusion were shown to be the result of complex social issues and not just of pedagogical failure. Although Willis's analysis focused on class rather than gender, his study paved new ground by linking the male students' cultures with wider structural processes of inequality.

Employing a similar methodology, Barrie Thorne's (1993) *Gender Play* developed social constructionist theorizing of gender in schools because she demonstrated that primary school students were active in creating and enforcing the gendered behaviors in the school she studied. Drawing on participant observations and interviews, Thorne showed that the reproduction of gender norms often occurred during children's play. Her work helped develop the understanding that gender is not the process of individual socialization nor the result of biological difference, but is in fact produced in part through the social interactions of groups of children.

The first book to critically examine the construction of masculinities as the prime focus of analysis, and the way in which masculinities intersect with secondary schooling in the United Kingdom, was *The Making of Men* by Mairtin Mac an Ghaill (1994). This work is important in many ways. First, by presenting a typology of masculinities, Mac an Ghaill empirically documented the existence of multiple masculinities within a school and the fact that boys in these groups had different attributes and aspirations. Second, Mac an Ghaill demonstrated how young men "become" heterosexual through their gendered displays. By deploying homophobia and acting tough, they simultaneously affirmed both their heterosexuality and their masculinity. Indeed, the boys in *The Making of Men* competed with one another for masculine capital, in much the way that Connell (1995) describes. Accordingly, this work also showed the heuristic utility of hegemonic masculinity theory.

Critical scholarship on the intersection of masculinities and education also sought to examine how cultural discourses about boys in school impacted upon the construction of masculinities in school settings. Schools are particularly potent sites for cultural fears about ongoing crises in masculinities, and arguably the most persistent discourse has been a form of crisis debate, as boys are repeatedly positioned as "failing" in schools (Epstein, Elwood, Hey, & Maw, 1998; Martino, Kehler, & Weaver-Hightower, 2009). Responding to feminist concerns about gender equality in schools, a masculinist backlash saw any improvement in girls' achievements in relation to boys, as boys' *underachievement* (Lingard, Martino, & Mills, 2008). In this supposed crisis, as Foster, Kimmel, and Skelton (2001, p. 4) argue, "boys are positioned as 'victims', specifically of: single (fatherless) families; female-dominated primary schooling; and feminism, which has enabled girls' successes." Accordingly, masculinity is regarded as continually at threat in schools, which serves as a conservative rhetorical move that seeks to protect male privilege (Lingard et al., 2008). Viewing masculinity as continually at threat shrouds the damaging aspects of masculinity in school cultures, which much critical scholarship on masculinity seeks to illuminate, examine, and contest.

THE PRESENCE OF HEGEMONIC MASCULINITY IN SCHOOL SETTINGS

The hierarchies of men described by hegemonic masculinity theory have been found in many societal institutions in Western countries (Barrett, 1996; Light & Kirk, 2000), and schools are particularly fertile sites for the investigation of the social processes of hegemonic masculinity (Connell & Messerschmidt, 2005; Martino, 1995). For example, in his study of a secondary school, Stoudt (2006) documents how the processes of hegemonic masculinity are entwined in the cultural and institutional practices of the school. He uses the lens of hegemonic masculinity to document how "normalized, subtle, hidden, and sometimes overt forms of male violence occur . . . every day" (p. 285). Rigid notions of masculinity were enforced through discursive regulation as well as physical and emotional violence. Stoudt also shows how, while severely limiting the types and styles of masculinity that are available in the school, the hegemonic processes enable many of the boys to gain from the patriarchal dividend, at the expense of female students and feminine-acting boys. Robinson (2005) also shows that some boys maintain their heteromasculine privilege through the sexual harassment of girls.

Salisbury and Jackson (1996) examine the processes of marginalization and domination that boys employ in their daily interactions in school. They argue that the sexist and homophobic language (and even sometimes violence) that many boys display is used because those boys feel compelled to act in accordance with the dominant modes of masculinity in school. They argue that the bullying, homophobia, and inability to relate emotionally are direct results of a toxic and vicious form of masculinity.

Although it is certainly true that toxic practices of masculinity can result from the processes of hegemonic masculinity (Connell & Messerschmidt, 2005), less damaging masculinities also proliferate in school settings. For example, Pascoe (2003) demonstrates how the archetype of "the Jock" maintains a hegemonic position in certain school cultures, but she also documents the ways in which boys shore up their masculinity in order to distance themselves from certain aspects of the jock masculinity. Pascoe (2003) writes, "When athleticism is not an option for boys, they draw on other masculine traits associated with the Jock, such as emphasized heterosexuality or dominance, to make up for what they lack in claims on masculinity through sports" (p. 1427).

In addition to drawing on masculine traits such as heterosexuality and violence, boys also associate themselves with students who are more popular than them in order to consolidate their masculine standing. Anderson (2005a) argues that this is most evident in nonathletic boys who support sporting teams, which allows them to gain prestige and privilege from sports even when they do not have the athletic or physical requirements to participate in the sport.

This affiliation with sports in order to gain masculine standing can be explained by Anderson's (2005a) concept of *masculine capital*. Similar to Becker's (1964) notion of human capital, where a person is socially esteemed because of skills or education, Anderson describes masculine capital as a form of currency with which boys buy immunity from stigma. By associating with highly masculinized sports, a boy can raise his masculine capital and provide himself with a level of protection from the marginalization and ridicule that traditionally occur between boys. This is also documented by McGuffey and Rich (1999), who show that athletic boys can occasionally engage in feminized activities because of the capital their sporting participation gives them. And although masculine capital can be raised by other means—for example, by wearing particular brands or styles of clothing, listening to particular types of music, and engaging in pastimes coded as masculine—sports are the most effective form of masculinity insurance (Anderson, 2005a; Pascoe, 2003).

One of the reasons athletics might be so effective in masculinizing boys is that it is a definer of masculinity in both schools and the wider culture (Burgess, Edwards, & Skinner, 2003; Messner, 1992). This is important because it can be argued that sports and education are the two institutions that are most influential in the lives of adolescents (Ferguson, 2000; Messner, 2009; Pollack, 1998). Pascoe (2003) and Anderson (2005a) highlight the centrality of sports in constructions of the Jock that frequently maintain dominance in school settings. Similarly, Light and Kirk (2000) demonstrate that the masculinities in the school they studied were primarily stratified in accordance with how closely boys embodied the practices of the rugby players in that school. Indeed, the argument for studying the intersection of sports, education, and masculinities was laid out by Connell in a recent article. There, Connell (2008b) argues that one must consider the "masculinity-making agendas" (p. 128) of any school, highlighting that physical education often becomes a focus for the reification of dominant masculinities (both within the school and at a cultural level) because of the associations between sports and masculinity (Hickey, 2008).

A thorough body of research employs hegemonic masculinity theory to examine the construction of masculinity in school cultures. However, considerable research exists that documents similar behaviors of marginalization and domination but which does not engage with Connell's theorizing (Pascoe, 2007; Youdell, 2004). Although there are theoretical and heuristic reasons not to employ Connell's theory (see Chapter 4, and Martin, 1998; Whitehead, 1999, 2002), the similarities among findings can be attributed to the homohysteric culture in which the research was conducted. As Anderson (2009) argues, it is the threat of marginalization and subordination that comes from being homosexualized in homohysteric cultures that produces the macho style of masculinity found in school settings.

THE HEGEMONY OF HETEROSEXUALITY IN SCHOOLS

Heterosexuality is privileged in schools through both structural mechanisms and cultural discourses. At the macro (structural) level, Epstein and Johnson (1998) demonstrate that state discourses determine the level and type of discussions concerning sexuality and gender in schools, showing the dynamic interplay between discourses of the media, the state, and individual schools. Through cultural analysis and ethnographic research, Epstein and Johnson examined the ways in which homophobic language in the media impacted upon school cultures and restricted what members of staff felt they were able to discuss with students.

Although it has now been repealed, Section 28 is perhaps the most famous British legislation to explicitly privilege heterosexuality. Widely understood to ban "the promotion of homosexuality in schools," it worked to silence much discussion of homosexuality, making teachers fearful of combating homophobia (Nixon & Givens, 2007). Evidencing its former power, Epstein (1994, p. 7) wrote:

> Some teachers believe that Section 28 does apply directly to their work and are, therefore, afraid of tackling issues of sexuality. Others have used it as a way of avoiding issues which they find uncomfortable and difficult to deal with. Yet others have, no doubt, welcomed it because it legitimated their own homophobia.

Epstein and Johnson (1998) develop this analysis with a discussion of the historical privileging of heterosexuality in school systems. They show how media and political discourses of sexuality and "the family" find particular resonance in schools, where marginalized sexualities are deemed to be a severe threat to the innocence of children, all of whom are assumed to be either heterosexual or asexual (Allen, 2007a; Renold, 2005).

Allen (2007a) also highlights the fact that although sexuality is continually discussed and enacted by students, the official discourse of schools constructs students as nonsexual. She argues that by ignoring homosexuality, failing to discuss sexual desire, emphasizing the risks of sex, and making pronouncements on the necessity of safe sex, schools delimit a particular form of heterosexuality that is to be esteemed—one that Epstein, O'Flynn, and Telford (2003) call "the straightest of straight versions" (p. 129).

The silencing of homosexuality is itself a political act. It is, as Butler (2006) describes, a political operation of hegemonic power "that works by claiming that it is apolitical, uncontroversial, undamaging and non-normative" (p. 532). In this framework, nonheterosexual identities are frequently omitted and obscured in subject curricula. For example, English and humanities subjects consistently avoid opportunities to discuss homosexuality (McCormack, 2011; Woody, 2003), and religious education, when not explicitly arguing that homosexuality is sinful (Hillier & Harrison, 2004), positions it as an "alternative" sexual lifestyle (Martino & Pallotta-Chiarolli, 2003).

The hegemony of heterosexuality is also consolidated through social inter-action. One of the most powerful ways in which this occurs is when people pre-sume that everyone else is heterosexual. Epstein and Johnson (1994) call this the "heterosexual presumption," arguing that it is so powerful that it is "compulsory in its insistent taken-for-grantedness" (p. 194). Indeed, the heterosexual presump-tion is an insidious form of "compulsory heterosexuality" (Rich, 1980) that nor-malizes heterosexuality by again making homosexuality invisible.

The hegemonic position of heterosexuality also impacts upon teachers and how they act in school settings (Ferfolja, 2007; McCormack, 2011). Many gay and lesbian teachers opt to hide their sexual identities in schools because they fear that coming out will damage their social and professional lives (Epstein & Johnson, 1998). I discuss elsewhere how the hegemonic dominance of heterosexuality stopped me from being open about my sexuality with students while I was study-ing for my teaching qualification (McCormack, 2011). My fear of contesting the heterosexual norms of the school led me to alter my gendered behaviors in order to (or in attempt to) conform to the version of heteromasculinity that was esteemed in the school. Indeed, the legacy of Section 28 is that teachers are still wary of discussing homosexuality with students. Nixon and Givens (2007) argue that although the removal of Section 28 was a totemic moment for the lesbian, gay, bisexual, and transgender community, and one that signified a marked change in how sexuality in schools was discussed at a policy level, talking about sexuality with students is still difficult for many gay teachers. Nixon and Givens show that student teachers feel a need to become established professionally before they can be open about their sexuality. One of the reasons for this has been the pervasive pres-ence of homophobia and homophobic language in schools (Ellis & High, 2004).

Homophobic Language in School Settings

The fundamental component of dominant masculinities in school cultures has traditionally been heterosexuality (Drummond, 2007; Mac an Ghaill, 1994; Skelton, 2001). Building on Mac an Ghaill's (1994) and Epstein and Johnson's (1994) scholarship, Nayak and Kehily (1996) discuss the simultaneous production of heterosexuality and masculinity, showing how adolescent boys traditionally deploy homophobia and present hyperheterosexualized versions of themselves in order to prove their heteromasculinity. Similarly, Frosh, Phoenix, and Pattman (2002) demonstrate how heterosexual boys construct an aggressive and orthodox form of masculinity in their social interactions in order to avoid being thought gay.

One way in which boys accomplish the presentation of a heterosexual identity is through the deployment of homophobic language (Chambers, Tincknell, & Van Loon, 2004; Plummer, 1999). There is no precise, generally accepted definition of homophobic language, nor is there one acknowledged way in which to conceptualize the use of homophobic utterances (Lalor & Rendle-Short, 2007; Pascoe, 2007; Thurlow, 2001). For now, I define homophobic language as antigay language that is intended to wound another person. The notion of the intent to wound is important here because it acknowledges that homophobic language is not used only against gay people; it is also used to regulate heterosexual boys' gendered behaviors (Mac an Ghaill, 1994; Pascoe, 2007). Homophobic language can be directed at any boy, and its usage is pernicious in both meaning and intent (Thurlow, 2001; Vicars, 2006).

The use of homophobic language serves two purposes. First, it is the easiest way to show intellectual and emotional antipathy toward homosexuality (Hillier & Harrison, 2004), distancing boys from anything perceived as feminine and/or gay (Plummer, 1999). Second, the discursive policing of orthodox masculinity promotes one's own masculine capital and sense of heteromasculinity (Epstein, 1993; Pascoe, 2007). As Harry (1992) comments, "[B]y viewing the victim as worthy of punishment for having violated gender norms, the offender . . . sees himself as rendering gender justice and reaffirming the natural order of gender appropriate behavior" (p. 116). Accordingly, Martino and Pallotta-Chiarolli (2003) argue that homophobic bullying is viewed as inevitable for boys who transgress the codes of orthodox masculinity.

Highlighting the operational aspects of homophobic language in discrimination, a number of scholars have shown that the primary way to subordinate a boy or young man is to call him a "fag" or accuse him of being gay, even if one does not believe this to be the case (McGuffey & Rich, 1999; Pascoe, 2007).

Pascoe (2007) provides a nuanced perspective of the use of homophobic language with her concept of "fag discourse." Here, the label "fag" is continually hurled between boys as they jockey for masculine position among peers. Although gay boys are most at risk from this discourse, Pascoe argues that all boys fear the "specter of the fag" (p. 71). This is because the epithet is used indiscriminately, even when there is no suspicion that a boy actually is gay. Copious use of the fag discourse occurs because the primary motive is to create a marginalized "other" through which one's own heteromasculinity is consolidated (Butler, 1990).

Pascoe (2007), however, comments that many of the boys who use fag discourse do not intellectualize homophobia. Accordingly, Pascoe's work is somewhat different from other frameworks of language and homophobia. This is because she demonstrates that it is possible for fag discourse to lose its sexualized meaning. If the intent and meaning of homophobia are stripped from the discursive use of "fag," the word will not overtly subordinate homosexuality, even though it might continue to promote a framework of homosexual stigma through discursive regulation of masculinity, particularly if it is directed at boys and men who have committed a gender transgression. I discuss these issues in more detail in Chapter 10.

Scholars have also shown how homophobia impacts students differently according to their race and class (Froyum, 2007; Taylor, 2007), and although the concept of homophobia has been critiqued for its psychologizing tendencies (Adam, 1998), I find that its sociological use continues to maintain heuristic utility (Anderson, 2009; Plummer, 2001).

Gay Students

The welfare of gay students is a difficult and underexamined area in sociological research. This is because until recently it has been very difficult to study gay students in meaningful numbers, as gay students would often stay closeted throughout their years at school. Exemplifying this, Epstein and Johnson (1998) did not interview openly gay students because "it was clearly not going to be possible deliberately to seek out lesbian/gay identified students within the schools where we were doing our observation" (p. 100). Accordingly, research on gay youth has tended to either present retrospective interviews with openly gay men and women who have left school (Flowers & Buston, 2001; Taylor, 2007) or examine students who have had particularly troubled educational lives (see Savin-Williams, 2001).

Research with openly gay students has, however, been undertaken, sometimes even during periods of high cultural homophobia. Reviewing the body of research on the school lives of gay students that was available at the time, Warwick, Aggleton, and Douglas (2001, p. 136) wrote that "many encounter discrimination, are victimized, and are confronted with homophobic verbal and physical bullying. Some will experience mental health problems, some will not. And, to a greater extent than young people in general, some will attempt and commit suicide."

There has also been substantial survey research on gay youth from psychological and quantitative perspectives (see D'Augelli & Hershberger, 1993; Ryan & Rivers, 2003; Wilkinson & Pearson, 2009). Demonstrating the negative psychological effects of homophobic bullying, Ian Rivers's work has been influential in bringing the importance of tackling homophobic bullying to a policy level (see Rivers, 1995, 2001, 2011). Rivers (1995) found that gay youth in schools experienced high levels of bullying, primarily taking the forms of name-calling, ridicule, and (less frequently) physical attacks. He documents that much of this bullying behavior occurred within school buildings, writing that "[l]arge numbers of participants recalled being tormented within their classrooms, along corridors and in the changing rooms before or after sports lessons" (p. 43). Perhaps unsurprisingly, then, research documents that gay students have elevated rates of absenteeism and leave school earlier in comparison to heterosexual students (Rivers, 2001; Warwick et al., 2001).

Research also shows that openly gay students employ a number of strategies to cope with these issues (Wilson et al., 2010). For example, Pascoe (2007) describes how gay students often self-segregate into areas in their school that they perceive as safe, such as drama and music classes. Research also shows how gay students attempt to build their own masculine capital: Epstein (1997) documents how one gay student (somewhat ironically) occasionally deployed homophobic epithets against nonmasculine boys as a way of protecting himself from homophobic bullying, and research has also shown that some gay students build muscle through exercise as a way of adopting one component of orthodox masculinity (Kimmel & Mahalik, 2005).

However, research also shows that a growing number of gay students contest homophobia in some instances (Anderson, 2000; McCormack, 2011; Plummer, 1999). For example, Youdell (2004) presents ethnographic moments on students who have been categorized into a stigmatized homosexual identity by their peers, yet who embrace this identity. She provides examples of the linguistic and bodily ways in which gay identities are marginalized, but she also shows how it is possible for students to reinscribe homosexuality as an identity of which to be proud. Furthermore, participation in Gay–Straight Alliances provides a safe social space for gay students to interact with their peers in (Walls, Kane, & Wisneski, 2010). These spaces also enable students to become politically engaged in issues of social justice and to actively campaign for social change (Russell, Muraco, Subramaniam, & Laub, 2009). As Miceli (2005) argues, Gay–Straight Alliances allow young people to assert a "positive, proud, and unapologetic self image" (p. 13).

THE DIVERSITY OF SCHOOL SETTINGS

Schools are not monolithic institutions in the cultural reproduction of sexual and gender norms. The type of school will affect the sexual and gendered identities within it. For example, schools might have different norms depending on whether they are single sex or co-educational and whether they are public/state or private. Perhaps the most significant variable is that schools have markedly different discourses of sexuality and gender depending on the age range of the students being taught (Epstein & Johnson, 1998; Epstein et al., 2003). For example, it has been shown that there are low levels of homophobic language in primary school settings (Renold, 2004; Thorne, 1993), but these levels increase greatly among boys aged 11 to 16 (Frosh et al., 2002; C. Jackson, 2006). Scholars suggest that this then decreases slightly when students reach the age of 16 to 18 (Aggleton, 1987; Plummer, 1999), although it is important to recognize that high levels of homophobia have been documented in schools with youth aged 16 to 18 as well (Epstein et al., 2003; Pascoe, 2007; Redman and Mac an Ghaill, 1997). And as discussed earlier, the high school does have its own unique institutional norms.

From a review of the literature on school cultures with high levels of homophobia, it is evident that certain traits transcend institutional contexts. Although the precise social dynamics will undoubtedly vary across schools, homohysteric cultures appear to have a particular set of characteristics. In such settings, homophobia is intellectualized by heterosexual boys, homophobic language is used to marginalize feminine boys, sports are central to the stratification of masculinities, boys must maintain emotional distance from each other and disengage from homosocial tactility, and boys engage in fighting and the sexual harassment of girls. These behaviors are the result of what Anderson (2009) calls a homohysteric culture. There exists very little research on how boys behave in a culture of inclusivity.

6

The Rise and Fall of Homophobia

This book demonstrates that homophobia maintains markedly less significance in twenty-first century Britain and America than it used to. In order to explore the significance of this claim, and in order to chart the importance of homophobia in different eras, it is necessary to adopt an historical perspective. In this chapter I demonstrate the rise of homophobia in the twentieth Century and then chart its fall over the past twenty or so years. In order to do this, one must first acknowledge the importance of the second industrial revolution in the bifurcation of gender roles in the early twentieth century (see Cancian, 1987; Williams, 1993). It was during this period that masculinity came to be constructed in opposition to femininity; that masculinity was associated with toughness and labor; and that men's strength became synonymous with their ability to earn a wage (Hartmann, 1976). It was also during this period that heterosexuality and masculinity became conflated in the cultural imagination (Anderson, 2009). It was because of this conflation that men started to police their behaviors in order to avoid being seen as gay (see Ibson, 2002). Following Anderson (2009), I argue that this fear of being socially perceived as gay—something called "homohysteria"—has been the primary reason for the elevated levels of homophobia in the latter half of the twentieth century.

It is my driving thesis that the changes to the stratification of masculinities I discuss in this research result from the fact that British youth culture is no longer homohysteric. In this chapter, I argue that the decline in homohysteria is principally the result of improved and improving attitudes toward homosexuality. This change in social attitudes is the result of a range of factors, including the success of the gay rights movement; the declining significance of religion; the implications of the AIDS epidemic; improving coverage of lesbian, gay, bisexual, and transgender (LGBT) issues in the media; and the expansion of the Internet. Accordingly, I first examine the rise of homophobia in recent decades, alongside the increased awareness of homosexuality, before discussing how matters have improved.

THE APEX OF HOMOPHOBIA

In the United States, the gay rights movement achieved national focus with the 1969 Stonewall Riots, in which gay men and drag queens rebelled against police brutality and persecution. Altman (1973) described the riots as the "Boston Tea Party of the gay movement" (p. 117), and Miller (1995) called them the birth of gay and lesbian liberation. This is because the event galvanized the LGBT community into political action. Indeed, the ramifications of the Stonewall Riots were felt internationally (Adam, Duyvendak, & Krouwel, 1999).

Despite having a tradition of less demonstrative social change, the British LGBT movement engaged in more radical forms of activism following the Stonewall Riots (Miller, 1995). In fact, a year after the riots, the Gay Liberation Front held marches and demonstrations in central London. These marches served two functions. First, they were designed to celebrate coming out and taking pride in one's sexuality. Second, they highlighted the existence of continued homophobic oppression. For example, although same-sex sex between two people was legalized in Britain in 1967 for adults aged 21 or over, the age of consent was made equal to that for heterosexual sex (16) only in 2001.

Although gains were made by LGBT activists in the 1960s and 1970s and identity politics continued to be used to contest homophobic oppression, homophobia greatly increased in U.S. and U.K. cultures in the 1980s (Loftus, 2001; Page & Shapiro, 1992). This was not simply a backlash against the achievements of the radical politics of this era. Instead, it was a "moralist" crusade.

Anderson (2009) argues that the AIDS epidemic was the primary reason for the spike in homophobia in the 1980s, because it made British and American cultures extremely homohysteric. AIDS contributed to the levels of homohysteria in two ways. First, the fact that closeted gay men began dying from the disease demonstrated that *anybody* could be gay. Even though the feminist gains of the 1970s had made homosexuality more visible, before AIDS it was still possible for social conservatives to believe that homosexuality was the disease of a strange group of outcasts, and that it did not exist within their own social networks. With family members, friends, and even Hollywood stars dying from AIDS, this illusion was shattered. Accordingly, the awareness of homosexuality greatly increased during this period. However, the second impact of AIDS was that it greatly stigmatized the gay community.

AIDS was born into an already homophobic social milieu, and it was branded as the "gay disease." This served only to further the social fear of homosexuals. Now, not only did the religious right perceive gay people as a threat to the heterosexual family, but they portrayed them as a threat to humanity. Rather than being considered as a legitimate social and sexual identity, homosexuality was itself equated to a disease (reminiscent of attitudes in the early 1900s). Accordingly, AIDS fostered great awareness of homosexuality combined with high levels of homophobia—a perfect storm for a homohysteric culture in which men would go to great lengths to be socially perceived as heterosexual.

Not only did AIDS have negative effects on the attitudes of the general public toward homosexuality, but it also influenced the gendered behaviors of both gay and straight men. For gay men, who were eager to distance themselves from the emaciated figures of AIDS sufferers, there was a turn to bodybuilding and the display of overly muscled bodies, a physical demonstration of health

(Halkitis, 1999; Petersen, 2011). This was accompanied by a move away from radical forms of contesting homophobia to a more assimilationist politics, in which gay men sought to conform to the norms of the wider heterosexual population (Weeks, 2007).

The high levels of homohysteria and the corresponding homophobia also resulted in a change in the gendered behaviors of heterosexual men (Anderson, 2009). Given the cultural conflation of femininity and homosexuality, straight men sought more explicit ways to portray themselves as masculine. Similar to muscular Christianity at the turn of the twentieth century, strong male physiques were associated with heterosexuality and virtue. This was reflected in the Hollywood iconography of the period: the muscle-bound figures of Stallone and Schwarzenegger filled cinemas as they destroyed enemies by means of their own physicality and indestructibility (Dyer, 1997).

Anderson (2009) further argues that the furor around the AIDS epidemic, and the vitriol aimed at gays and lesbians because of it, combined with a homophobic political culture to exacerbate the anti-gay sentiment of the 1980s. Indeed, the so-called moral majority of American and British culture that condemned homosexuality and AIDS was stoked by politicians who sought political gain from these oppressions. Ronald Reagan and Margaret Thatcher were popular leaders elected by conservative voters, and even though it has been suggested that they were not particularly homophobic themselves, they played to their base by supporting homophobic policies and initiatives (Cretney, 2006). For example, it was Thatcher's government that introduced Section 28 to British schools.

The final component that made the 1980s the apex of homophobia in modern Western culture was the role of religion (Hunter, 1991). In the United States, the religious right became a political force as evangelical Christianity was channeled into the living rooms of families through the televangelism of Pat Robertson, Jerry Falwell, and other homophobes. Although religion has tended to be less extroverted in the United Kingdom, it nonetheless had anti-gay influence both through the media and through bishops who sit in the British Parliament. The synthesis of these factors resulted in an extremely homohysteric culture. Not only were people aware that anybody could be gay, but there was incredible stigma attached to homosexuality. The homophobic media and political culture made it possible for the anti-gay agenda to be promoted with little visible resistance.

It has also been argued that economic changes, specifically the deindustrialization of the United Kingdom and United States, influenced attitudes toward homosexuality (Mizen, 2004; O'Donnell & Sharpe, 2000). However, I suggest that the influence of this is overstated. The argument is that in the 1970s and early 1980s, working class young men were structured into manual labor that, although low-paying, provided job stability, as well as a work environment suffused with traditional notions of masculinity (Willis, 1977). Unable to gain entrance to higher education or the middle class professions, working class young men found moving into manual labor to be a key way for them to demonstrate their transition into adulthood (France, 2007). However, this pathway to adulthood all but vanished as a result of the deindustrialization that occurred in the 1980s and the corresponding mass unemployment of that time (O'Donnell & Sharpe, 2000). It is argued that at that point young working class men turned to homophobia and violence as alternative means of demonstrating their adult masculinity.

Although the changing employment patterns of this period undoubtedly had an impact on the esteemed gendered behaviors of working class British youth (McDowell, 1991; Mizen, 2004), it is important not to place too much emphasis on the role of economic conditions when explaining macho forms of masculinity in the 1980s and 1990s. Although many white working class youth who were economically marginalized and socially excluded in the 1980s might have used homophobia, misogyny, and aggression to demonstrate their own masculinity and entry into adulthood, homophobia in the 1980s was high among middle class men and women as well. In other words, economic conditions do not explain the change in attitudes toward homosexuality that occurred across social demographic groups. This suggests that the other factors I discussed are primarily responsible for the rise in homophobia.

A ZEITGEIST OF DECREASING HOMOPHOBIA

Since the mid-1980s, the time period that Anderson (2009) documents as the most homophobic in Western cultures, attitudes regarding homosexuality have changed drastically. It used to be the case, as Epstein and Johnson (1998) documented, that schools avoided discussion of sexuality because they feared negative responses from parents and the media. Similarly, until its repeal in 2003, Section 28 prohibited the "promotion of homosexuality" in schools. Yet there has been a marked change in how homosexuality is discussed in schools, and this transformation is manifest in the governmental documents about sexuality in schools. For example, these have included guidance on sex and relationships education that includes the recognition of diversity in types of families, information on how to combat homophobic bullying, and strategies for schools to embed proactive ways of preventing homophobia and promoting inclusivity (Atkinson & DePalma, 2008).

The most revolutionary policy directive in the United Kingdom has been the new Single Equalities Act, introduced in 2010. According to this policy, all workplaces are legally compelled to promote inclusivity and diversity of sexual orientation, as well as gender, disability, and race. This legal imperative has been adopted by OfSTED, the British school inspectorate. Schools now failing to protect LGBT students will receive poor inspection reports, and might even be placed in "special measures." Although it is too soon for research to examine the impact of this new law, improving school environments for LGBT youth have nonetheless been documented in Britain, as well as in other English-speaking countries.

Positive attitudes toward homosexuality are increasingly prevalent in British schools (Jones & Clarke, 2007). This has corresponded with a wider range of acceptable gendered behaviors for male students. For example, Swain (2006b) documents the ways in which boys can ascribe to their own "personalized" masculinity without being homosexualized in English schools. In Canada, Kehler (2007, 2009) also describes the ways in which heterosexual students are more able to engage in emotional bonding without being homosexualized. In the United States, Miceli (2005) documents the increasing number of Gay–Straight Alliances, which provide safe spaces for the growing numbers of openly gay students in U.S. high schools (see also Russell, Muraco, Subramaniam, & Laub, 2009).

It is also important to note that some recent research on masculinities in educational settings has not focused on homophobia. For example, both Jackson and Dempster (2009) and Francis, Skelton, and Read (2010) discuss the construction of masculinities in schools, but neither article discusses the impact of homophobia. The implication is that the levels of homophobia in these settings were not high enough to warrant analysis.

Attitudes toward homosexuality have also been shown to be improving in universities. Taulke-Johnson (2008) describes the ways in which gay students' experiences of university are increasingly positive and shows that they do not view themselves as victims of homophobia. Similarly, Anderson and McGuire (2010) document that players on an elite university rugby team espouse pro-gay attitudes and are socially inclusive of gay friends. In forthcoming research, Bush, Anderson, and Carr also evidence an absence of homophobia among undergraduate students studying for sport degrees at an elite university. Similar positive attitudes are also being documented in the United States, where gay students are socially accepted and included by their peers (Adams, 2011; Adams & Anderson, 2011; Anderson, 2011c).

Although some research published in nonacademic sources continues to argue that schools are highly homophobic, most of these studies lack both the methodological and the analytical rigor required to contribute to academic discussion of homophobia in schools (Guasp, 2008; Hunt & Jensen, 2007). It is also worth noting that those who report the most homophobia are often tied to organizations designed to prevent it. For example, Stonewall (the United Kingdom's largest LGBT advocacy group) still argues that there is an "epidemic" of homophobia in schools. However, in doing so, it damages both its own credibility and potentially the experiences of closeted students who are attempting to assess the homophobia of their school environment.

In the United States, the *School Climate Survey* (Kosciw, Greytak, Diaz, & Bartkiewicz, 2009), published on behalf of the gay rights advocacy group GLSEN, documents troublingly high levels of homophobia among school-attending youth, in terms of homophobic language as well as heteronormative practices that lead to hostile school cultures. They show that 61% of participants felt unsafe in school because of their sexual orientation, 72% of students heard homophobic remarks frequently, and 53% of participants had experienced some form of cyberbullying. Although I am skeptical of the ability of quantitative research to appreciate the complexity and nuance of issues of sexuality, there are nonetheless a number of factors that help explain the results of the GLSEN study.

First, although it is more rigorous methodologically than Stonewall's research, there are still issues of reliability and validity. The primary issue concerns how

GLSEN selects those they survey. For example, the GLSEN study draws heavily from those who have attended gay youth groups—young people who are more likely to have experienced problems in school (Savin-Williams, 2001). Also, the report does not provide a breakdown of homophobia by different regions (the "red state/blue state" issue). Finally, the participants of the study were between 13 and 18 years of age and attending a K–12 (secondary) school during the 2008–2009 school year. Research shows that younger students are more homophobic than 16- to 18-year-olds, so comparisons with this older age bracket are limited (Poteat, Espelage, & Koenig, 2009). All of these issues mean that the report is likely to overestimate the levels of homophobia of American high schools. Thus, while the GLSEN study provides cause for concern, it is not evidence of a homophobic zeitgeist sweeping U.S. schools.

It is also worth highlighting that *positive* outcomes can be seen in the GLSEN study. Almost 50% of participants said that their school had a Gay–Straight Alliance or other, similar supportive club. Furthermore, nearly half of all students had access to content about homosexuality in their school libraries—something the study calls "inclusive curricular resources" (Kosciw et al., 2009, p. 58). Almost all students commented that they had access to a member of staff who was supportive of LGBT issues. Given that this report was designed to highlight continued issues for LGBT youth in schools, closer inspection of the findings suggests that schools are becoming more inclusive, in accordance with other research on the issue (Anderson, 2009; Savin-Williams, 2005).

Schools are not the only orthodox institution in which there is strong evidence that levels of homophobia have declined. For example, research shows that cultural homophobia has decreased in multiple sports settings in recent years (Anderson, 2011b, 2011c; Anderson & McGuire, 2010; Harris & Clayton, 2007; Price & Parker, 2003; Markula & Pringle, 2005; Southall, Nagel, Anderson, Polite, & Southall, 2009). In 2005, Anderson used in-depth interviews with 68 openly gay athletes to document how men are increasingly emerging from their athletic closets to contest orthodox scripts of masculinity. He shows that athletes are coming out because of the gay-positive attitudes they assess among their teammates. In a recent update of this research, Anderson (2011b) documents that the experiences of openly gay athletes are continuing to improve. Furthermore, he shows that whereas these positive experiences were once limited to high-achieving players who maintained high masculine and sporting capital, gay athletes who are not central to the team's success are also having very positive experiences when they come out.

A growing body of academic research argues that the decrease in cultural homophobia has also occurred in the wider British and American culture (Anderson, 2009; Sherkat, Powell-Williams, Maddox & de Vries, 2011). In *The World We Have Won*, Weeks (2007) charts the changing social landscape for gays and lesbians in the United Kingdom. Although he is careful to highlight the fact that the privileging of heterosexuality persists in multiple forms, and although he uses a global perspective to contextualize the Western concept of gay rights,

Weeks highlights the improved social, political, and legal context for gays and lesbians in the twenty-first century.

This improved social context is also explicated by McNair's (2002) book, *Striptease Culture*. In it, McNair argues that because of a proliferation of media discourses on sexuality (in no small part the result of the Internet), there has been a "democratisation of desire." This has provided gay men and women with increased visibility, greater recognition, and more sympathetic and positive media portrayals (Netzley, 2010). In this context, the greater visibility of LGBT people and issues is both evidence of and a reason for decreasing homophobia.

Anderson (2009) provides further evidence of improved cultural attitudes toward homosexuality by examining data from the past 30 years' worth of *British Social Attitudes* surveys. In 1987, 64% of people thought that homosexuality was "always wrong," but this figure had dropped to 24% by 2006. Anderson also uses ethnographic studies to document how the changing attitudes toward homosexuality in Britain materialize in the gendered behaviors of male youth, showing that different multiple archetypes of masculinity can be esteemed in the same setting. He shows that men can engage in physical intimacy with other men without threat to their socially perceived heterosexual identities. Indeed, recent research by Anderson, Adams, and Rivers (2010) shows that young heterosexual men in Britain are kissing each other as a demonstration of love. These men do not interpret the kisses as indicative of same-sex desire, and they are not concerned about whether other people view them in this way.

I suggest that the decrease in homophobia among heterosexual young men can be understood as a virtuous circle of decreasing homophobia and expanded gendered behaviors. As homophobia declines, more tactile and intimate behaviors are available to men, who discover that these taboo behaviors actually have positive effects. This leads to a further decrease in homophobia as same-sex intimacy loses its stigma. It is this virtuous circle that helps explain the speed of changing attitudes toward homophobia. Accordingly, although the seminal literature on masculinities in education documents high levels of homophobia and the esteeming of orthodox masculinity, contemporary research suggests that levels of homophobia have significantly decreased, and that a more varied set of gendered behaviors is becoming available to male youth.

EXPLAINING THE DECREASE IN HOMOPHOBIA

The Success of the Gay Rights Movement

One of the key reasons for the dramatic improvement in attitudes toward homosexuality over the past few decades has been the success of the identity politics of the gay rights movement (Bernstein, 1997). Plummer (2006) argues that it is through identity politics that a new culture of LGBT rights has emerged in both Britain and the United States. One of the key ways in which this has occurred is through the visibility of gay identity. As the power of the media in influencing opinions was recognized, gays and lesbians fought to be seen and heard in newspapers and on television. Yet when openly gay male characters first appeared on television screens, they were critiqued for conforming to stereotypes of gay men, being desexualized by not having boyfriends nor displaying the same level of sexual activity as straight couples, and being marginal rather than central characters (Walters, 2001).

However, dramatic changes have occurred in the past ten years. In the United Kingdom, every major British soap now features a gay person as a regular character whose sexuality is no longer central to storylines. Gay comedians including Graham Norton, Paul O'Grady, and Alan Carr host prime-time chat shows on the major television channels, and an openly transsexual woman, Nadia, won a series of the television show *Big Brother*. As more and more celebrities come out (from Ricky Martin to Dale Winton), the reaction in British culture is increasingly, "So what?" This is also true in the United States, which has seen greater numbers of more positive portrayals of LGBT characters (Netzley, 2010).

This has corresponded with other forms of progress in the media. Kian and Anderson (2009) document that media portrayals of openly gay sportsmen are increasingly positive—something borne out in the United Kingdom by the press response to openly gay professional athletes Stephen Davies (in cricket), Gareth Thomas (in rugby), and Anton Hysen (in soccer). There has also been a positive change in how the media discusses heterosexual men. Providing a genealogy of the term "metrosexuality," David Coad (2008) documents how the way men are portrayed in the media has become more inclusive, with the result that there is less cultural coercion for men to act according to one archetype of masculinity.

The rise in gay visibility is not restricted to the media. As Weeks (2007, p. 146) notes, "in the arts, theatre, politics, trade unions, academia, business, television, journalism, the police . . . there are now openly gay people in prominent places." And in addition to an openly gay presence, Weeks highlights the ordinariness of these gay people's everyday experiences. This supports Savin-Williams's (2005) argument that gay youth in the United States have increasingly positive experiences and should not be viewed as an "at risk" group.

Despite a history of criminalization of "gay behaviors," there have been several recent legal victories in Britain and the United States. In 2002, the U.S. Supreme Court ruled that antisodomy laws are unconstitutional, and in 2010 the U.S. Congress laid out a mechanism for repealing the "Don't Ask, Don't Tell" policy prohibiting gays from serving openly in the military, with the policy ending in September, 2011. There have been myriad other municipal and state victories for LGBT people in other U.S. states. Things are more positive in the United Kingdom. In Britain, it is illegal to be fired for being gay, and gay men and lesbians are allowed to serve openly in the military. Furthermore, gay couples can adopt children and maintain all the rights of marriage through civil partnership. Accordingly, in most respects, gay men and women have legal equality with heterosexuals. This removes one key form of the stigmatization of homosexuality (Rubin, 1984; Weeks, 2007).

The Role of the Internet

Advancements in technology have also greatly influenced how people live in the twenty-first century (Nagel, 2003; O'Connell Davidson, 2005; Plummer, 2003). In a process known as globalization, cheap international flights and new forms of communication have allowed people to travel the world and gain experiences of different countries and cultures. Furthermore, with the mass expansion of the Internet, it is possible to experience a diverse range of cultures—including sexual cultures—without leaving one's home.

The role of the Internet is particularly important to the stratification of sexuality and gender in society (Valkenburg & Peter, 2008). For LGBT youth, it has provided a safe space for them to begin to explore their sexual identities. For example, Gray (2009) documents the ways in which sexual-minority youth in rural areas of the United States use the Internet as a way of making friends, finding partners, and developing their own sexual identity. Harper et al. (2009) suggest that it also makes the coming out experience less fraught. When talking to strangers in anonymous chat rooms, gay and lesbian youth seek advice on how to come out, trialing the strategies they will use when disclosing their sexual identity to friends and family.

The Internet also gives more control to young LGBT people as they explore sex. They increasingly organize "hook-ups" on the Internet or use Web cams to have virtual sex. This method of obtaining sex is so successful that research in the United Kingdom shows that a large majority of British men now find their first sexual partner by using the Internet (Bolding, Davis, Hart, Sherr, & Elford, 2007).

The Internet has also had great influence on the gendered and sexual lives of young heterosexual men. Indeed, it provides *all* young people who have access to computers with a level of autonomy from parents and other adults, enabling them to explore and express their own identities in ways their parents do not know about and might not like (Robards, 2010). As young people readily express their sexual identities on Facebook, much of the cultural taboo about asking a person's sexuality is vanishing among youth.

McNair (2002) highlights the power of the Internet in changing the structural and cultural organization of the sexual. He writes, "[T]o a much greater extent than in previous technological leaps, the internet has globalized the porn industry, and eroded the capacity of individual nation states to police the consumption of sexually explicit material by their citizens" (p. 57). Adopting a pro-porn feminist position (see also Rubin, 1993a), McNair argues that the Internet has been instrumental in democratizing desire, opening up sexual and gender positions that had previously been regulated by nation-states and geographically determined community standards. Anderson (2011a) highlights that the panoply of sexual images and videos that young heterosexuals find on the Internet expands their minds. Indeed, he argues that theInternet has been "instrumental in exposing the forbidden fruit of homosexual sex, commodifying and normalizing it in the process" (2009, p. 6).

Although debate rages in popular culture about the role of the Internet in social life (Elliot & Lemert, 2006; Weeks, 2007), it has undoubtedly been influential in decreasing the levels of homophobia in Western cultures (Anderson, 2011a; McNair, 2002). Whether to proclaim their sexual identity and forge new friendships on social networking sites or to watch porn and organize hook-ups, the Internet has been used prodigiously by young people to expand sexual and social horizons (Bogle, 2008; Hillier & Harrison, 2007).

Economics and Emerging Adulthood

I have argued that economic conditions had little influence on the elevated levels of homophobia in the 1980s, but it is worth highlighting that more recent changes in economic conditions would support a decrease in homophobia among working class youth. Whereas the deindustrialization of British society saw manual labor and manufacturing jobs relocated overseas, a resurgent service sector fueled a new range of job opportunities for young working-class men in the 1990s and 2000s. Unable to enter the middle class, masculinized world of finance, these young men instead worked in more feminized occupations, such as tourism, leisure, and service sectors (McDowell, 2003). Accordingly, white working class youth were placed in jobs in which they were compelled to act in opposition to the laddish, aggressive masculinity that was prevalent in the 1980s and early 1990s (Francis, 1999; Salisbury & Jackson, 1996).

Importantly, as these young men engaged in this work and took pride in their newfound employment, they recalibrated their understandings of feminized actions so that they were compatible with their masculine sense of self. In this new context, working in factories and industrial jobs became archaic and anachronistic rather than something to aspire to, as male youth enjoyed the relative freedom and autonomy that the feminized service sectors offered (Kenway & Kraack, 2004). Although some working class youth continue to be marginalized from deindustrialized jobs (Nixon, 2009), many others have reexamined their gendered identities in light of working within a feminized terrain (see also Anderson, 2008b).

The other key factor concerning economic conditions that has helped in the development of more positive attitudes toward homosexuality is a delayed entry into adulthood. Arnett (2004) identifies a social trend that instead of entering the work place and starting a family, today's 16- to 26-year-old white men forge close friendships with their male peers. He identifies a changing social dynamic that accompanies increasingly flexible (and insecure) career paths, alongside a lessening of restrictive sexual morality. Instead of building a career, these men play video games, talk sports, and watch porn (see also Kimmel, 2008). Arnett (2000, 2004) calls this phase of life "emerging adulthood." Recognizing that when young people leave home today they do not automatically take on the roles and responsibilities of adulthood, Arnett (2004) writes the following:

> For today's young people, the road to adulthood is a long one. They leave home at age 18 or 19, but most do not marry, become parents, and find a long-term job until at least their late twenties. From their late teens to their

late twenties they explore the possibilities available to them in love and work, and move gradually toward making enduring choices. Such freedom to explore different options is exciting, and this period is a time of high hopes and big dreams. (p. 3)

This, then, means that in a culture of decreasing homophobia, young men today have the time and space to engage in a panoply of behaviors, experiencing new sexual, gendered, and emotional sensations and feelings. This period of emerging adulthood provides the physical time and space to engage in new gendered behaviors, while the culture of decreased homophobia ensures the intellectual and emotional freedom to do so.

PART III

The Declining Significance of Homophobia

7

Decreasing Homohysteria

In this chapter I document the seismic shift that has occurred in attitudes toward homosexuality within the informal school cultures at the three research sites. I find that heterosexual boys intellectualize and espouse pro-gay attitudes. This is supported by the experiences of openly gay students, as well as by the absence of homophobic language. In addition to this, I explicate the ways in which boys are physically tactile with each other, demonstrating that they do not fear being homosexualized in these settings. Accordingly, I present empirical findings on the gendered behaviors of male high school students that contrast with older literature (e.g., Mac an Ghaill, 1994; Martino & Pallotta-Chiarolli, 2003; Salisbury & Jackson, 1996). I then discuss the implications that this has for theorizing masculinity construction in these high schools.

MASCULINITIES IN HOMOHYSTERIC SCHOOL CULTURES

Previous research has established that high levels of homophobia are common-place throughout educational institutions in the United Kingdom (Ellis & High, 2004; Epstein & Johnson, 1998). Ethnographic investigations also demonstrate that homophobia is a central mechanism in the maintenance of male students' heteromasculine identities (Mac an Ghaill, 1994; Pascoe, 2007). Thus, rather than being reproduced through personal prejudice, homophobia often serves as a form of heterosexual and masculine social currency (Plummer, 1999) Homosexual suspicion is effective in relegating boys in the masculine hierarchy because any-one's heterosexuality can be questioned in a homophobic culture (Anderson, 2008a).

Anderson (2009) develops the concept of homohysteria in order to understand the power of cultural homophobia in regulating masculinities. As I discuss in Chapter 4, homohysteria is defined as the cultural fear of being homosexualized, and high levels of homohysteria often cause boys to avoid any association with homosexuality. Homohysteria is a particularly useful concept here because it his-torically contextualizes levels of homophobia and theorizes how changing levels of homophobia will impact on the construction of masculinities in any given cul-ture. For example, in periods of high homohysteria, the discursive and physical regulation of other boys' behaviors results in one archetype of masculinity being esteemed above all others (Connell, 1995). Boys who most closely embody this standard are accorded the most social capital, whereas those who behave in ways that conflict with this valorized form of masculinity are marginalized.

However, Anderson (2009) argues that as the level of homohysteria declines, the mandates of the hegemonic form of masculinity hold less cultural sway. Inclusive masculinity theory argues that with a decrease in homohysteria comes a marked expansion in the range of permissible behaviors for boys and men. The regulative mechanisms of hegemonic masculinity—physical domination and discursive marginalization (Connell & Messerschmidt, 2005)—are no longer present or lose utility in such a setting. This means that although some boys will continue to maintain personal homophobia, its expression will be stigmatized in their peer group (Anderson, 2009).

There are four main ways in which the influence of high levels of homohysteria on boys' gendered behaviors is made evident. One consistent finding is that boys *intellectualize homophobic attitudes* in order to avoid being homosexualized. They talk of their "disgust" of homosexuality, calling it unnatural, immoral, or suggesting that it goes against religious doctrine (Hillier & Harrison, 2004). Those boys who support gay students and/or gay rights are homosexualized and ostracized within the school community for their association with homosexuality (Anderson, 2000; Plummer, 1999).

The second way is that boys *marginalize and harass gay students*. Heterosexual male students avoid contact with gay students, and they also bully and harass their peers because of their perceived or actual sexual identity (Epstein & Johnson, 1998; Plummer, 1999). Accordingly, many gay students report negative school experiences, ranging from being ostracized to verbal harassment and physical assault (Rivers & Cowie, 2006; Warwick, Aggleton, & Douglas, 2001); this is also true of heterosexual boys who are feminine or who do not conform to traditional notions of masculinity (Mac an Ghaill, 1994).

Boys are also encouraged to *disengage from homosocial tactility*, because this is also homosexualizing in homohysteric settings (Derlega, et al., 1989; Floyd, 2000). Accordingly, high levels of homohysteria mean that boys are "prohibited from holding hands, softly hugging, caressing, or kissing" (Anderson, 2009, p. 8). With the exception of certain team sports, physical touch is normally limited to fighting and acts of aggression (Ferguson, 2000). This means that when heterosexual boys "inappropriately" touch one another, they normally find it necessary to publicly defend their heterosexuality through homophobia and other heterosexualizing behaviors (Plummer, 1999).

Finally, boys *employ homophobic language* in order to distance themselves from homosexuality (Chambers, Tincknell, & Van Loon, 2004; Thurlow 2001). This serves two purposes. First, homophobic epithets help boys distance themselves from anything perceived as feminine and/or gay (Epstein, 1997; Plummer, 1999). Second, the discursive policing of orthodox sexual and gender norms promotes one's own heteromasculine capital (Epstein, 1993; Frosh, Phoenix, & Pattman, 2002; Mac an Ghaill, 1994). Accordingly, homohysteria has a negative impact on both the attitudes and the behaviors of heterosexual boys, meaning that it is important to examine the continued significance of homohysteria in school settings.

INTELLECTUAL ACCEPTANCE OF HOMOSEXUALITY

Colin is a popular and sporty student at Standard High. When talking about gay rights, Colin stated, "I believe in equality for gays. I mean, you wouldn't treat them any differently, would you?" In fact, all of the boys interviewed at Standard High openly supported gay rights. Jack's support of gay rights was unequivocal. He said, "I believe that gay people should be equal in society. Anything else is wrong. I mean, if you love someone, what does it matter if it's a man or a woman?" Evidencing how normal these positive attitudes toward homosexuality are, Nick was unable to provide a reason for his pro-gay attitude. Confused, he asked, "Well, why wouldn't you support gay rights?"

Pro-gay attitudes were also held by students at Religious High. Lee said, "I have no problem with gay people. Gay, straight, what does it matter?" Geoffrey commented, "In my book, there's nothing wrong with being gay." Nine of the twenty-two boys interviewed related this to their contact with openly gay students at the college. For example, Alex said, "Since coming here, I've met gay guys. They're cool, and so is them being gay." Similarly, Zak commented, "One of my mates is gay, of course there's nothing wrong with it."

Even those students who appear less comfortable discussing homosexuality espoused pro-gay attitudes. For example, Dean said, "I don't see what's wrong with homosexuality. I wouldn't want to do anything gay, but then I'm straight." Cooper added, "It's not my thing, right? But I'm not against it." What is notable for a religious college, however, is that the argument that homosexuality is against religious doctrine maintained no support among the boys I talked to (cf. Hillier & Harrison, 2004). Geoffrey said, "I know it's a religious college, but no one cares about that. None of my friends go to church." Lewis said, "I think homophobia is homophobia, and no one buys the religion stuff anyway."

The intellectual acceptance of homosexuality is also demonstrated by participants' responses to hearing about my own homophobic school experience. For example, one day at Standard High, while walking with Nick and Rob to get soda from the local shop and discussing what it means to be homophobic, Nick asked about homophobia at my school. I discussed my experiences of pervasive homophobic language, and Nick replied, ". . . that's just excessive. It's like racism used to be." Rob agreed, adding, "That's out of order; I know you wouldn't find that here." The expression of homophobia was a surprise to these students, and it was stigmatized at Standard High.

The stigmatization of homophobia occurred at Religious High, too. For example, Dominic said, "I think it's actually homophobia that's bad now. If you were homophobic, you would be too embarrassed to say anything." Craig, a charismatic and sporty student, commented, "I knew guys who were homophobic back in school. But you come here, and meet gay guys, and you grow up." Anthony agreed, saying, "You just realize it's stupid." James commented, "It's Neanderthal. Who cares whether someone's gay? I mean, get over it."

The least progressive attitudes to homosexuality were held by boys at Fallback High, who had all experienced troubled family and/or educational lives. Even here, though, none of the students intellectualized homophobia. Phil said, "You're born gay or straight. So we shouldn't try and change people. I don't have a problem with it." When asked about gay people, Perry replied, "I'm not bothered, mate." However, a minority of students (three in total) expressed only tolerance for homosexuality. For example, Charlie commented, "It's their choice. I don't care what other people do if it doesn't affect me." Jamie showed slightly more ambivalence, saying, "I don't want to know about it, but they can do what they want." Nonetheless, these responses are noteworthy because it has been suggested that boys with social and economic problems maintain high levels of homophobia (Froyum, 2007).

It should also be noted that there are no openly gay students at Fallback High. This means that these students might not have socialized with gay boys their own age, a factor that research suggests is beneficial to acquiring pro-gay attitudes (Adams & Anderson, 2011; Smith, Axelton, & Saucier, 2009). Although it is quite possible that gay students opted to leave Fallback School at the age of 16, the small population size (of only 18 male students) means it is not significant that there are no openly gay students in this cohort.

In addition to espousing pro-gay attitudes, many boys embraced things that are socially coded as feminine or gay. For example, in the common room at Standard High, posters advertised auditions for the popular youth television show *Skins*. The production company was seeking both main characters and extras for the new series of the show, and this caused considerable excitement among many of the boys. "Are you trying out for the auditions?" Sam asked Matt as he entered the common room. "Definitely, man, wouldn't miss it, I even know what I'm going to wear," he replied. Later, Kai, Joe, and Jack were discussing the auditions. Joe said, "See, you should have done drama like me, you'd stand more of a chance." Kai laughed and said, "They'll just see my style and know they've got to have me. I mean, who could turn this down!"

Although research documents that acting and drama are feminized or homosexualized activities (Pascoe, 2007), these boys were free to express interest in and excitement about acting auditions in this setting. Although the popularity of the show might be a mitigating factor in this case, the freedom to associate with things that are socially coded as feminine or gay is also evidenced by the proclamation of a song that is socially coded as gay as an unofficial school anthem.

"Barbie Girl" is a camp 1990s song that was played regularly in the common room. It imagines life as a Barbie doll ("I'm a Barbie girl, in a Barbie world. Life in plastic, it's fantastic"). One time, Rob danced to the song, one hand in the air, the other pulling his T-shirt up his torso. I asked him why the song is played so often. He laughed, answering, "You could say it's our school anthem." Indeed, students were often seen dancing to the song, and it was played with almost monotonous frequency.

The students were aware that the song has gay associations. Sam said, "It's brilliant. It's pretty gay, too!" Jack added, "I guess we grew up with it, so it's always been a song everyone likes. Then it was in an episode of *Family Guy*, which was funny because, you know, we were already playing it." When I commented that the song is viewed as gay in the wider culture, Jack smiled, saying, "Yeah, so what? Who cares if it's gay?" Although irony might be involved when students claim the song as a school anthem, it demonstrates that these boys do not fear being homosexualized by association with things that are socially coded as gay.

Students' understandings of homophobia also point to the intellectual acceptance of homosexuality. While asking students at Standard High to discuss their understandings of anti-gay prejudice, it became apparent that although the terms "heteronormativity" and "heterosexism" were alien to the students, some of the concepts were not. Chiefly, the students at Standard High *redefined* aspects of institutionalized heteronormativity under the rubric of homophobia. In other words, what academics call heteronormativity (Atkinson & DePalma, 2009; Epstein & Johnson, 1994; Ferfolja, 2007) the students called homophobia. This is more than just a reflection of a limited vocabulary—they had identified the institutional exclusion of discussions about homosexuality as homophobia.

Evidencing this, while I was conversing with a group of students during recess, Justin asked about my impressions of Standard High, saying, "So, do you think this school is bad for homophobia?" I replied, "No, not really. I wish my time at school was a bit more like it." Justin looked a little perplexed and asked, "Don't you find it homophobic?" When I inquired about what he meant, Justin responded by highlighting that there are no openly gay teachers, and that "gay stuff is never spoken about in lessons." Nick added, "Yeah, I asked Mrs. Jones something once about homosexuality, and she told us not to ask those questions."

Another day, I discussed the homophobia present at my school, saying that the boys were called gay if they even touched each other. "Really?" Martin said. "That's just stupid." Rob added, "So you think [Standard High] is good? What about there being no gay teachers?" At other times, participants would comment to me about the lack of openly gay sportsmen, or the way in which openly gay pop stars such as Will Young are treated differently. In total, at least 15 boys discussed with me types of heteronormative practice as evidence of homophobia. Accordingly, it appears that at least some students are growing increasingly aware of the complex manner in which heteronormativity operates at Standard High. However, they identify this privileging of heterosexuality as a form of homophobia. This suggests that not only are homophobic attitudes being suppressed, but these students have intellectualized pro-gay attitudes and have even begun to critically interrogate at least some dominant sexual norms.

This intellectual acceptance of homosexuality is significant for three reasons. First, even though it is possible that students were overstating their advocacy of gay rights, this is still markedly different from a time when students had to explicitly proclaim homophobic attitudes in order to maintain a heterosexual identity (Frosh, Phoenix, & Pattman, 2002; Mac an Ghaill, 1994; Salisbury & Jackson, 1996). Second, it appears that at both Religious High and Standard High, homophobia, rather than homosexuality, is stigmatized. Although this might result in homophobic attitudes being forced underground (which I would argue is no bad thing in itself), this still serves as evidence that homophobia maintains less cultural sway with the majority of students at these institutions (Epstein & Johnson, 1998; Pascoe, 2007). Third, substantial evidence exists that attitudes and behavior are closely correlated, meaning that these attitudes are a strong indication that these boys will behave in ways that support gay students (Farley, 1997; Loftus, 2001).

SOCIAL INCLUSION OF GAY STUDENTS

The social inclusion of gay students is another key way of documenting that a culture is not homohysteric. Religious High has the most openly gay students, all of whom report positive experiences at the school. For example, Keith said, "Being gay just isn't that much of an issue. It's cool." Greg also commented about the inclusivity of heterosexual students:

> I was a bit worried about the religious thing at first, but it's good here. I think coming out may have helped me make friends. Once people knew I was gay, I could be more relaxed around them. I could be more myself.

Lesbian students have similar experiences. Maxine commented, "No one cared when I said I was a lesbian. My friends weren't surprised, and no one else seems bothered." Similarly, Erica said, "I've never got hassle for being a lesbian. People either think it's cool or they don't care."

Not only did gay students report being happy at Religious High, but they were also socially included in the mainstream workings of the high school. For example, Max was elected student president when he was 16. However, during the election, rather than viewing his gay identity as a hindrance, Max made his homosexuality a part of his campaign. Not only were his posters framed with rainbow borders, but he was pictured in only his underwear; the byline for the poster read, "Vote Max . . . because he'll do anything you ask him to" (see Fig. 7.1). In addition to this, in his campaign speech, Max included an argument that his homosexuality helps him better understand issues of equality. Max was applauded at the end of his speech, and as he left the hall after the event, several athletic boys gathered around, congratulating him. One commented, "Mate, you're such a homo," and another said, "You're so gay. You've got my vote." Max laughed, saying, "I'm gay for all of you."

Max's election is particularly noteworthy because whereas the literature suggests that openly gay students can be popular only if they embody orthodox notions of masculinity (Epstein, 1997; Pascoe, 2007), Max exhibits flamboyant mannerisms and self-identifies as a queen. Max is not the only camp student at Religious High, either. Thomas would frequently wear a woman's belt over his shirt. He said, "I'm quite alternative in how I dress. But people don't care. No one's

For Freedom, Fairness and Fun!

Vote MaX Morris

For Student Union PRESIDENT!

"Because he'll do anything you ask him to!...

...well, almost anything."

Figure 7.1 Max's poster for Student President.

hassled me, but I do get the odd funny look." I asked whether he ever felt isolated or excluded at Religious High. "Not really," he replied, "I've got my friends, my group I'm happy with. No one bullies me or anything." Laughing, he said, "They just think I'm really, *really* gay."

In addition to being camp and dressing flamboyantly, openly gay students freely talked about their sexuality and sex lives. Max said, "I talk about sex all the time. That's partly because I like to talk about it, but straight guys ask me questions about gay sex, too." Eddie also commented,

I talk about sex with my straight mates. One time, I gave my best mate Helen advice on how to give head. The next day, her boyfriend came up and hugged me. I asked him what that was about, and he said, "For what you told Helen yesterday."

The inclusivity at Religious High is also evidenced by the reception Ross received when he came out as transsexual (female-to-male). First identifying as a lesbian, Ross later told friends that he was going to change his name and start using the male pronoun. He said, "I lost some friends when I said that. They just gradually started seeing me less and less. But I've made new friends, too." Ross maintained that he has not been bullied or harassed since coming out, a claim supported by my participant observations—I often saw Ross in the canteen and other social areas, and I never observed him being bullied or marginalized. It is possible that those students who distanced themselves from Ross might have maintained transphobia, but the level of Ross's social inclusion is remarkable when compared to that experienced by others (Grossman & D'Augelli, 2006).

There are no openly gay students present at Fallback High. However, many students there have had previous contact with gay males. While being interviewed, Stuart spoke about his older brother's gay friend:

> My brother's best mate came out a few years ago. He's 'round the house all the time at the moment, because he can't get a fucking job. He's a cool guy, though he always beats me at *Street Fighter* [a computer game].

Several other students reported a similar level of contact with gay people. For example, Phil said, "Yeah, I've had a gay friend. His parents moved, though, so we don't see each other much now." Conversely, no participants indicated that they had distanced themselves from friends or family because they knew them to be gay.

At Standard High, there is only one openly gay student. Tom is quiet and hard-working, and he does not maintain high masculine or social capital. However, he is not marginalized in the school. Discussing his school experience, Tom said, "Guys don't bully each other here, and no one would be homophobic. I'm happy at [Standard High]." Tom said that he does not feel subordinated by his peers, commenting that although he was bullied "a little" with homophobic language in earlier years, this does not happen in the high school. "I like it here. The other guys are cool with it. I've got my friends and nobody is bothered." Tom has only two close friends at Standard High, but he insisted that this was because he spends most of his time in the library, and not because he is gay. "I'm a quiet guy. That's just who I am," he said. Indeed, many of the boys at Standard High are keen to be inclusive of Tom.

Sam, a large, muscular, heterosexual student, said that he is friendly with Tom. "Whenever I see him around, I say hi. He's a nice guy." When I asked Sam whether Tom's homosexuality makes him less popular, he responded, "No. That's irrelevant. He's just a quiet guy. I think he's here to work more than have fun." Joe provided another example of this inclusivity when he told me that he once felt bad seeing Tom sitting alone on a bus. Knowing about Tom's shyness, he summoned two friends, and together the boys sat with Tom for the rest of their journey. Joe said, "He was all on his own. I mean, I couldn't just let him sit there." Of the 12 students interviewed, 5 discussed how they are friendly with Tom, giving examples of how they have included him in their social activities.

My participant observations support the interview data, as I observed several instances of boys with high levels of popularity including Tom in their activities, even though Tom was not part of their friendship group. For example, one lunch break, Colin and Grant were leaving the college grounds to get some food from the local shop. Seeing Tom ahead, Grant shouted, "Hey Tom, you going to the shop? Wait up, we'll walk with you." The boys then spoke amiably together as they made the 15-minute round trip. This is a typical example of the many small acts of inclusion extended toward Tom by boys whom Tom did not identify as friends.

Richard is the only student who identifies as heterosexual but who is suspected to be gay by some of his peers. Even here, though, other heterosexual students argued that Richard must be straight because he had not openly self-identified as gay. In a conversation in the common room, Grant asked Ethan and Adi whether they thought Richard might be gay. Grant said, "I don't think he is. I just wondered." Adi replied, "Well, he could be, I suppose. But he'd tell us if he was." Ethan agreed, saying, "Yeah, why wouldn't he?" It is noteworthy, however, that (to my knowledge) none of the boys has ever asked Richard about his sexuality.

It is also important to note that the boys' questioning of Richard's sexuality did not seem to affect their interactions with him. For example, Grant was talking with Richard when he, for no apparent reason, leaned over and kissed Grant on the cheek. Grant lurched away and (through laughter and a smile) said, "Stop that." Richard momentarily raised his eyebrows and then returned Grant's smile. The two boys then continued with their conversation. Although Grant's telling Richard to "stop that" was a method of consolidating his heterosexual identity, particularly when coupled with moving his head away, it is noteworthy that Grant did not attempt to heterosexualize himself, nor did he stigmatize Richard for his behavior. When I asked Grant later whether he was bothered by the kiss, he said that he was not, adding, "It just took me by surprise."

The social acceptance of homosexuality at all three sites is also evidenced by participants' reactions to my coming out as gay. Near the end of the third week of data collection at each site, I would casually mention my homosexuality in a naturally occurring conversation. For example, at Standard High, I first came out when asked about my plans for the weekend, when I named the club I was planning on attending. One of the students asked, "Isn't that a gay club?" I answered, "Yeah, that's why I'm going there." Adi then asked, "What's it like in there? Is it any different from a straight club?" After we discussed this for a while, the conversation moved on to other students' weekend plans.

Students asked a variety of questions about my sexuality. At all three high schools, no student expressed any negative feeling or attitude in my presence. Although some students seemed surprised, no questions indicated hostility, and no student appeared uncomfortable about this knowledge. It is possible that more homophobic students avoided me once I came out, but I have no evidence to suggest that this was the case. Of course, the acceptance of me as a gay man into the social networks of students does not demonstrate that gay students will be accepted in the same manner. It is, however, further evidence that these heterosexual male students are happy to associate with gay boys and men, in contrast to what the literature has traditionally shown.

HOMOSOCIAL TACTILITY

Research has traditionally shown that physical tactility between boys is limited, because its homosexualizing potential relegates boys in masculine hierarchies (Anderson, 2009; Floyd, 2000; Ibson, 2002). That is, being physically close to another boy can be interpreted by others as indicative of desiring same-sex sex. An exception to this has been sports, in which the elevated levels of masculine capital that athletes maintain permit some forms of same-sex touching (Messner, 1992; Pronger, 1990). However, boys at these high schools are very tactile with each other. At Standard High, where students profess pro-gay attitudes and denounce homophobia, there is a great deal of physical closeness between boys. For example, one afternoon, Adi was sitting with his legs resting on Ryan's lap. Ryan played with Adi's laces, not destructively tying knots but gently tying and untying his shoe. Adjacent to them, Sam sat in Liam's lap while talking with Martin, who was slowly and tenderly stroking Rob's leg. His hand traced up and down Rob's thigh. There was no apparent reason for this touching, except to serve as a sign of affection. Even though it occurred in a busy common room, it was not commented on by any student.

As another example, Jack was seated on the windowsill of the common room, his feet placed on the seat of a chair that rested against the wall. Nick started talking to Jack about their plans for the weekend, and he rested his hands on Jack's knees. Jack, who was wearing shorts, seemed oblivious to this. As Nick leaned forward to emphasize his point, he ran his hands up Jack's thighs and back down again. His actions were seen by many, but challenged by none.

Jack is often tactile with his friends. Another day, having been overseas for the weekend, Jack was catching up with his peers. He saw his closest friend, Tim, enter the common room, and shouted out, "Timmo!" Tim ran across the room, flinging his Topman satchel onto one of the nearby chairs. As Tim approached, Jack jumped into an embrace with Tim. Jack's legs wrapped around Tim's waist, and he flung his arms around Tim's head. Tim caught Jack and held him up by grasping Jack around his lower waist. Exaggeratedly kissing Tim on the top of the head, Jack shouted, "Timmo, where were you all weekend, I missed ya!" As Tim set Jack down so that he was standing, the two talked about their weekend in a style best described as gossiping. They then walked off to their lesson, deep in conversation.

The tactility of the 16- to 18-year-old boys is a frequent and regular phenomenon at Standard High, and it occurs beyond the social context of the common room. For example, in assembly one day, Ethan was sitting behind Liam. Unsolicited, Ethan leaned forward and gave Liam a back rub. Liam turned around, smiling, and said, "That's great, just go a bit lower." In gym class, several boys were sitting in the sun, waiting for a tennis court. There were not enough chairs for everyone, and Kai was left standing up. Nick said, "Kai, come sit on my lap." Kai sat down, and Nick put his arms around Kai's waist. The boys continued to discuss who should play with whom, and no one was concerned by the tactility.

Another day, Colin asked Sam (who was wearing shorts), "Have you been shaving your legs?" Sam replied, "No. I've got hair, it's just blond." In order to investigate, Colin moved closer, running his hand up and down Sam's leg. "They look good," he said. The discussion then attracted Grant's attention, who confirmed, "They do look good." Another time, Richard was stroking the back of Nick's hair, gently rubbing the nape of his neck and discussing Nick's bad attempt at hair dyeing. Ethan also touched Nick's hair, saying, "Yeah, it's really dry." Nick responded, "I know. I had to put loads of conditioner in it!" None of this raised homosexualizing or feminizing sentiment.

In an example that highlights the normalcy of such physical intimacy, Ben and Eli, who do not maintain high levels of popularity, were standing in a corner of the common room. As they talked, they were casually holding hands, with their fingers laced together. Ben then moved his head toward Eli's ear, speaking to him for about a minute. His mouth was so close that it appeared his lips were touching Eli's ear. Halfway through the exchange, Ben changed his embrace, placing an arm around Eli's waist and a hand on Eli's stomach. Although the informal ethnographic approach prevents an exploration of statistical data on rates of touching (cf. Field, 1999), I observed a large majority of boys (over two-thirds) engaging in at least one of the forms of homosocial tactility described above.

As easily as these behaviors could be coded as gay, there is no evidence to suggest that the students view them as such. Coding these acts of homosocial tactility as an expression or indication of sexual desire is problematic for several reasons, including that one would have to assume that almost all of the boys at Standard High maintain same-sex desire. Thus, a more reasonable explanation is that these boys are enjoying the emotional and behavioral intimacy afforded to them in an environment free of explicit homophobia (see Anderson, 2008a).

Physical tactility is also exhibited at Religious High, and again it is not accompanied by homophobic language. Here, boys tend to hug each other on special occasions, embracing for several seconds. For example, in an English lesson that occurred at the start of the day, James entered late. The teacher, who knew it was James's birthday, said, "Well, I suppose we'll let you off this time; happy birthday." Rather than immediately sitting down, however, James hugged each of his male friends for approximately three seconds. This was done in a gentle and friendly manner, with each of James's friends commenting, "Happy birthday, mate," or some similar phase. The class then proceeded with the lesson.

Physical closeness at Religious High tends to be less exuberant than the tactility found at Standard High. For example, Zak and Anthony were seated together in the sun, listening to music. Their arms occasionally touched as they talked. However, they did not engage in the prolonged tactility that is evident at Standard High. This is most likely because the majority of students at Standard High have known each other since they were 12 years old. At Religious High, in contrast, students come from various secondary schools, and friendship groups therefore have not had the chance to develop in the same way.

There is much less physical tactility at Fallback High. There are two reasons for this. The first is that, similar to Religious High, the students have known one another for only one year, and so most of the friendships are relatively new. Second, Fallback High is comprised of a small group of troubled male students. For example, Aiden, Jamie, and Charlie embody a traditional archetype of masculinity and are in the same classes as those students who are more feminine and inclusive. These students, who occasionally pat each other on the back and sit close together, are likely inhibited by the more orthodox views of their classmates.

Although the culture at Fallback High is not homohysteric, and although these students do not harass their more inclusive classmates, the presence of orthodox students likely prevents the expression of more tactile behaviors.

Other forms of less intimate physical tactility occur at Fallback High, too. For example, students often drew pictures on each other's hands and arms. Sometimes these were in the form of masculinized tattoos, most often on the upper arm, but students also drew random pictures (such as cartoon characters) on each other's hands and forearms. This required that the boy drawing the picture softly hold the other boy's hand. There was no apparent hierarchy in who drew pictures on whom, and most boys were relaxed and happy to be drawn on. The main purpose of this activity appeared to be to pass time when students were bored, but it also served as a homosocial bonding technique. Aiden and Charlie were the only boys whom I did not observe engaging in any form of homosocial tactility.

At all three sites, it is a normal and everyday occurrence for students to be in close proximity to each other in lessons. For example, around a computer, students often shared the same seat or perched on another student's lap. Similarly, boys frequently rested their chin on the shoulder of a boy in front of the computer monitor in order to view the screen. Likewise, if boys were sharing a textbook, they often sat very close together to view the book. This tactility was not an active statement of pro-gay beliefs, nor was it part of exuberant displays of friendship; instead, it was the normalized action for boys at these schools.

Further supporting a softening of boys' behaviors, there had been no physical fight at Religious High or Standard High for the whole of the academic year. Students at both schools attributed this to the view that fighting was no longer part of "being a man." Sam said, "It just wouldn't be cool. Fighting sucks." Jack agreed, saying, "Guys are now more laid back—they depend on their wit, rather than strength." At Fallback High, although fights are rare, Jamie and Charlie were in a fistfight earlier in the year. Even so, this is the exception, and the aggression and dominance often associated with teenage boys is not present at any school (cf. Stoudt, 2006). I suggest that boys do not have to present themselves as aggressive and violent because they do not fear being homosexualized in these settings.

ABSENCE OF HOMOPHOBIC LANGUAGE

The frequent use of homophobic language in school settings is a well-established academic finding (see Ellis & High, 2004; Plummer, 1999). However, there is no homophobic language at Standard High or Religious High, and homophobic pejoratives are only very occasionally used by a minority of students at Fallback High; I observed homophobic language a total of three times at Fallback High, and this occurred only within the same group of three boys.

Homophobia is regarded as a sign of immaturity at Standard High. Matt said that someone who uses homophobic pejoratives would be policed by his peers. "He wouldn't keep at it for long," he said; "It's just childish." Justin added, "When I was in middle school, some kids would say 'that's gay' around the playground, but they wouldn't get away with it anymore. We'd tell them it's not on." Sam agreed: "You might find that [homophobic language] before, but not here. It's just not acceptable anymore."

Tom, the openly gay student at Standard High, said that he did not hear any homophobic language. "No, I don't hear any. People don't care that I'm gay. It's fine." Part of this is because many heterosexual students equate homophobic pejoratives with racism. Nick said, "Look, racism is unacceptable. I think saying nasty stuff about gays is just as bad." Joe added, "I would never say 'poof' or 'queer' or other words like that. It's wrong. I mean, I wouldn't say racist stuff either." All of the students interviewed at Standard High explicitly stated that they view anti-gay language to be unacceptable. Participant observations at Standard High support these statements: not only was there a total absence of homophobic language, but the word "gay" was used only in discussions about homosexuality.

Homophobic language is stigmatized at Religious High as well. Eddie and Greg, who are both openly gay, said they do not hear homophobic language. Eddie said, "It's fine, there really isn't any anti-gay stuff. Being gay isn't even an issue any more." Greg agreed: "It's just cool here, being gay is fine." The openly gay student president, Max, said, "There's so little homophobia here, and everyone's so open. I love it."

These views are further supported by the way in which heterosexual boys discuss the openly gay students at Religious High. For example, although he is popular, Greg is disliked by some of his classmates who view him as "really arrogant." Lewis said, "You either love him or hate him. And I don't love him." What is notable, however, is that these students do not use Greg's homosexuality as a way of attacking him. In fact, homosexuality is never used as an insult, even by people who dislike individual gay students. Participant observations at Religious High also document a complete absence of homophobic language, although some students use the phrase "that's so gay." I critically examine this in Chapter 10, but I highlight that there is no intent to wound with the use of this particular phrase (Lalor & Rendle-Short, 2007; Rasmussen, 2004).

The situation at Fallback High is more complicated. Although most students do not use homophobic language, I observed Aiden, Jamie, and Charlie (who embody a traditional archetype of masculinity) employing homophobic pejoratives once each. For example, when discussing whether he should get his hair cut, Aiden said, "But then I might look like a poof." When I asked Aiden in an interview about his use of anti-gay language, he argued that it does not represent personal homophobia:

I don't have anything against gays, you know. Like, it doesn't bother me that you're gay. But my dad says nasty stuff about gays all the time, and so those words for me just slip out. I don't mean to be homophobic.

Clearly, this is one time when knowledge of my sexuality could have influenced what Aiden said. However, his lack of personal homophobia is supported by the multiple times that Aiden socialized with me during data collection—I had lunch with Aiden on average once a week. Throughout my time at Fallback High, I only heard homophobic language a total of three times. Rather than indicating homophobic attitudes and behaviors, I suggest that this use of language can be explained through cultural lag (Ogburn, 1950), whereby a person's use of language lags behind his or her change in attitudes.

Further highlighting the stigmatization of homophobia, there is no evidence to suggest that using homophobic pejoratives in this manner raises one's masculine capital. Indeed, most students at Fallback High disapprove of homophobic language. Phil said, "It's dumb when Aiden says things like that, but what can you do?" Similarly, Dan commented, "It really annoys me when those guys use that language. It's so stupid."

The near-total absence of homophobic language, and its rare use by a minority of students in Fallback High, indicates a decrease in the power of homophobic language in all three settings; this is particularly true when the findings here are compared to previous research (Ellis & High, 2004; Salisbury & Jackson, 1996). Supporting this assertion, there were times when students at Fallback High might have been expected to engage in homophobic language but did not. Students frequently discuss boys they dislike, some of whom transgress heteromasculine norms, but they do not use homophobic language. For example, Aiden, Jamie, and Dan were talking about Seth, a former student at Fallback High. Dan said, "Do you remember when we caught him dancing in that room?" Jamie laughed, adding, "Yeah, he had his hair gelled up and was dancing to some musical—*Grease*, or something." Aidan asked, "Wasn't he wearing leather trousers, too?" Even though I probed their reaction to this, no homophobic epithets were deployed. The infrequency with which homophobic language is publicly used at Fallback High supports the notion that homohysteria maintains less significance in this setting.

In order to see whether participants were altering their behaviors in response to my presence, I spoke to canteen workers and other staff at all three high schools who spend time in student social areas but who maintain little authority over students. They all said that the absence of homophobia was normal in the setting. This is also true of the key informants at each site. Accordingly, the data shows that homophobic language has fallen out of usage and has even become stigmatized in these high schools. In addition to being an important finding in its own right, this stigmatization of homophobia indicates that these high school cultures are not homohysteric.

EXCEPTIONAL HIGH SCHOOLS?

A potential criticism of these findings is that I have stumbled upon unique sites, and that institutional factors cause the dynamics of gender and sexuality to be different here than in (most) other schools. I first addressed this issue by collecting data at three schools, two of which were strategically chosen because they were expected to have elevated rates of homophobia. However, I also control for this by examining for a culture of *decreasing* homophobia at Standard High, the site where students espoused the most pro-gay attitudes.

In order to conditionally explore whether there has been a culture of declining homophobia at Standard High, I interviewed three former gay students: Luke (24) and Matt (22), who were closeted at Standard High, and Alistair (20), who was openly gay when he attended the school. The informants were located through existing social networks of current students, and they make a case for decreasing homophobia at Standard High.

Luke argued that homophobia prevented him from coming out: "There was just no way I would have come out then. Are you kidding?" He said that he heard anti-gay epithets on a daily basis, and that such language was never questioned by teaching staff. Luke said, "If you did something wrong, someone would call you a 'fucking poof,' and the teachers didn't care." This use of homophobic language is similar to what Thurlow (2001) describes, wherein the intensifier "fucking" demonstrates the intent to marginalize the subject of the abuse.

Matt, who was also closeted at school, was more ambivalent about levels of homophobia. He said, "My friends probably would have been fine, but I wouldn't exactly have been supported. Some guys were pretty homophobic." Matt also questioned whether he should have come out at Standard High. "I got to university, came out, and made these gay friends. Some of them had been out at school and it had been fine. It got me thinking if I shouldn't have been a bit braver."

Alistair, the youngest of the former students, said that homophobia had less influence on his school experience. "When I came out, it was a bit of an issue at first, but most kids were fine with it." He said, "A few students hassled me, but I told my form teacher, and she sorted them out. I was aware of the occasional nasty joke, and that upset me. But I'm definitely glad I came out."

These narratives suggest that there has been a withering away of homophobia in Standard High in recent years, and that I have not simply stumbled upon a unique group of students. Results from these interviews cannot be stated absolutely, but they suggest decreasing homophobia within this particular setting. Given that homophobia is of decreased significance across all three sites, and that there is evidence to suggest that homophobia has decreased at Standard High over the past few years, this supports the validity of the findings. That is, the measures undertaken in order to check for spatial and temporal uniqueness indicate that the attitudes toward homosexuality and gay students at these sites will have relevance to other schools with similar demographics.

I emphasize that I am discussing overt homophobia; this includes the marginalization of gay students, the use of homophobic language, and negative attitudes about gay men. And, according to these measures, it is *homophobia* that is stigmatized at these schools today. Thus, rather than homophobia being an integral part of masculinity in the way that Kimmel (1994) describes, heterosexual male students instead argue that homophobia is a sign of immaturity.

GAY-FRIENDLY HIGH SCHOOLS

Research on school cultures shows that boys' gendered behaviors are structured by a restrictive heteromasculine ethos that is heavily policed by homophobic language (Mac an Ghaill, 1994; Plummer, 1999). This research suggests that because homosexuality is stigmatized, boys distance themselves from anything coded as feminine or gay (Pollack, 1998). Anderson (2009) describes such a cultural zeitgeist as "homohysteric," and his concept of homohysteria is particularly salient for this research because it recognizes levels of homophobia as historically and spatially situated, making it possible to theorize about and examine the impact of different levels of homophobia on boys' gendered behaviors.

My research, however, finds three British high schools to be very gay friendly. This chapter demonstrates that the significance of homohysteria in these three settings is markedly different from what the academic literature describes. The boys' social inclusion of gay students and their intellectual acceptance of homosexuality show that most of them do not fear being homosexualized. Perhaps the best evidence of the lack of homohysteria was the near-total absence of homophobic language. At Standard High and Religious High, there was no anti-gay abuse whatsoever, and the rare use of homophobic pejoratives at Fallback High was met with disapproval from other students. Quite simply, these are gay-friendly high schools.

It is possible that my open discussion of my sexuality might have influenced some students to hide their own homophobia, but it is notable that the frequency and style of homophobic language did not change with the disclosure of my sexuality at any of the three research sites. It is also important to note that with over 1,000 students at Religious High, many students did not know who I was when I was walking around the school grounds and observing student interactions. This means that it is unlikely that they were changing their behaviors in my presence. Finally, the remarkable level of physical tactility between heterosexual male students is also evidence that these school cultures were not homohysteric, because it demonstrates that boys do not fear being homosexualized for such behavior (cf. Ibson, 2002; Pollack, 1998).

At first, I sought to explain these behaviors through social capital, thinking that high levels of masculine capital could buy immunity for some boys (Anderson, 2005a; Pascoe, 2003). However, participant observations showed that these inclusive behaviors were not limited to boys of any one definable group. Instead, regardless of the boys' popularity (see Chapter 9), and without the implication of same-sex desire, physical intimacy was present among and between boys of all social groups and masculine archetypes.

The gendered behaviors of the boys in these settings, where homohysteria maintained little significance, are best described by Anderson's (2009) inclusive masculinity theory. This is because inclusive masculinity theory provides a framework for understanding the gendered dynamics of times and places where overt homophobia has diminished—something that Connell's (1987, 1995) work fails to address. And here, where boys did not show signs that they feared being perceived as gay, inclusive attitudes were esteemed, and many archetypes of masculinity were equally validated.

The findings described in this chapter are important because they demonstrate that these are gay-friendly high schools. Homosexual suspicion is no longer an effective way of relegating boys in the masculine hierarchy, and boys do not fear being perceived as gay in these settings. Accordingly, these findings are at variance with the near-homogenous view put forth in the literature that educational settings have high levels of homophobia. This is an important finding in and of itself. However, there is further utility in these findings: they enable an examination of sexual and gender dynamics in settings where homophobia is not a fundamental policing mechanism. Accordingly, in the following chapters I explore how the absence of overt homophobia affects the maintenance of heterosexual identities, I examine the social organization of male peer group culture, and I present a new model for understanding the use of homosexually themed language.

8

Heterosexual Recuperation

In this chapter I examine the ways in which the boys at Standard High reproduce and regulate their heterosexual identities without using homophobic language. Whereas previous research shows that boys maintain masculinity through vociferously deploying homophobic pejoratives, this is not the case at Standard High. The demonstrations of physical and emotional closeness that I document in Chapter 7 most frequently occur without any form of heterosexual boundary maintenance work. However, even in this inclusive setting, I find that boys maintain their heterosexual identities through a social process that I conceptualize as *heterosexual recuperation*.

In Chapter 7, I argue that inclusive masculinity theory best captures the social dynamics of these settings, because the esteemed attributes of participants do not rely on the marginalization and domination of others (Anderson, 2009). However, inclusive masculinity theory does not examine the mechanisms through which heterosexual identities are maintained in inclusive settings. Accordingly, I contribute to inclusive masculinity theory by detailing the ways in which the boundaries of heterosexual identities are strengthened through the concept of heterosexual recuperation. I also show that the absence of overt homophobia leads to heterosexuality being consolidated in these schools. Accordingly, in this chapter, I develop a conceptual framework for understanding some of the empirical findings documented in the preceding chapter. For this analysis, I limit the data to those collected from Standard High because I spent the most time collecting data there, and the analysis was devised inductively at that site.

HETERONORMATIVITY AND HOW BOYS MANAGE
THEIR HETEROSEXUAL IDENTITIES

Considerable research links the operations of homophobia, heteronormativity, and sexuality in the production and maintenance of gendered identities (Kimmel, 2005; Plummer, 1999). Yet research often underplays the complex, multidimensional interaction of sexuality and gender. As Jackson (2006, p. 106) writes, "Sexuality, gender and heterosexuality intersect in variable ways within and between different dimensions of the social."

At an institutional level, schools have been shown to produce their own sexual and gendered oppression (Allen, 2007a; Atkinson & DePalma, 2009; Nixon, 2010). Educational policies and school curricula privilege heterosexuality while simultaneously ignoring all other sexual identities (Epstein & Johnson, 1998). For example, Ferfolja (2007) demonstrates that heterosexuality is privileged in 13 Australian schools through the institutional silencing and omission of gay identities, and she argues that this reproduces homophobic prejudice. Indeed, institutionally sanctioned cultures of homophobia severely diminish the social freedoms and learning environment of sexual minorities, and many gay students remain stigmatized in school systems across Western cultures (Epstein, O'Flynn, & Telford, 2003; Pascoe, 2007; Ryan & Rivers, 2003).

However, the boundaries of legitimized heterosexual masculine identities have also been shown to be policed through a range of (sometimes brutal) discursive and behavioral practices (Chambers, Tincknell, & Van Loon, 2004; Mac an Ghaill, 1994; Steinberg, Epstein, & Johnson, 1997). Indeed, the stigma attached to homosexuality leads boys to use an array of heterosexual boundary maintenance techniques to publicly defend their heterosexual identities. The primary way in which boys do this is through homophobia (Pascoe, 2007; Plummer, 1999).

Other forms of heterosexual boundary maintenance exist, too. For example, Redman and Mac an Ghaill (1997) discuss "intellectual muscularity," whereby a heterosexual masculinity is presented through the "ability to 'push people around intellectually' " (p. 169). Heterosexuality is also confirmed through physical muscularity and sporting success (Anderson, 2005a; Pronger, 1990), as well as via the competitive use of ritualistic insults and verbal game-play (Pascoe, 2007). Huuki, Manninen, and Sunnari (2010) also describe the heterosexual boundary maintenance work of boys who ironically proclaim same-sex desire but then consolidate their heterosexuality through the use of homophobic language immediately after.

However, all of these processes of heterosexual boundary maintenance have occurred in homohysteric settings (Plummer, 1999; Redman & Mac an Ghaill, 1997). Indeed, the fact that the majority of research examining the policing and maintenance of heterosexual boundaries has occurred in homohysteric settings has caused Anderson (2009) to suggest that existing sexuality and gender theories fail to capture how heterosexual boundaries are policed in homophobia-free settings, in which gay students are socially included, homophobic language is absent, and heterosexual students do not intellectualize negative attitudes about sexual minorities.

I add to existing gender and sexuality scholarship by conceptualizing *heterosexual recuperation* as a heuristic tool for understanding the strategies boys use to establish and maintain heterosexual identities without invoking homophobia. I delineate two forms of heterosexual recuperation, recognizing that these are not necessarily exhaustive of the ways in which boys can recoup their heterosexuality. *Conquestial recuperation* conceptualizes the ways in which boys boast of their heterosexual desires or conquests (Mac an Ghaill, 1994), and *ironic recuperation* describes a satirical proclamation of same-sex desire or a gay identity made in order to maintain a heterosexual identity (Huuki et al., 2010; Kaplan, 2005).

Both forms of heterosexual recuperation are used when boys fear that their heterosexuality is under question. For example, boys might deploy heterosexual recuperation after they perform a gender-transgressive behavior (Pascoe, 2007). Heterosexual recuperation therefore serves as a boundary-making activity, consolidating heterosexual masculinities and potentially esteeming heterosexuality in the process.

LIMITED HETEROSEXUAL RECUPERATION

Previous research on the gendered terrain of acceptable masculine behaviors has shown that when boys transgress heteromasculine boundaries, they normally find it necessary to publicly defend their heterosexuality through homophobia and/or other heterosexualizing behaviors (Epstein, 1997; Salisbury & Jackson, 1996). Unique to this study, however, is that even in the absence of homophobia, there is still only a limited amount of heterosexual recuperation used by participants.

Conquestial Recuperation

An example of conquestial heterosexual recuperation comes from Chris, who is known for his provocative humor. One day, between lessons, Chris asked whether Tom Cruise is gay. Jack responded, "I don't know, but there is a really funny clip of him talking about Scientology on the Internet." Chris replied, "I'm still on the Jenna Jameson one." Here, Chris employed the common knowledge that Jenna Jameson is a female porn star, thus framing himself as heterosexual.

Another day, Justin, Kai, and Ryan were sitting in the common room. They were talking about a house party they had attended the previous night, which Kai left early to have sex with his girlfriend. Justin said, "Kai, you're such an idiot leaving when you did! You missed the vodka, the best music, everything!" Kai shrugged his shoulders, smiled, and said, "I'm the one who got laid last night." Justin laughed and said, "Fair point. I can't ever imagine turning down sex. I mean, I want it *all* the time. I just can't get enough." Ryan added, "Seriously. I'm just always horny. When I get a girlfriend, she can have it whenever she likes." In this discussion, the boys discuss their heterosexual potency as a way of maintaining their heterosexual identity.

The use of conquestial recuperation is linked with popular television shows such as *Family Guy* and *The Inbetweeners*. In both of these shows, male characters discuss their sexual desires in humorous (and sometimes aggressive) ways that consolidate their heterosexual identity. Interestingly, the boys at Standard High use far less conquestial recuperation and use it in a less aggressive (and some might argue misogynistic) manner than these television shows. The use of conquestial recuperation was infrequent, occurring on average slightly less than once a week.

It is also important to note that although boys sometimes used conquestial recuperation to consolidate their heterosexuality, this occurred in a setting where heterosexual boys' attitudes to women appeared to be improved compared to what other literature suggests (Chambers et al., 2004; Robinson, 2005). Male students did not express misogynistic attitudes, and girls who had had sex with several boys were not stigmatized for having done so. For example, one free period, Tim, Liam, and Grant (three of the most outgoing boys) walked into the common room and overheard a group of girls discussing oral sex. The boys crossed to the other side of the common room, where they continued their conversation. They did not label the girls as sluts or whores, as previous research suggests they might have (Lees, 1993).

This example is typical of the way in which boys at Standard High do not publicly invoke misogyny. Although I did not have access to the boys' private sexual talk (in which the sexual objectification of women as well as conquestial recuperation is perhaps more likely to occur), girls at Standard High appear to have greater freedom from sexualized harassment than other research suggests (cf. Epstein, 1996; Robinson, 2005). When conquestial recuperation is used, it does not occur alongside overt forms of misogyny.

It is also noteworthy that although many boys have sexualized discussions about girls, boys who do not present hyperheterosexual versions of themselves (that is, those who do not engage in conquestial recuperation) are not stigmatized for their lack of overt heterosexuality. For example, Ethan attended a costume party, where a girl offered him oral sex. His friends told me that he declined the offer, saying, "He couldn't be bothered to take his costume off." Yet when telling this story, none of the boys questioned Steve's heterosexuality. Affirming this, later that afternoon, Steve walked past a group of boys, and one called out to him, "Mr. Lazy." Although Steve was clearly being made fun of, he was not homosexualized for rejecting heterosexual sex. Furthermore, Steve did not attempt to recuperate his heterosexuality in front of his peers.

Ironic Recuperation

The more frequent use of heterosexual recuperation at Standard High comes through irony. Ironic recuperation is sometimes used to enable boys to engage in close physical contact. As an example of this, Joe and Tim (two of the most popular students) walked up to a group of boys who had congregated in the center of the common room. Joe stood behind Tim, hugging him around the neck. Joe then lowered his arms to Tim's waist and rested his head on Tim's shoulders. A moment later, Joe jumped up and down, energetically shouting, "I'm horny! Let's wrestle! I'm horny!" Tim laughed and fell to the ground, squashing Joe beneath him. The boys laid motionless for a few seconds before Tim got up and then helped Joe to his feet.

I interpret this as the recuperation of heterosexuality through ironic behaviors, and I also suggest that the tactility of the hug, and the lack of overt homophobia, distances it from orthodox forms of heterosexual boundary management. Both students are socially perceived as maintaining a heterosexual identity, the main reasons for this being that Joe has a girlfriend and Tim is known for having had casual sex with multiple girls.

There are several examples of this form of heterosexual boundary maintenance. One day in the common room, Adi was giving Ryan a back massage. Ryan said, "That's so good." Adi smiled, saying, "I know how to please a man." Ryan laughed and said, "Go harder. Harder." By ironically mimicking same-sex sex, these boys consolidated their heterosexual standing. Another day, Sam and Kai were queuing for food in the common room. Sam rested his arms around Kai's neck and gently leaned on him for support. Sam then said, "Hey, are you wearing aftershave? You smell good." Kai responded, "Yeah, Hugo Boss. Good, isn't it?" Sam replied, "Sure is. Good, and sexy." Sam then started grinding against Kai, who laughed and said, "I wore it for you." While these examples document heterosexual boundary maintenance following physical touch, it should be noted that a great deal of homosocial tactility occurs without this mechanism, as discussed in Chapter 7.

Ironic heterosexual recuperation also serves as a strategy to enable emotional bonding between friends. An example of this is when Justin, an extroverted boy, gave Martin several presents for his birthday. About 25 students gathered to watch Martin open the gifts and blow out the cake's candle. Halfway through, Martin became emotionally overwhelmed by his best friend's generosity. He stood and hugged Justin, embracing him in front of the crowd. When another boy said, "That's sweet," Justin performed for the students who had congregated around them, exclaiming, "I'm turned on. I'm turned on." Everyone laughed with him, but the boys did not unlock their embrace for another few seconds. This highlights the way in which ironic heterosexual recuperation permits an expanded (but still restricted) level of emotional and physical intimacy. By shouting "I'm turned on," Martin and Justin were not regulated by others for their intimacy. However, the boys nonetheless limited their own public display of emotional intimacy by employing ironic recuperation.

Ironic recuperation also occurs when heterosexual students jokingly proclaim a close friend to be their boyfriend. One day, Simon and Ben were in the common room as Joe entered and shouted, "Come on, Ben, you're late for lesson." Ben exclaimed, "Shit. I've got to dash, Simon. Laters, boyfriend." In interview, Tim said, "I joke a fair bit that me and Jack are boyfriends. Everyone knows we're not, but we spend so much time together, and he's my best mate, we almost are." Tim acknowledges the playful component of this language use, adding "We play up to it a bit. I'll kiss him on the head or the cheek when I haven't seen him for a while, or he'll tap me on my butt when I give him a hug."

There are also several boys at Standard High who call their close friends "lover" and "boyfriend." For example, as Rob and Liam were leaving school, Rob said, "See you tomorrow, lover." Liam responded by saying "Yeah, Rob, you will." In total, approximately 20 boys regularly used the terms "boyfriend" and "lover" as a way of addressing their close friends.

Interviews and participant observations show that these ironic proclamations are not taken seriously by students. Given that they are only ever used between close friends, they can be interpreted as a way of combining close emotional bonds with heterosexual identities. The ironic pronouncement demonstrates that although emotional closeness between boys is much expanded in these settings (see Chapter 9), some students nevertheless seek to consolidate their heterosexual identity through joking in this manner.

Even so, other students argue that this use of heterosexual recuperation demonstrates their positive attitude toward homosexuality. Discussing how he calls his best friend his boyfriend, Tim said,

> I think we do it because we're so at ease with it, you know. I mean, Tom [an openly gay student] doesn't care, I know he thinks it's cool. And he should, it's our way of saying we're cool with it, you know?

Ben also argued that his pro-gay attitudes are compatible with this use of language: "I'm not saying that I do it to show that I'm pro-gay, but if I was homophobic there's no way I would call my mates boyfriend."

Whereas some boys use ironic recuperation after public expressions of intimacy, most male students are open about the emotional relationships they have with their friends. For example, Ryan referred to his friendship with Adi as a "bromance," a media term coined by skater David Carnie in the 1990s to explain close male friendships (see also Adams, 2011). Ryan said, "Adi's my go-to guy, I love him to pieces." He added, "We're like J.D. and Turk from *Scrubs*. You know, Adi's got a girlfriend, but he's been with her for six months. We've been best friends for six years. We've got a bromance going on."

Ryan was the only participant to refer to his closest friendship as a bromance. Many other students were happy to say that they love their friends. Ben said, "Eli's my best mate, and I love him. I can trust him with what's important." When I asked whether he has ever told Eli this, Ben replied, "Yeah, I've told him how important he is to me. He's my best friend, after all." Tim said, "I love my friends, and I could rely on them if I needed to." At Standard High, the proclamation of love for a friend was interpreted and esteemed as a sign of emotional closeness. It did not connote same-sex desire. And while this open expression of emotional intimacy has been documented among younger (Way, 2011) and older (Anderson, 2009) male friends, my research is the first to show it is an important part of friendship among 16-18 year old male youth.

THE IMPACT OF HETEROSEXUAL RECUPERATION

The absence of overt homophobia at Standard High permitted new theorizing about the boundary-making practices of heterosexuality. Accordingly, I identified heterosexual recuperation as the chief mechanism for maintaining heterosexual boundaries without invoking homophobia. I highlight, however, that heterosexual recuperation can continue to privilege heterosexuality, implicitly marginalizing gay identities. However, some students argue that this use of language is indicative of pro-gay attitudes. Indeed, although I demarcate the focus to *overt* homophobia in this research, it would be a mischaracterization to label hetero-sexual recuperation as covert homophobia. This is because, as Plummer (1999, p. 134) argues when discussing what he calls implicit homophobia, covert homo-phobia implies an intent on behalf of participants of which I had no evidence. Indeed, this chapter shows that the privileging of heterosexuality can exist even in a group of youth who are intellectually opposed to homophobia. This is institu-tionalized heteronormativity, in that it can exist despite the desire of participants to eradicate it.

Although I suggest that heterosexual recuperation consists of mechanisms used to (re)make a heterosexual identity, I also highlight that the ironic form serves as a social mechanism enabling boys to expand (and even break) the tightly policed gendered boundaries described by masculinities literature. That is, ironic recuperation provides boys with a specific strategy by which they can enact other-wise transgressive behaviors without threat to their socially perceived hetero-sexual identities. Whereas only boys and men with high masculine capital have previously been permitted to transgress gender norms (Anderson, 2005a; McGuffey & Rich, 1999; Pascoe, 2003), ironic recuperation is a mechanism that the majority of boys can use.

The relative rarity of heterosexual recuperation in these settings is particu-larly noteworthy. As discussed in Chapter 7, physical tactility and emotional inti-macy frequently occurred without any palpable form of heterosexual boundary maintenance. This means that even with the decrease in homophobia and the cor-responding expansion of acceptable gendered behaviors, it appears that hetero-sexuality is *more* consolidated at Standard High.

Elaborating on this, scholars researching settings with high homophobia explicate the fragmented and precarious nature of heterosexual identity construc-tion and maintenance, suggesting that just one gender transgression can homo-sexualize a boy (Anderson, 2008a; Pascoe, 2007; Youdell, 2004). Yet at Standard High, boys were socially perceived as gay only if they publicly identified as such. Thus, in this setting, decreased homophobia strengthened the boundaries of heterosexual identity, while simultaneously permitting individuals to move out-side of them. This means that decreased homophobia does not necessarily result in a dissipation of sexual identities.

It is interesting to note that heterosexual recuperation was performed only by boys in these settings. Although girls undoubtedly have a range of heterosexual boundary maintenance techniques of their own (Lees, 1993; McRobbie, 1989), my observations documented that my conceptualization of heterosexual recupera-tion was enacted only by boys. Of course, it is possible that girls demonstrate these behaviors in private, but it is also possible that the gendered nature of hetero-sexual recuperation is attributable to the historical conflation of heterosexuality and masculinity, and to the prominent position that homophobia has had in the regulation of heterosexual masculinities.

This chapter also does not examine the impact that heterosexual recuperation has on women, but I draw some conclusions based on my data. The most perti-nent example here is of Chris's proclamation about watching porn (when he talked about Jenna Jameson). Research in school cultures has argued that the highly sexualized and public discussion of women as sex objects can contribute to misogynistic attitudes and behaviors (Lees, 1993; Robinson, 2005). However, this research occurred in homohysteric cultures and featured much more aggressive and degrading language than that found at Standard High. Whereas some scholars might argue that Chris's use of a woman porn star to frame himself as heterosexual is inherently misogynistic, I demur from this view, as it requires an antiporn standpoint that should not be accepted without empirical evidence of a socionegative impact (see Nussbaum, 1995; Rubin, 1993a). Accordingly, further research is required in order to assess the impact of conquestial recuperation on girls in school cultures.

9

Popularity without Oppression

In this chapter I detail how the heterosexual boys at Standard High maintain the attributes of inclusive masculinity beyond pro-gay attitudes, and I explicate the social dynamics of the male peer group cultures in this setting. Contrasting with what the literature traditionally shows (Cillessen & Rose, 2005; Mac an Ghaill, 1994), I document that practices of subordination and marginalization are not used to obtain popularity or masculine standing in this setting. At Standard High, boys ascribing to different masculine archetypes (e.g., jocks, emos, geeks) can all maintain high social status.

Nonetheless, a social hierarchy exists. Rather than being ranked by masculine capital, however, boys are instead stratified by "popularity." I show that this ranking of boys is determined by their possession of a number of variables, namely, charisma, authenticity, emotional support, and social fluidity. Accordingly, I show the ways in which popularity is maintained, examining the social matrix of a setting where I document inclusive masculinities to be numerically dominant.

In this chapter, I again limit the data to those collected from Standard High. This is because I spent the most time collecting data at Standard High, and the conceptual framework presented in this chapter was devised inductively at that site. Data collection at the other high schools focused more on the impact of homohysteria than it did on understandings of popularity and friendship in each setting, although it should also be highlighted that no data from these sites contradicted the analysis presented here. Furthermore, the purpose of this section is to examine the social dynamics of an inclusive masculinity setting, rather than attempt to generalize across a particular demographic of heterosexual male students. Finally, in terms of exploring the social dynamics of friendship networks, Standard High proved to be the optimal setting. This is because Fallback High, with only 18 male students, was too small to enable an exploration of these social dynamics, and Religious High, with over 1,000 students, was effectively too large. Accordingly, although many of the findings are likely applicable to the other sites, I restrict the analysis to Standard High.

HIERARCHIES OF MASCULINITY AND POPULARITY

Hegemonic masculinity theory has traditionally been used to understand how boys and men are stratified in a setting. In discussing this theory, Connell (1995) describes two key mechanisms that produce a hierarchical stratification of boys: *domination*, which conceptualizes the material acts that subordinate specific groups of boys and men, and *marginalization*, which represents the discursive challenging of the legitimacy of particular masculinities. She argues that these processes combine to produce only one culturally esteemed form of masculinity, and that the social esteem in which a boy is held is directly correlated to how closely he models this archetype of masculinity (Pascoe, 2003; Stoudt, 2006).

These processes of oppression are used by boys and men to maintain or improve their position within male hierarchies—to make them more popular. And with heteromasculinity traditionally privileged, boys are forced to distance themselves from homosexuality and femininity (Connell, 1987; Pronger, 1990). Accordingly, homophobia, violence, and misogyny have regularly been shown to be integral aspects of the dominant mode of masculinity, as well as required attributes for maintaining popularity (Mac an Ghaill, 1994; Vaillancourt, Hymel, & McDougall, 2003).

I have already discussed at length the role homophobia plays in policing the boundaries of acceptable masculine behaviors (see also Anderson, 2009). There are, however, other social mechanisms that regulate gendered behaviors as well. Bullying is one of the social processes that boys use to consolidate the stratification of the masculine hierarchy (Martino & Pallotta-Chiarolli, 2003; Rivers, Duncan, & Besag, 2007). By punishing those boys who exhibit behaviors that are not socially condoned, it also serves to bring "deviant" boys back in line with the norms of a particular setting (Steinberg, Epstein, & Johnson, 1997). This limits the range of permissible behaviors available to boys. Indeed, the rules of masculinity are so restrictive that Mac an Ghaill (1994, p. 56) describes them as limiting boys' legitimate interests to "three F's": football, fighting, and fucking. Francis (1999) describes a slightly expanded list of acceptable behaviors, including "'having a laugh,' alcohol consumption, disruptive behavior, objectifying women, and an interest in pastimes and subjects constructed as masculine" (p. 357).

The most esteemed form of masculinity has often been known, particularly in American settings, by the label "jock" (Anderson, 2005a; Sabo & Runfola, 1980). Pascoe (2003, p. 1426) comments, "Jocks are considered the highest ranking position in the social order." She explicates the link between the Jock, popularity, and the processes of hegemonic masculinity, arguing that "[t]o be a Jock is to emphasize dominance over others, whether it be on the field or in the social world, as can be seen by their position on the social hierarchy" (p. 1426). As in the majority of research on the intersection of masculinity, homophobia, and popularity, one boy's privilege and popularity is maintained at the expense of another's marginalization (Connell, 1989; Francis, 1999).

A substantial amount of research examines the intersection of homophobia, popularity, and masculinity (C. Jackson, 2006; Mac an Ghaill, 1994; Warrington & Younger, 2011). However, there is notably little scholarship on the social hierarchies of heterosexual boys and men in settings where overt homophobia is absent. For example, although Carolyn Jackson (2006) partially examines the popularity rankings of male students, she focuses on how popularity is interlinked with (homophobic) orthodox masculinity.

The focus on "laddish" behaviors prevents the multiplicity of masculinities that exist in school settings from being fully recognized. As Lyng (2009) argues, this means that empirical studies of secondary schools do not "grasp the variety of student groups and the relations between them" (p. 463). In order to overcome one aspect of this issue, it is necessary to investigate the social processes by which boys are stratified when homophobia is absent. Accordingly, I theorize the social processes of the ranking of boys in a school setting where I empirically demonstrate that inclusive masculinities numerically predominate.

STANDARD HIGH AS AN INCLUSIVE MASCULINITY SETTING

Inclusive masculinity theory identifies homophobia as the key mechanism in regulating and stratifying masculinities in a homohysteric setting. However, Anderson also argues that as homohysteria declines, boys and men adopt more inclusive attitudes toward women, as well as toward boys and men who do not embody orthodox masculinity (Anderson, 2008a, 2008b, 2008c). At Standard High, with the processes of marginalization and domination absent from boys' social interaction, inclusive attitudes and behaviors are found in a number of ways. This is most notable with respect to homophobic language, which is never used by participants at this school. Indeed, the term "gay" is never used aggressively, and is used only in its literal sense when referring to homosexuality. Homophobic pejoratives have fallen out of usage altogether.

Other tenets of orthodox masculinity hold less significance at Standard High, too. As discussed in Chapter 8, boys rarely employ misogynistic language or engage in behaviors that sexually degrade women (cf. Chambers, Tincknell, & Van Loon, 2004; Robinson, 2005). The (hetero)sexualized discussions of sex tend to focus on the boys' own potency, rather than girls' traditionally stigmatized behaviors. Although discussion of one's heterosexual potency is also found in traditional forms of masculinity (Mac an Ghaill, 1994), these discussions at Standard High are notable in that they are not used to marginalize or dominate other students. Although this might have socionegative effects in relation to misogyny, it is further evidence that students do not marginalize or bully each other.

In further contrast to boys' talk about sex in homohysteric settings, male students at Standard High are able to discuss sexual organs honestly and openly without regulation. For example, during a free period, Richard and Jack were sitting in the common room with their friends Lucy and Helen. Ostensibly working on an English assignment, they started to talk about sex and penis size. Lucy commented that she and her boyfriend had decided to have sex for the first time, and that she did not know what size his penis was—"I mean, how big are they generally?" Richard said, "I think they're about six centimeters aren't they?" and Jack said, "I always thought it was five inches?" Helen then asked, "Is that when they're floppy, or when they're hard?" The discussion proceeded in a similar vein for several minutes before the students returned to the English assignment. Aside from the surprising lack of knowledge about the issue, as well as the absence of banter or joking, this example demonstrates that these boys can show ignorance about basic issues around sex without being marginalized for their lack of knowledge (cf. Salisbury & Jackson, 1996).

Corresponding to the lack of aggression and fighting at Standard High, boys are also not as concerned with being seen as "hard" as previous literature suggests they might (Gard, 2001; C. Jackson, 2006; Wellard, 2006). Indeed, these boys are not marginalized for demonstrating weakness or fear. For example, Steve, Kai, Grant, and Colin discussed being scared of dogs. Kai said, "I love all dogs, the big ones are the best." Colin disagreed, saying, "No, I hate them. They're just too demanding, and when they lick you, yuck!" Steve commented that he is scared of dogs, and he discussed an incident that was traumatic for him as a child: "When I was really young, I was in this park and I was chased around by this big dog. I was, like, running around the park, screaming." Concerned, Grant asked him whether he was bitten. Steve said, "No, no, I think it just licked me actually." The boys all laughed at this, including Steve. Grant then said, while giving Steve an exuberant hug, "You've got me now, mate. I'll protect you!" Here, Steve is able to present himself as scared and vulnerable without regulation of his masculinity. Instead, he finds that his friends joke with him and provide emotional support.

Finally, a requisite characteristic for boys at Standard High is that they are inclusive of other boys. There are countless examples of this, but particularly note-worthy is the active inclusion of Tom, the openly gay student. I discuss this in Chapter 7, providing examples of several heterosexual male students actively including Tom in their daily endeavors. However, inclusion goes beyond accep-tance of lesbian, gay, bisexual, and transgender students. The boys also play sports together, regardless of their athletic ability. For example, Daniel is not particularly popular at Standard High, and he walks with a limp. Nonetheless, as he was pass-ing a group of sporty boys who were playing tennis, they asked him to join their game. Whereas this invitation would once perhaps have been designed to humili-ate Daniel, these boys were sincere in their offer. They welcomed him to the court, and, after rallying back and forth for several shots, Rob offered Daniel advice on improving his serve. Afterward, Rob commented to me, "If we were playing another school and it was competitive, you want your best team. But if it's just for fun, then anyone can play. Why not?" So whereas boys once avoided association with marginalized or less popular students, this is not the case at Standard High. Instead, these inclusive acts have been normalized, with friendliness both expected and esteemed. These changes in what behaviors are socially valued influence what constitutes popularity for young men. Accordingly, I examine how boys in this inclusive setting are stratified according to popularity.

A POPULARITY RANKING AT STANDARD HIGH

Boys are no longer stratified according to an aggressive and domineering form of masculine dominance at Standard High, yet a hierarchy of boys is still evident. Put simply, certain boys are more popular than others. This popularity, however, is not maintained through peer diminution, domination, or risk-taking behaviors (cf. Stoudt, 2006; Warrington & Younger, 2011). Instead, many boys ascribing to a wide range of masculine archetypes can maintain popularity. These boys come from both privileged backgrounds and areas of socioeconomic disadvantage; they include students of various ethnicities and boys of various athletic abilities. Dominant discourse is based on white, middle-class norms, yet these attributes do not stratify boys *within* the school. Instead, a boy's popularity is dependent on the extent to which he maintains other characteristics. In this hierarchy, I identify four main categories of behavior that increase one's popularity at Standard High: charisma, authenticity, emotional support, and social fluidity.

It should be recognized that popularity is a somewhat nebulous concept (Cillessen & Rose, 2005). At one level, popularity is self-evident to the extent that it is visible as a set of relations between peers (Adler & Adler, 1998). However, popularity is also firmly entrenched in discourses of race, class, gender, and sexuality and despite the complexities behind this deceptively simple term, popularity remains a useful and enduring concept. Indeed, Francis, Skelton, and Read (2010, p. 3) comment that "for all its fragility and inherent contradiction, the concept bears great resonance and recognition in schools." The participants in this research discuss popularity themselves, and it effectively describes the social dynamics of Standard High.

Charisma

A boy's popularity at Standard High is primarily maintained by his entertaining his peers through high-octane, energetic behaviors (see Harris, 2010). Accordingly, *charisma* denotes the extroverted and "fun-loving" acts that increase popularity. For example, the primary entertainment in the common room one week was based on the use of a skateboard. Different boys would use it to perform tricks, each trying to outperform the others. The success of the trick, however, was less important than the energy and exuberance with which it was executed. The most popular performances were the funniest and most physical, not necessarily the most skilled. Thus, boys displaying the most charisma received the most praise.

Charisma has always been important in boys' behaviors, but here it is found without the violent or aggressive acts usually associated with teenage boys (Robinson, 2005; Salisbury & Jackson, 1996). For example, one day, Jack, Joe, and Oli entered the common room, where loud music was playing. Hearing it, they jumped on two empty tables in the middle of the common room and started dancing and singing along. After a crowd has gathered, Joe laid on his back, cradling his legs in his arms. Oli and Jack spun him around for several seconds, and the other students chanted Joe's name. Dizzy, Joe jumped off the table and stumbled. The other students cheered, and Oli stopped him from bumping into a wall. This example is typical of esteemed masculine behaviors at Standard High: the students are energetic, but fundamentally unaggressive.

Charisma is also important when the boys play sports. For example, a group of students often play an informal game of cricket during their lunch break. The players always want a good bowler because this ensures that everyone gets a chance at batting. However, even though Ben has the most skill, the favorite bowler is Jack. This is because although Ben ensures a fast (though not too fast) turnover of batters, Jack provides more entertainment when bowling. Whereas Ben concentrates on his bowling, Jack uses his charisma to entertain the other players in various ways. He imitates famous cricketers, moves in funny ways, and banters with other players. Jack is esteemed for his extroverted behaviors when playing cricket, and he is always a central player in these informal games.

Although charisma is often linked with extroversion, it is also important among students who are less outgoing. Boys who spend their time in the music rooms at lunch, for example, exhibit a more restrained form of charisma. These boys will play music together or listen to each other's performances. Musicianship is an important factor, but boys are also esteemed when they weave humor into their performance. Harry is particularly popular for the way he plays classical music in different styles on the piano (playing Bach, for example, in both classical and jazz styles). Although these students would not dance on tables in the common room or engage in other extroverted activities, the extent to which they can entertain their peers is nonetheless key in determining their popularity.

The centrality of charisma in rankings of popularity is also supported by interviews, and all boys make reference to it in some form. Paul, a quiet student who plays in a rock band, highlights the importance of charisma to popularity: "The bigger the character you are, the higher up you are." He added, "Take Joe, he's really out there. But he's popular because he's a big character." Sam agreed, "I would be more popular if I was loud and outgoing, but that's not really me." Rob suggested that this is because extroverted behaviors raise the spirits of *all* students. "Say it's a wet and rainy day and everyone's down," he said, "You can always rely on someone doing something, just to make everyone laugh again, and feel a bit better."

Authenticity

The most popular boys at Standard High are also seen by other students as genuine and open. I conceptualize this characteristic by the variable *authenticity*. Indeed, the presentation of a "truthful" and "honest" self is a valued attribute for boys at Standard High. For example, Jack argued that authenticity is highly important. "It is ultimately about comfortability with yourself," he said, "and a lot of guys are a lot less secure than they portray." When talking about popularity in interviews, ten of the twelve boys comment that it is important in determining popularity.

One way in which authenticity is displayed is through clothing. The most esteemed clothing style is that of a group of sporty students who dress to display their physique (Filiault & Drummond, 2009). They wear tight T-shirts and low-slung trousers, revealing their underwear. Although this dominant clothing style exists at Standard High, several popular boys differ from this norm. For example, Jack wears garish clothes. Even though style is highly valued, his difference is championed, and his popularity high. This is partly attributable to his charisma, but it is also due to his self-confident, individualistic fashion choices. Similarly, Grant wears clothes symbolic of lower-class groups, and Nick wears sports clothes. These clothing choices correspond with the students' self-image, and they therefore display authenticity through their difference, helping the boys to maintain their popularity.

However, whereas authenticity cements the popularity of the more charismatic boys, it is also important for those who lack charisma because it provides these boys with an opportunity to increase their popularity. For example, while talking about differences between students, Rob commented, "Take Sam; he's a bit different. But I got to know him, and he's really cool. I like his individuality."

The importance of authenticity is also demonstrated by the fact that boys who follow their own interests are respected for doing so. Grant said, "Some guys don't dance on tables and stuff, but that's them. They want to get on with their work, and I respect them for that." Grant's statement is supported by participant observations.

Standard High has silent workrooms where students can choose to study when they do not have lessons. Students have to cross the common room to reach these workrooms, and many low-ranking students, including Tom, spend their free time in them. Yet I did not observe students being heckled or bullied for going to these rooms; rather, their work ethic was praised. Justin said, "I wouldn't do it. I mean, I don't think it's fun. But good for them if they want to get good grades." Unlike in other research (cf. C. Jackson, 2006), boys do not have to distance themselves from hard work in order to maintain popularity (see also Francis, Skelton, & Read, 2010).

The importance of authenticity in popularity rankings is further evidenced by discussions of boys deemed lacking in it. For example, Jack suggested that Ben does not maintain authenticity. Jack said, "I know he's insecure, but he comes across as false." When asked about Ben, Steve agreed, saying, "It's annoying. He talks about football loads, but I know he's not really into it. I don't know why he pretends." Colin concurred, "Yeah, he tries too hard. He's a good guy, but he puts too much effort in." Accordingly, Ben's lack of authenticity limits his popularity.

Emotional Support

The giving of *emotional support* between boys is an ordinary interaction at Standard High; boys regularly offer each other reassurance and advice. Indeed, boys at Standard High maintain that support is a crucial part of friendship. In interviews, several boys said that their friends provide emotional comfort and practical help. Discussing his friends, Rob said, "I could have a serious chat with any of them, but at the same time still have a laugh." Tim agreed, saying, "I talk to my best friends about everything—if I've got girlfriend trouble, or when I'm upset or stressed. It's really important for me to be able to do that." Boys speak of their close friendships openly, without the threat of being feminized for doing so (Harris, 2010; Kehler, 2007).

As Tim suggests, boys also support each other in times of stress. For example, Steve had been learning to drive for several months. Before taking his road test, a group of friends publicly offer him support. Oli said, "I know you'll pass first time, you're really good," and Matt said, "Good luck, man, I'll be thinking of you." As Steve prepared to leave, Grant embraced him for several seconds and says, "I know you can do it."

Boys also provide assurance to each other in public events such as assemblies and music performances. Even though ritualized events like these have tradition-ally been scenes for the (re)establishment of masculine hierarchies (Pascoe, 2007), this is not the case at Standard High. An example of this is the election of "student officers." Each candidate was required to give a three-minute speech in assembly, and each was applauded as he or she stepped up to the platform to argue for his or her election. Simon, who is somewhat socially awkward and not particularly pop-ular, spoke hesitantly, making several mistakes. Nonetheless, he was equally applauded by his peers. Later, in the common room, Simon walked past a group of the most popular students. Grant called out, "Well done, Simon. It was good," and Rob added, "Yeah, it's not easy to do." There was no heckling, and the boys praised Simon's willingness to take part.

The election of "head boy" (the most important student officer position, along-side that of head girl) highlights the esteem in which emotional support is held at Standard High. Colin, a popular and sporty student, discussed how he considered running for head boy because of the encouragement of his friends:

I was quite touched by how many people said I should run. All my mates thought I should do it, basically because I'm a good listener and I help my mates out when they're going through a bad patch. But in the end I thought Simon would be better at it, he's probably smarter than me and cares more about the issues, so we all supported him instead.

Even though Colin decided against running, he was encouraged to run in part because of the way he supports his friends. Furthermore, he then supported another student who he knew really wanted the position.

As a demonstration of the importance of emotional support, if it is judged by peers that a boy has not offered the right level of support, he is reprimanded for his behavior. For example, Ben was discussing with his friends the opportunity he had been given by an art teacher to help paint a mural in the common room. Ben said, "I think I will. I mean, I want to leave my mark on the school." As Justin and Kai were suggesting that this was a good opportunity, Joe joined the conversation by commenting, "You can paint it with my dick!" However, no one laughed at this, and there was a short silence until Kai commented, "Joe, don't be harsh, it sounds cool." Joe looked perturbed and quickly replied, "Oh, sorry man. You've got to go for it. I mean, you love that kind of stuff." Here, Joe was regulated for the cavalier and somewhat aggressive manner in which he contributed to the discussion. His failed attempt at humor resulted in his demonstrating his support of Ben so as not to lose social standing.

Social Fluidity

Research shows that boys' friendship groups are traditionally fragmented into heavily insulated social cliques (Mac an Ghaill, 1994; Stoudt, 2006). In contrast, boys at Standard High valorize the ability to socialize with a range of students. Complementing both inclusivity and support, *social fluidity* denotes the ease with which students can move between social groups, and how well they can befriend a broad range of peers.

The privileging of social fluidity means that there are no real cliques at Standard High, only groups of friends. That is, although friendship groups exist, they lack the exclusivity, competitiveness, and rivalry that characterize many social cliques (Adler & Adler, 1995). Furthermore, although these distinct friendship groups exist, there is often overlap between them. Nick said, "I'm friends with the sporty lot, yeah, but also other guys. I spend time with each, and that's important to me." Sam had a similar view of social groupings: "I'm friends with lots of guys. In fact, you'll see me hang out with different guys each week. It's not like you can only have one group of friends. That would be dumb."

Many boys value this sociability. For example, in the last week of the summer term, approximately two-thirds of the students organized a five-day holiday together to the same seaside resort. About ten students carefully planned the trip, ensuring that the whole group would stay near one another. Rob, one of the main organizers, said, "It's important we go as a group, so we can all celebrate the end of the year together."

House parties are also a regular occurrence at Standard High. Tim is a member of the school football team, and one of the most popular boys at the school. He regularly hosted house parties on weekends when his parents were out of town. Yet rather than these being exclusive events, all students were invited. Tim said,

> I just shout out in the common room that a party is on, and I put it on my Facebook. Everyone's invited, but normally it's about 20 or 30 people who turn up—my main group of friends, and then their friends as well. But people do turn up who aren't in the main group, and that's cool. The more the merrier.

Boys who are not part of Tim's friendship group spoke positively about these parties. Chris said, "I go occasionally. I don't mind missing them because I'm not that close to Tim, but sometimes my girlfriend wants to go, and I always have a good time when I'm there." Simon commented, "I went to a couple, and it was fun to hang out with the guys, but everyone got so drunk and that's not my thing, so I don't go anymore."

In addition to having a large number or broad range of friends, social fluidity also involves being able to socialize with boys who are not part of one's own friendship group. For example, Rob presented himself as able to spend time with anyone, saying, "I love spending time with my friends in the common room. But if my friends aren't there, I can talk to guys I don't really know, just make conversation with them."

Students with less popularity agree. Paul, who perceives himself as being on the periphery of several groups, said, "When you enter the common room and your friends aren't there, you can just talk to other people. I'd be more popular if I did that more, but I find chatting to people I don't know difficult." At this level, social fluidity blurs somewhat with charisma. This is because charismatic boys are better socially equipped to talk to people beyond their friendship group. Of significance, however, is that popular boys who do not socialize beyond their immediate social network do not rank as highly as boys who maintain a broad range of friends. Notably, the most popular boys desire to mix with all students, and participant observations show that the most popular boys are also happy to have less popular students join their group of friends.

BEING UNPOPULAR? A HIERARCHY WITHOUT HEGEMONY

The stratification of masculinities traditionally found in schools has been shown to be maintained by marginalizing students and stigmatizing particular boys as *un*masculine (Connell, 1989; Mac an Ghaill, 1994; Stoudt, 2006). This is not the case with the popularity stratification found at Standard High. The ranking system there is not used by students to stigmatize their peers—it is not a *negative* ranking system. That is, although some boys at Standard High might maintain little popularity, they are not labeled as unpopular or socially ostracized by their peers. When asked whether anyone is unpopular, Grant said, "No, we all get along pretty well. I might not like everyone, but there's nobody I hate." Jack concurred, saying, "There are a few guys I can think of who don't have many friends, but I wouldn't say they were unpopular, no."

The boys recognize, however, that certain behaviors are unacceptable at Standard High. Rob said, "It wouldn't be O.K. if someone was rude all the time, or upset people." Oli added, "Well, if you bullied someone, that would be bad." Nick summed up the boys' views by saying, "Basically you'd be unpopular if you were really mean to someone." Participant observation supports these statements. I did not come across a single student who was ostracized or labeled as unpopular in my six months at the school. Indeed, the one time I witnessed a boy harassing another student (for sitting in his seat), other boys confronted the aggressor, who later apologized for his behavior. It seems that defying the tenets of inclusive masculinity is the only way to be unpopular at Standard High.

Students who are not particularly popular also appear happy with their position in the popularity ranking. For example, Sam recognized that he would be more popular if he were more extroverted, but he commented, "That's not really me. I'm happy with my friends, and I don't want to be more popular." Indeed, the less popular students do not desire to be like the more popular boys. Paul said, "There are plenty of guys more popular than me, but that's because I'm not a joker. And it suits me fine." Similarly, Kai commented, "Look at Tim, he's really cool. But I like my friends and my group. I don't want to change." Accordingly, this is a social hierarchy without hegemony, and new conceptual tools are required in order to understand its maintenance.

Popularity in an Inclusive Setting

Research on school cultures shows that many boys' social groupings are stratified in accordance with a masculine hierarchy that is based on exclusion, homophobia, and antifemininity (C. Jackson, 2006; Phoenix, Frosh, & Pattman, 2003). In such a setting, heterosexual boys must conform to restrictive gender norms if they desire to maintain masculine status. However, this chapter describes how boys at Standard High positioned themselves against homophobia; they did not publicly engage in misogyny, and they did not exhibit aggressive or violent behaviors. Offering fresh insight into the gendered behaviors of boys in school settings, this chapter supports Anderson's inclusive masculinity theory by showing that the set of acceptable masculine behaviors is greatly expanded in settings where homophobia is absent. When boys cease to be homophobic, misogynistic, and aggressive, multiple forms of masculinity can prosper, and masculine capital no longer serves as the main determinant in the stratification of boys.

Inclusive masculinity theory does not, however, explain how boys are ranked in an inclusive setting. This chapter conceptualizes a popularity ranking of boys consisting of four variables: charisma, authenticity, emotional support, and social fluidity. It highlights that whereas toxic practices of masculinity have been shown to exist in many settings in the past (Connell & Messerschmidt, 2005), the boys in my research engage in sociopositive acts that do not harm others.

An important conceptual finding of this research is that boys who provided emotional support were esteemed for doing so at Standard High. This stands in contrast with much existing literature. For example, Brannon (1976) highlighted how a man must be a "sturdy oak," and Pollack (1998) showed that a code exists to severely restrict the emotional freedoms of boys. Yet the emotional support demonstrated in this study highlights how the understanding of boys as emotionally illiterate is based on work that is over a decade old, and I question the extent to which seminal work from a more homophobic era speaks to contemporary youth. And although Way's (2011) important book documented emotional intimacy between young boys diminishing as they enter late adolescence and emerging adulthood, I suggest that this is the result of her participants living in a homohysteric setting and so her findings, with working class black and Latino youth, are not comparable with white middle class youth in the United Kingdom.

The issue of authenticity has also been raised by other scholars. Lyng (2009) characterizes this by arguing that students have particular masculine styles that they are expected to embody in a consistent manner. She writes:

> Students have shared social notions of and implicit rules for what performances, preferences, and other signifiers fit well together within one style, and ... being able to display through practice the knowledge of these rules is essential to being rendered a socially competent student. (p. 467)

Although her research occurred in a more homohysteric setting than Standard High, it shows that charisma has often been an important trait for boys to maintain.

The social fluidity of male students is also an important and somewhat counterintuitive finding. Research on masculinities and student friendship groups demonstrates the ways in which friendship groups are consolidated by the exclusion of ostracized students (Poteat, Espelage, & Green, 2007; Stoudt, 2006), yet this chapter suggests that this is not the case in settings of low homohysteria. In Standard High, the ability to socialize across friendship groups was an attribute that raised one's popularity. Accordingly, it is necessary to contextualize processes of exclusion as dependent on existing within highly homohysteric cultures. Indeed, not all boys are esteemed for exhibiting homophobic, misogynistic, and violent behaviors, and we therefore need a new approach for understanding male hierarchies in schools.

10

Homosexually Themed Language

In preceding chapters I have documented that homophobic language is nearly totally absent in the three high schools studied. I also show that these high schools are not homohysteric and that pro-gay attitudes are espoused by heterosexual male students. However, it is not known what happens to the discursive practices of boys and men who have traditionally maintained high degrees of homophobia in settings where overt homophobia has become socially unacceptable. Indeed, I found that the existing frameworks that conceptualize homosexually themed language did not help understand the use of language in these schools. Accordingly, in this chapter I review the ways in which homophobic language has been conceptualized, and I provide a model for understanding the spectrum of its evolving usage.

UNDERSTANDING HOMOPHOBIC LANGUAGE

Although a multitude of social forces construct and regulate hierarchies of sexuality and gender, language serves as the currency through which ideas and social norms are (re)produced (Cameron & Kulick, 2003; Kiesling, 2007). This is particularly true in schools, where young people engage in a plethora of verbal exchanges in order to consolidate their gendered and sexual identities (Thorne & Luria, 1986). This can range from the playing of "cooties" to homophobic name-calling. Accordingly, the prevalence and varied meanings of homophobic and homosexually themed language are of fundamental importance in understanding the regulation and stratification of sexuality and gender in school systems (Plummer, 1999).

The use of homophobic language is an increasingly important issue in both cultural and political realms. However, compared to the diverse academic literature on the topic (McCormack & Anderson, 2010; Pascoe, 2005; Rasmussen, 2004), understanding of the issue is all too frequently based on a simplistic conceptualization of language that is (or is not) homophobic. This can lead to an exaggeration of the prevalence of homophobic language in contemporary cultures. This is because many people have been brought up in a culture in which the majority of colloquial language relating to homosexuality has been homophobic, making people at risk of hearing homophobia in language whether it is there or not.

This is problematic because a fear of homophobia (even when the fear is unwarranted) can lead to gay people deciding to stay in the closet (Anderson, 2002). In order to clarify what makes language homophobic, I argue that the literature documents two requisite features: (1) it is said with pernicious intent, and (2) it has a negative social effect.

The first requirement of homophobic language, pernicious intent, recognizes that the speaker is intending to degrade or marginalize a person or behavior by use of the association with homosexuality. Armstrong (1997) argued that hostility and the devaluation of homosexuality are "implicit in the usage of homophobic terms" (p. 328). Thurlow (2001) furthered this argument by examining "intensifiers"—words such as "fucking" that demonstrate a desire to wound a person. He found that homophobic language was accompanied by an intensifier more frequently than any other form of insult in school settings—for example, saying "you fucking poof" rather than "you poof."

Further evidence of the pernicious intent of homophobic language is provided by a consideration of its role in bullying. Rivers (1996) found that verbal abuse was the most common form of bullying practice leveled at gays and lesbians, and homophobic language has also been frequently used by bullies of heterosexual students (Rivers, 1995; Douglas, Warwick, Kemp, Whitty, & Aggleton, 1999). Given that bullying is the marginalization of a person by more powerful peers, the frequent use of homophobic language in bullying behaviors is clear evidence of its pernicious intent.

Bullying also evidences the second component of homophobic language: it maintains negative social effect. Gay and lesbian adults often speak of the emotional trauma caused by homophobic bullying in their youth (Flowers & Buston, 2001), and research also highlights the socionegative impact that this has on students; this includes elevated rates of absenteeism, social isolation, and higher drop-out rates (Warwick, Aggleton, & Douglas, 2001). Homophobic bullying has also led to elevated levels of suicide among gay youth (D'Augelli, Hershberger, & Pilkington, 2001), although recent research suggests that lesbian, gay, bisexual, and transgender suicide rates might now be comparable to those of urban heterosexual youth (Mustanski, Garofalo, & Emerson, 2010).

Even when homophobic language is not intended to marginalize another person (instead castigating a behavior or action), it nonetheless reproduces homophobia because users still intend to stigmatize same-sex desire (Hillier & Harrison, 2004; Rubin, 1984). For example, using explicitly anti-gay epithets to regulate heterosexual boys who do not conform to orthodox gender stereotypes reproduces the hierarchical stratification of all masculinities, as well as harming the recipient of the abuse. Accordingly, homophobic language can contribute to a hostile school culture for all male youth.

Although pernicious intent and negative social effect are the two key factors that have been used to determine whether language is homophobic or not, implicit in most of the academic research on the subject is an assumption that this homophobic language is said within a homophobic environment. That is, homophobic language has occurred in schools where students have homophobic attitudes and gay students are closeted or marginalized. Some scholars documented the homophobic culture (Mac an Ghaill, 1994), whereas others assumed its presence (Ellis & High, 2004; Thurlow, 2001).

The assumption of a homophobic environment is understandable given that the vast majority of the research on homophobic language occurred between 1980 and 2000, when British and American cultures were homohysteric and homophobic (Anderson, 2009; Loftus, 2001). Yet the marked decrease in levels of homophobia of recent years necessitates that this assumption be made explicit in order for the cultural context to be recognized. Accordingly, I propose an additional factor for analyzing homophobic language: a homophobic environment. In Fig. 10.1 I provide a framework for understanding the components of homophobic language.

This linking of environment with effect and intent helps to historically contextualize the conceptualization of homophobic language that so accurately captured the social dynamics of the 1980s and 1990s (see Epstein, 1997; Mac an Ghaill, 1994; Salisbury & Jackson, 1996). However, more recent research on the use of homosexually themed language has highlighted complexities that do not readily fit into this framework of homophobic language.

THE CHANGING USE OF LANGUAGE

In 2005, C. J. Pascoe introduced the concept of "fag discourse" into discussions of homophobic language. Building on Thorne and Luria's (1986) notion of "fag talk,"

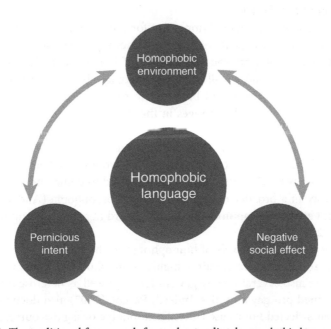

Figure 10.1 The traditional framework for understanding homophobic language.

fag discourse conceptualized a particularly *gendered* form of homophobia. Here, the purpose was not necessarily to regulate sexuality, but instead to regulate boys' behaviors. Importantly, Pascoe distinguished the use of the word "fag" from the use of anti-gay pejoratives such as "queer" and "poof" because "fag" no longer had explicit associations with sexuality for many of the participants in her study.

Although the observation about the gendered nature of homophobia built on the work of British scholars of masculinity (Epstein, 1997; Mac an Ghaill, 1994), an important difference is that Pascoe (2005, 2007) documented the ways in which "fag" was used as a pernicious insult that regulated gender without intending to marginalize same-sex identities. For example, Pascoe (2005) highlighted that "some boys took pains to say that 'fag' is not about sexuality" (p. 336), and she later argued that "fag" refers to "any sort of behavior defined as unmasculine" (Pascoe, 2007, p. 57). Accordingly, fag discourse conceptualizes the use of anti-gay epithets because of antipathy toward gender non-conformity, not homosexuality.

Pascoe also highlighted that the intent was not *necessarily* pernicious, even if it frequently was. As Pascoe (2007) commented, "[F]ag talk and fag imitations serve as a discourse with which boys discipline themselves and each other through joking relationships" (p. 54). With Pascoe's fag discourse and these "joking relationships," the notion of intent is far more complex than with homophobic language. Although there is always an intent to regulate something (be it sexuality or gender, a person or a behavior), the type of intention varies with fag discourse. This intent can be to wound someone, but it could also be to castigate a behavior or even just competitively joke with friends. Indeed, use of the word "fag" seems almost habitual, as a "compulsive" (p. 86) part of boys' interactions. It should be clear, however, that this nuance is not recognized in the pernicious-intent component of homophobic language.

Pascoe's work was considered important for the significance it had in furthering understanding of the gendered nature of homophobia. However, most academics failed to appreciate the significance of her work in documenting the *changing* nature of homosexually themed language. Because pernicious intent was still sometimes evident, and because the social effect was often extremely negative, they overlooked the changes in the use of language that fag discourse conceptualized. Accordingly, despite the subtle changes in intent and effect, scholars continued to label fag discourse as part of the traditional framework of homophobic language (e.g. Bortolin, 2010). This would have been appropriate in the 1980s and 1990s, when the word "fag" was used to demonstrate disgust with homosexuality in a broader culture of extreme homophobia (Anderson, 2009), but it did not accurately capture the use of the word in a different cultural context (see Fig. 10.2).

It is easy to read high levels of homophobia in the school where Pascoe collected data, and there were certainly highly homophobic aspects of the setting. Yet there were also several openly gay students, as well as heterosexual students who maintained pro-gay attitudes. Indeed, Pascoe (2007) also documented that many students elected not to use either homophobic or fag discourse. She wrote, "I was stunned at the myriad opportunities to levy the epithet and the seeming

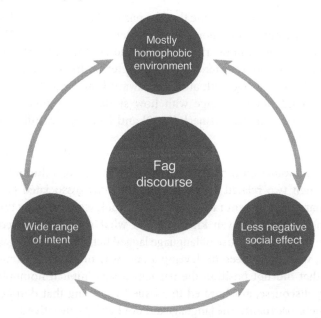

Figure 10.2 A framework for understanding fag discourse.

refusal by these boys, gay and straight, to invoke it" (p. 79). This is something not documented in previous research, and it is evidence of a less homophobic environment.

Although it does document differences from the framework of homophobic language, Pascoe's work has not been the final development in understanding homosexually themed language. This is because, as I discuss throughout this book, homophobia has continued to decrease at a rapid rate since Pascoe's study. Although many researchers acknowledge this (Richardson, 2010; Swain, 2006b; Weeks, 2007), it has yet to be examined how homosexually themed language operates in a pro-gay environment.

In an attempt to address this lack of engagement with changing cultural attitudes, I coauthored an article with Eric Anderson that sought to understand how the effect of homosexually themed language varied according to the social context (McCormack & Anderson, 2010). In that article, we develop the concept of "gay discourse" in order to understand the use of language that has a homosexual theme but which is not homophobic as described in my framework above. This concept emerged from our ethnographic data with heterosexual rugby players who espoused pro-gay attitudes and had openly gay friends but who nonetheless used phrases like "don't be gay" and "that's so gay." They asserted that this position was consistent because "gay" had two meanings—it referred to sexuality in some contexts and meant "rubbish" in others (see Lalor & Rendle-Short, 2007)—and they argued that the two meanings were wholly independent of each other.

Some scholars continue to argue that the phrase "that's so gay" is homophobic despite decreasing cultural homophobia (see DePalma & Jennett, 2010; Sanders, 2008). Yet they do this without critical investigation of the attitudes of those using the language. As a result, they tend to mischaracterize the phrase as homophobic because they do not engage with attitudes toward homosexuality. Equally problematic, they tend not to engage with how students interpret this discourse (Adams, Anderson, and McCormack [2010] and Lalor and Rendle-Short [2007] are notable exceptions).

However, in our research, Anderson and I explained this use of language by viewing the phenomenon through Ogburn's (1950) lens of cultural lag. Cultural lag occurs when two related social variables become dissociated because their meanings change at different rates. In this case, adolescents employ this language without consideration or even knowledge of what it once conveyed. In other words, these rugby players' use of language lagged behind their pro-gay attitudes. Accordingly, we felt the need to develop a new way of understanding their language, one that did not position the participants as implicit homophobes. Our concept, gay discourse, ameliorated this issue by arguing that despite implicitly privileging heterosexuality, the language did not have the negative social effects of either homophobic language or fag discourse. Figure 10.3 conceptualizes this in a way that draws out the difference as compared to homophobic language. With a more inclusive environment and an absence of pernicious intent, the social effects of this language are far less negative.

This framework was useful in understanding the dynamics and implications of the phrase "that's so gay." However, it was less effective in explaining another use

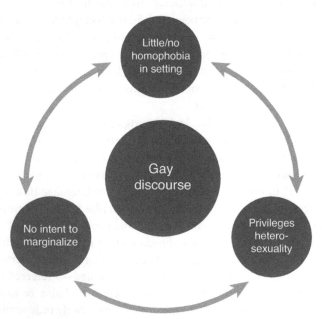

Figure 10.3 A new framework for understanding gay discourse.

of the homosexually themed language of these players: as a form of social bonding. In greeting one another, the men would often say "Hey, gay boy" or "Hey, sister." This language was used between friends in a welcoming manner. We argued that this language could continue to privilege heterosexuality because of the framework of homosexual stigma that used to exist in rugby. Unfortunately, we were falling back on the same assumption of context that we accused others of doing in labeling "that's so gay" as homophobic, a position that was aided by the fact that there were no openly gay athletes to judge this use of language. Still, we did not have evidence that this privileged heterosexuality, and should not therefore have drawn the conclusions that we did.

The lack of negative social effect is also found in sports settings. Anderson's (2011b) most recent examination of the experiences of openly gay male athletes finds that they do not attribute anti-gay sentiment to the phrase "that's so gay." Indeed, one of his respondents argued, "You can't judge homophobia that way. . . . The word has different meanings and most of the time it's not got anything to do with gay" (p. 128). Furthermore, all of his participants argued that use of the words "gay" and "fag" were not indicative of homophobia. They also did not use the prevalence of the word as a determining factor when deciding to come out. Accordingly, the negativity in the use of homosexually themed language has been expunged in these instances.

My research at Religious, Standard, and Fallback High presents a unique opportunity: the chance to examine the use of homosexually themed language in both the absence of homophobia and the presence of gay peers. I am unaware of any other research that investigates such a setting. Accordingly, in the rest of this chapter, I explore the use of homosexually themed language at the three schools, examining how the language fits within the frameworks explicated here. I then develop a new concept of "pro-gay language" in order to understand the playful use of homosexually themed language that bonds heterosexual and gay peers. Finally, I develop a model for understanding the evolution of homosexually themed language that should be of use to teachers and practitioners in understanding the meanings and effects of specific instances of homosexually-themed language.

THE USE OF GAY DISCOURSE

When reading media reports and recent academic literature, it is possible to get the impression that the phrase "that's so gay" is ubiquitous and inescapable in British and American schools (Hunt & Jensen, 2007; Kimmel, 2008). However, in my research I found that the phrase was not used at all at Standard High or Fallback High. It was, however, used by some of the boys at Religious High. For example, when given a great deal of homework to complete over the weekend, Jonathan complained, "That's so gay! When am I supposed to go out?" And when Zak realized that he left his book at home, he muttered, "So gay."

It is hard to quantify the usage of this language. Some boys, like Zak, used the phrase frequently (more than once a week), whereas others did so rarely.

Other boys never used it. Collectively, my research notes indicate that I heard the phrase approximately twice a week. Although this is not a methodologically rigorous statistic, it suggests that the use of this phrase is less regular than other research documents (Ellis & High, 2004).

When I asked boys at Religious High about the "gay" content of this language, participants maintained that it is decidedly not homophobic (see McCormack & Anderson, 2010). They argued that their pro-gay attitudes prevented it from being interpreted as such. Zak said, "I say it all the time. But I don't mean anything by it. I've got gay friends." Alex added, "It isn't meant homophobically. When I say 'that's so gay,' I don't mean homosexual." Lewis was insulted by the suggestion that the phrase could be interpreted as homophobic. He said, "What? So saying 'It's so gay that I got homework' means that I think my homework is a guy and is attracted to other guys? That doesn't make any sense."

In addition to maintaining pro-gay attitudes, several students believed that it is acceptable for them to use the phrase "that's so gay" because their gay peers use it too. For example, when asked why he uses the word "gay," Lewis said, "It doesn't mean 'gay' in that way. Look, Greg says it, and he's gay. Why can't I, if he can?" This is something that gay students agreed with. Eddie, who is gay, said, "I don't mind straight people saying 'that's so gay.' I say it, so it would be hypocritical if I had an issue with it." Greg also agreed with this argument.

The negative social effect of gay discourse is quite limited. I argue that it privileges heterosexuality above gay identity because of the implicit association of homosexuality with negative expressions, feelings, or attitudes. Although the word "gay" now clearly has two independent meanings, use of the phrase "that's so gay" implicitly and perhaps inevitably draws on the history of stigma associated with homosexuality. In this framework, homosexuality might be acceptable, but it is not as desirable as heterosexuality.

In order to understand the limited extent of this negative effect, it is important to recognize that the word "gay" has been used as an expression of displeasure without intent to reflect or transmit homophobia in many contemporary youth settings (Adams et al., 2010; Lalor & Rendle-Short, 2007; McCormack & Anderson, 2010). These articles support my participants' contention that their language does not demonstrate homophobia, or even reference homosexuality. From their perspective, it "simply" serves as a cathartic expression of dissatisfaction.

PRO-GAY LANGUAGE

Thus far, the use of homosexually themed language at these schools has corresponded with the discursive practices of the rugby players with whom Eric Anderson and I devised the concept of gay discourse (McCormack & Anderson, 2010). However, in a manner previously undocumented in school and sports settings, gay and straight students at Religious High use certain types of homosexually themed language as a way of socially bonding with each other. Again, this most frequently draws on traditional notions of heteromasculinity, but it does so in a playful and friendly manner. For example, Max, the openly gay student president, was working alongside Cooper and James in an English lesson. While Cooper was doodling in his book, he looked up and asked Max, "Is this really gay what I'm doing?" Max started laughing and said, "Yeah, it's pretty gay." Another time, Greg was playing catch with Lewis and some other heterosexual friends. As Lewis threw the ball, it slipped out of his hand, travelling only a few meters. Greg shouted, "Lewis! You're gayer than me!" This form of bantering between heterosexual and gay peers was a regular occurrence within established friendship groups. Not only did it bond students together, but it also appeared to expunge some of the negativity from these words, perhaps consolidating the dual meanings of the word "gay." Accordingly, I call this "pro-gay language."

However, pro-gay language is not used only to bond gay and straight peers as in the examples above. The other key form of pro-gay language is when heterosexual male students casually call their close friends "lover" or "boyfriend." In Chapter 8, I identify this as a form of ironic heterosexual recuperation. For example, at Standard High, Liam and Rob would knowingly play on the close friendship they maintained, calling each other "boyfriend" "for a laugh." However, there were considerably more times when boys employed this language out of homosocial affection, without any discernible attempt to consolidate their heterosexual standing. This occurred at all three schools.

At Fallback High, for example, Phil and Dan would regularly address each other as "lover" or "boyfriend." They called each other "babes" and "my lover" daily, particularly when planning social activities. For example, Dan said, "Hey, my lover, are you coming 'round mine after school today?" Phil replied, "Sure, babes, you know I wouldn't miss it." These two boys maintained the closest friendship at Fallback High, and regularly socialized together in their free time.

Proclaiming close friends as boyfriends is understood by students as a way of demonstrating emotional intimacy. Phil said, "Yeah, I call him boyfriend and stuff, but that's just a way of saying he's my best mate." Similarly, Dave commented, "I'll sometimes call my best mates 'lover' or something. It's just a way of saying, 'I love you,' really." Importantly, these students did not think that labeling each other this way would homosexualize them. For example, Dan said, "I think it's pretty obvious. It doesn't mean I fancy Phil, it means he's my best mate. No one's got confused so far, anyway." And at Religious High, Dave said, "People know I'm straight, so it's not a question of being attracted to him. It's about loving him." Accordingly, I define pro-gay language as the use of homosexually themed language to bond people together in sociopositive ways or to demonstrate pro-gay attitudes.

The ability of boys to express their emotions in such an open way is clearly a positive development, and mirrors the findings of Way (2011) among younger African-American and Latino boys in the United States. Of further importance though, is that just as homophobic language once contributed to a homophobic school environment, this form of pro-gay language now helps promote gay-friendly cultures of inclusivity.

A MODEL OF HOMOSEXUALLY THEMED DISCOURSE

In this section, I present an empirically grounded model for conceptualizing all forms of homosexually themed language. In order to highlight the differences in meaning and effect, I conceptualized gay discourse as distinct from homophobic language. Homophobic language is well documented in the academic literature (Plummer, 1999), and I have argued that it is defined by pernicious intent, a homophobic environment, and having a negative social effect. In contrast, gay discourse lacks any intent to marginalize or wound and as a result has little if any negative social effect. Some scholars might, however, argue that it continues to promote heteronormativity. Although I think that this is unlikely, I suspect that this is one instance in which distinguishing the causal effects of language is nearly impossible.

In addition to the use of gay discourse, I also documented instances of male students using homosexually themed language in ways that have a sociopositive effect, calling this pro-gay language. First, this form of language was used as a way of bonding heterosexual and gay students. Second, it was used by heterosexual friends as a way of demonstrating their emotional intimacy. Importantly, none of this was accompanied by heterosexual recuperation or homophobia, and these students did not appear to be worried about being considered gay because of it.

In this model, I foreground the importance of the cultural context in understanding language. This is because the social environment is pivotal for discerning the intent of language, how it is interpreted, and the social effects it has. To explain this, I highlight that no phrase is necessarily part of a particular category. For example, when I was a closeted school student I heard the phrase "that's so gay" frequently, and it was one of the reasons that I decided to stay in the closet: I interpreted the phrase as deeply homophobic, and it had negative emotional effects on me. But I attended a highly homophobic school where the phrase "that's so gay" was heard alongside homophobic pejoratives such as "poof," "shirtlifter," and "bender." Students growing up at Religious High today hear the same phrase differently. The point is that the phrase "that's so gay" is not *necessarily* homophobic, nor does it have to be a part of gay discourse—the categorization of language will depend on the cultural context. Thus, I argue that homohysteria is the key factor in determining the type of social environment. In cultures of high homohysteria, the same language has different effects.

RELATING THE MODEL TO HOMOHYSTERIA

In Fig. 10.4, I situate cultural context as central to understanding and categorizing types of homosexually themed language. First, in a highly homohysteric culture, boys use homophobic language to consolidate their own heterosexual identity and masculine standing (Plummer, 1999). In this stage, homosexually themed language is indeed homophobic, as it is used with pernicious intent and has a very negative social effect.

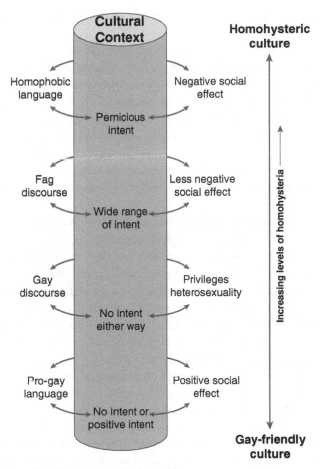

Figure 10.4 A model of homosexually themed language.

The second framework, fag discourse, occurs in settings that are slightly less homohysteric. Here, it is likely that many gay students have negative school experiences and that the setting is homophobic, but it is also likely that there will be students who support gay rights (and probably even some openly gay students). In this stage, some young men who use fag discourse will insist that it is not meant to stigmatize homosexuality, whereas others will use it with pernicious intent. It will continue to have negative social effects, however, including the regulation and restriction of acceptable masculine behaviors, because the intent of the language use is not always clear (Anderson, 2002).

In the third framework, gay discourse occurs in settings where young men are not particularly concerned about whether they are socially perceived as gay. In these settings of low homohysteria, boys say phrases like "that's so gay" as expressions of dissatisfaction and frustration. Importantly, there is no intent to marginalize or wound people with this use of language, and although this is not necessarily pro-gay, young men maintain that the word "gay" does not connote same-sex desire in this context.

Finally, in gay-friendly cultures such as the high schools discussed in this book, students are not part of a homohysteric culture. Although they might prefer to be thought heterosexual, they do not police their behaviors in order to live up to a heteromasculine ideal. In such a setting, homosexually themed language is used in a way that has *positive* social effects. Sometimes pro-gay language is used without any specific intention, but it is also used as a mechanism for bonding students by demonstrating emotional intimacy or the inclusion of openly gay students. The fun and fundamentally friendly way in which this language is used—that is, the ease these students have with gay peers—helps contribute to the creation of a gay-friendly environment.

It is worth emphasizing that the use of language is always complex and tricky. There will be some overlap between types of language, as well as exceptions to the framework. For example, although a person can use homophobic language in a gay-friendly setting, this would be an anomalous result and would not fit with general conceptualizations of homophobic language in the wider literature. For example, if a student were to shout, "You fucking poof" at another boy in a gay-friendly high school (like Standard High), it is highly likely that that student would be reprimanded by students and teachers alike, and (apart from the impact it would have on the recipient) it would have marginal, if any, negative social effect on the broader culture. Likewise, saying "that's so gay" in a highly homophobic setting would probably be interpreted as homophobic, whereas this would not be the case in a gay-friendly school. In understanding this form of language, context is all-important (see Davies, 1999; McCormack & Anderson, 2010). It should also be noted that Fig. 10.4 does not provide an exhaustive list of words or phrases with a homosexual theme. It does, however, provide a framework by which to judge other forms of language. One example of this is the phrase "no homo" (see Brown, 2011). Originating in hip-hop culture, it has received commentary in the media from leading scholars such as Pat Griffin and Michael Kimmel. "No homo" is used when men transgress traditional heteromasculine boundaries as a way of consolidating their heterosexual identities—it is a form of heterosexual recuperation. In her blog, Pat Griffin (2009) is particularly scathing about this use of language, viewing it as homophobic, writing, "[T]hese words can become weapons that provoke fragile peers to suicide or murder." However, drawing on Pascoe's (2007) work, Michael Kimmel (2009) suggests that "no homo" is a sign of progress, writing that the phrase "reflects the significant decline in homophobia among straight men in the United States today."

In my model, I suggest that "no homo" is akin to gay discourse. As Kimmel argues, there is no actual intent to stigmatize feminine behaviors or homosexuality; rather there is a recognition that a particular behavior might code a person as gay. Indeed, it can even be used as a technique to *expand* heteromasculine boundaries, effectively enabling someone to say, "I'm straight, but I love you." Indeed, one could argue about whether it is "homosexually themed" at all—that it is instead a statement of one's own heterosexuality, without being homophobic.

But this nitpicking aside, although "no homo" privileges heterosexuality, it is hard to see it as homophobic. Accordingly, this model can be used as a framework for understanding new manifestations of homosexually themed language as they arise.

It is my hope that this new model will help teachers, students, and scholars understand and identify different forms of homosexually themed language, and that by categorizing it appropriately, it ensures that we are all more able to appropriately judge the extent to which particular schools are homophobic, gay friendly, or somewhere in between.

11

Gay-Friendly High Schools

In this book I examine the changing attitudes and behaviors of heterosexual male youth in British high schools. Given the corresponding evidence of positive experiences of lesbian, gay, bisexual, and transgender (LGBT) students in these settings, it is reasonable to call them *gay-friendly high schools*. For example, Max made his sexuality a part of his successful campaign to be student president, using his charisma, flamboyance, and intellect to play with issues of sexuality—flirting with straight friends, kissing his gay peers, and campaigning for LGBT issues. Other gay students also reported positive, homophobia-free school experiences.

The main focus of this book has been to explicate the ways in which heterosexual students are gay friendly—espousing pro-gay attitudes, being inclusive of gay students, condemning homophobia, and having close friendships with gay students. There is a total absence of evidence suggesting that homophobia is present or esteemed, and interviews and participant observations of all students demonstrate gay-friendliness. Sexuality simply is not an issue in determining a student's popularity in these schools, and happiness and mental health are no longer predicated upon being heterosexual (see Savin-Williams, 2005). It is not an overstatement to argue that these male youth are redefining heterosexuality and masculinity for their generation. Asking why this is the case—why and how things have changed so much—is an interesting and important question.

It is tempting to look for institutional factors (such as school policies or influential teachers) to explain these results, particularly because they deviate from what one might expect. However, I could find no outstanding reasons why the inclusive behaviors of these boys should be radically different from those of male students in other schools. There has been, for example, no openly gay teacher in any of these high schools in recent years. No comprehensive gay sensitivity training programs have been put in place, and no other institutional pro-gay initiatives exist (see Beckett, Tweed, and Fisher [1999] for what this might look like). Indeed, as discussed in Chapter 7, some boys at Standard High critique their school's policies and curricula as being homophobic.

Furthermore, there are contrasting policies between the schools, indicating that institutional factors play little part. For example, the antibullying and equal opportunities policies at Standard High and Religious High do not reference sexual orientation, whereas those at Fallback High do. Similarly, despite its religious ethos, Religious High is the only site that has resources on homosexuality in its library and medical center. These differences do not, however, correlate to the varying levels of homohysteria at each school. This suggests that cultural factors play the key role in the decreased levels of homohysteria found in these research sites, not institutional perspectives. Indeed, it would be deeply problematic to ignore the markedly different political, cultural, and legal landscape that exists for LGBT people in the United Kingdom today (McNair, 2002; Weeks, 2007), as well as the fact that boys and young men in Britain are able to engage in a broader range of gendered behaviors than had previously been the case (Anderson, 2009; Anderson & McGuire, 2010; Swain, 2006b).

My argument is that social change has occurred among these youth as a result of how they engage in wider cultural discourses, rather than through institutional norms. That is, contemporary attitudes toward homosexuality in the United Kingdom are markedly different compared to those that existed when the seminal literature on homophobia in schools was undertaken (Epstein, 1997; Francis, 1999; Mac an Ghaill, 1994). This corresponds with Weeks's (2007) argument that social change regarding sexuality has largely been the result of the collective action of individual people, calling this change part of "the world we have won." He writes,

The momentum is positive, and largely due to one essential feature of this new world: grass-roots agency is central to the direction we are moving in. Increasingly the contemporary world is a world we are making for ourselves, part of the long process of the democratisation of everyday life. (p. x)

It is important to note, however, that since I collected the data for this research, there have been further shifts toward inclusivity in institutional directives. In the United Kingdom, OfSTED, the school inspectorate, has made the equalities agenda a key issue that schools must address. Sexual orientation is one of the named equalities that schools must protect, and failure to do this can result in the school failing inspection. Crucially, the new framework is no longer concerned with simply tackling discrimination. Rather, schools must also promote inclusivity and diversity. In this regard, OfSTED has shifted from a reactive approach, compelling schools to tackle homophobic bullying when it occurs, to a proactive one where schools must be able to demonstrate the ways in which they have promoted diversity and inclusivity. I suggest that this policy shift is the result of a recognition that attitudes toward homosexuality have fundamentally changed in the wider culture.

However, it is important to stress that although I argue that these institutional changes have not been causative factors in evincing pro-gay attitudes, they are important to have, and they are fundamentally *necessary* if schools are to be guaranteed safe spaces for LGBT students. School policies need to align with school culture in this regard. That is, even if these policy and curricular changes do not make students pro-gay, they are a powerful statement of inclusivity and equality, and the effect of this on LGBT youth should not be underestimated.

Even without policy change, things are moving in the right direction. This is a product of these students' engagement in youth culture, in which more inclusive attitudes have prevailed (Anderson, 2009; McNair, 2002). The Internet has been an environment where such views have developed and flourished. For example, the vast majority of students belong to social networking sites such as Facebook. On such sites, boys are asked to identify the gender to which they are attracted, increasing the visibility of homosexuality. Boys also post photos of their nights out, their holidays, and other important and mundane aspects of their life. As Anderson (2009) finds happening with his participants, this normalizes homosocial bonding—these boys post photos of drunken antics in which they hug and kiss each other. Further demonstrating the normalcy of tactility, there are many photos on these profile pages of boys who have engaged in similar acts of homosocial closeness, including hugging and sharing beds together. These Facebook photos also include pictures of boys kissing on the cheek and lips, much like Anderson, Adams, and Rivers (2010) describe happening in UK university settings.

It is important to note that the only three boys to engage in homophobic language in my research had minimal engagement with contemporary culture. These three students did not belong to social networking sites and used the Internet only for their schoolwork. They watched television only for its soccer coverage, and they did not listen to contemporary music (preferring 1990s bands like Nirvana instead). They did not buy their clothes in high street stores, and although they occasionally ventured into the nearby city, they spent most of their leisure time in Standard Town. It seems that their lack of engagement with contemporary culture is closely linked to their more orthodox masculine behaviors. This is clearly affected by their class background, and it points to the problems of some working-class, disaffected youth who do not (or cannot) engage in the wider cultural changes occurring around them. Having rejected a more global youth culture, these students are more likely to adopt the homophobia of their fathers.

If positive attitudes do come from engagement with youth culture, it might help explain why higher levels of homophobia have previously been recorded with younger students (Phoenix, Frosh, & Pattman, 2003; Plummer, 1999). Several of my participants discussed some level of homophobia in earlier years of schooling, although whether the diminishment of homophobia is because of the maturity of aging students or because of corresponding decreasing homohysteria over time is unclear.

As a further complicating factor, these high schools have their own institutional context, which is the result of boys' electing to stay in full-time education after the age of 16 in the United Kingdom (although this age has been extended to 18 since data was collected). This self-selection factor means that some of the more disruptive boys will have left these educational settings. This is a point of difference from high schools in the United States, where compulsory education continues until the age of 18.

Although it is likely that this self-selection issue will result in some homophobic youth leaving these schools, a more important issue is the cultural context in which the schools are located. That is, the higher levels of homophobia that

Pascoe (2007) finds are likely attributable to data collection that occurred in a more homophobic period of time, in a more homophobic country: her research was conducted several years earlier than mine, and American culture tends to be more homophobic than that of the United Kingdom (Anderson 2009).

The effect of these issues of selection has, however, been limited through the inclusion of Fallback High, which was specifically chosen because its students are working-class, disaffected youth who have had troubled educational experiences. Furthermore, the student body at Religious High comprises a diverse group of students, from many class backgrounds and with a wide range of academic abilities. Simply stated, these students are not an elite group of privileged young men.

It is also important to recognize the homophobia that was present in British high schools in the past (Epstein, O'Flynn, & Telford, 2003). For example, Redman and Mac an Ghaill (1997) documented high levels of homophobia in these sites. They showed that even though high school boys adopted gendered behaviors that distinguished them from younger boys, these new forms were still based in homophobia, misogyny, and aggression. The postcompulsory element of high school education did not lead to a gender utopia. Indeed, evidence of a historical change in attitudes toward homosexuality is also found in Chapter 7, in which I describe interviews with students who used to attend Standard High, who state that it had been homophobic in years gone by. Accordingly, I argue that cultural change is the primary reason for the diminished influence of homohysteria in these settings.

It is, after all, a seemingly obvious conclusion that the rise in gay visibility and the increasing ordinariness of homosexuality will have a positive impact on heterosexual men (Netzley, 2010; Savin-Williams, 2005; Walters, 2001). Weeks (2007) describes the positive advances in attitudes toward homosexuality as "the inevitable reality," and he argues that these changes have "broken through the coils of power to enhance individual autonomy, freedom of choice and more egalitarian patterns of relationships" (p. 7). Although levels of homophobia will continue to vary according to geography, race, class, and other forms of social context, the decline in homohysteria in my research appears to primarily be the result of wider cultural, political, and legal changes regarding declining homophobia more broadly.

GAY-FRIENDLY HIGH SCHOOLS IN A GLOBAL PERSPECTIVE

Data collection for this research occurred in the south of England, a place that many readers might think is more liberal than other parts of the globe. Indeed, there is a well-known North/South divide in the United Kingdom, and the North is deemed less inclusive of gender and sexual diversity than the South. This divide has similarities with the red state/blue state split in the United States, in which it is generally found that those states that always vote Republican (red) are less gay friendly than the (blue) Democrat-voting states. With both examples, although they maintain some truth, these generalizations act only as a framework (see Gray, 2009). Manchester, for example, is a Northern city in the United Kingdom, yet it vies for the status of Britain's gay capital alongside London and Brighton. Similarly, there are rural areas in the South of England where poverty persists and attitudes might be more conservative. All this is to say that we cannot be sure which attitudes will prevail where.

The key point is that caution must be used when considering geographical position. I urge readers to treat the North of the United Kingdom with an open mind. Do not assume that kids from grey Northern cities will be more homophobic than reported here. Before my research, people assumed that kids all over England were homophobic; it might be equally mistaken to presume homophobia in the North. Indeed, in my own conversations with young men from the North of England, I have found stories that are less divergent than one might expect. For example, in the fall of 2010, I spoke to a gay fresher at the University of Brighton who went to school in a small Northern town. I was struck by how closely his school experiences mirrored those of the boys I encountered in my research. Although multiple conversations like this are not systematic evidence of gay-friendly high schools, it certainly highlights the error of assuming homophobia among male youth in a particular region.

A similar question of generalizability (i.e., the applicability of my findings to other places) is the extent to which these findings can cross the Atlantic to America and other Anglophone countries, including Canada and Australia. When I discussed this issue with masculinities scholar Eric Anderson, he commented that the United Kingdom seems to be about ten years ahead of the United States and Australia on issues of sexuality and gender. Watching political and cultural battles in the United States and Australia from afar and talking to academics about this issue, this seems like a good starting point, but it is also important to emphasize the positive change that has been occurring in these countries, too.

Ritch Savin-Williams has documented a changing social zeitgeist in relation to gay youth and their experiences of wider society. In 2005, Savin-Williams wrote *The New Gay Teenager*, an important book that showed great changes in the treatment and life experiences of sexual-minority youth. It was a controversial work because it argued that increasing numbers of nonheterosexual youth are rejecting identity categories (particularly the categories "lesbian," "gay," "bisexual," and "transgendered") and are instead going about enjoying their sexual lives without using (or at least with less use of) identity labels. He argued that gay youth had become "banal" in their ordinariness, and that they do not suffer the discrimination of previous generations.

It is my view that Savin-Williams's work powerfully captures a major change in American culture. However, his work also overstates some areas of change, particularly with regard to the speed with which sexual-minority youth are casting off sexual labels. For this reason, I think his work should be read in tandem with Eric Anderson's (2009) book, *Inclusive Masculinity*. Anderson and Savin-Williams address the same social phenomenon—decreasing homophobia among youth—from two different angles: the impact on gay youth (Savin-Williams) and the impact on straight men (Anderson). Reading them alongside each other provides an important and new perspective for understanding the impact of the zeitgeist of decreasing homophobia on young people more generally.

Regarding the likelihood of finding gay-friendly high schools in the United States, Savin-Williams (2005) suggests that the chances are high. He discusses a "dramatic cultural shift" in both sports and education:

> High school honor student and varsity athlete Jason Fasi asks his teammates for signatures in support of forming a Gay-Straight Alliance group at Mission Viejo, California. They sign. No one beats him up, no one shies away from dressing next to him, and no one heckles him. Two Ohio high school heterosexual runners wear flashy rainbow socks, symbolic of gay pride, during a state track meet to show support for their two gay teammates. . . . Two Illinois girls are voted the school's "cutest couple" by their fellow high school seniors. (p. 199)

Similarly, since developing inclusive masculinity theory, Anderson has continued to undertake ethnographies that examine attitudes toward sexuality and gender among British and American college men. In an article in the *Archives of Sexual Behavior*, Anderson, Adams, and Rivers (2010) show that British men are kissing each other as a sign of affection, normally on the lips, but sometimes even with tongues. These kisses are considered a homosocial sign of friendship, and are not coded as sexual by the men who kiss. Significantly, participants recognize that people witnessing the kiss will not know whether it is a sexual kiss between partners or a social one between friends. Homohysteria has declined so much among youth in Britain that these men simply do not care.

Anderson shows that similar, though less pronounced, changes are present in the United States as well. In an article examining the masculinities of college athletes at a Catholic university in the Midwest, Anderson (2011c) finds almost no homophobia, and those few men who maintain some personal homophobia recognize it as an issue that they need to reconcile. Importantly, Anderson does not find that these attitudes are due to a liberalizing university setting; rather, he reports that most of these men had these attitudes while at high school. Anderson links these findings to broader cultural attitudes. He writes,

> A June 4, 2010 Gallup poll (Gallup.com) shows that young American men (18-49) are the fastest rising demographic in accepting homophobia, having gained 20% in the previous four years. In fact, they are shown to be less homophobic than women of the same age when asked if homosexuality was "morally acceptable," with 62% responding that it is. (p. 16)

This statistical finding supports the joint argument that Anderson, Savin-Williams, and I develop. This 62% figure (which is likely much higher among 18-year-olds, given the range in ages from 18 to 49) highlights that a cultural shift has already occurred. Indeed, a recent survey by the Pubilc Religion Research institute found that almost half (44%) of evangelical aged under 29 support gay marriage.

If women are now more homophobic than men in a period in which levels of homophobia have decreased in both cohorts (see Altmeyer, 2001; Loftus, 2001), and if evangelical Christians are becoming increasingly supportive of gay rights, this is a serious challenge to conventional understandings of the construction of masculinity that tied homophobia inextricably to masculinity (see Kimmel, 1994; Nayak & Kehily, 1996).

However, we still have a long distance to travel. The Gay, Lesbian and Straight Education Network (GLSEN), a charity that campaigns for sexuality equality in U.S. schools, produced *The 2009 National School Climate Survey*, which sought to examine the experience of LGBT youth in U.S. schools (Kosciw, Gretak, Diaz, & Bartkieicz, 2009). This is a substantive (and substantial) document highlighting issues that LGBT youth face in many educational institutions. It shows that sexuality equality has certainly not been achieved across the board. However, although they do highlight bullying and homophobic language, they also document improvements that have been made, suggesting that between 2007 and 2009 there were "small but significant decreases in frequencies of verbal harassment, physical harassment and physical assault," as well as marked improvements in the numbers and effectiveness of Gay–Straight Alliances, supportive educators, curricular resources, and school harassment and assault policies.

I also suggest that some of these results would be dramatically improved if my model of homosexually themed language were used. That is, the study interprets phrases like "that's so gay" as homophobic, and takes the use of such language as evidence of a hostile school culture. One of the main problems with quantitative research on sexuality is that it cannot take account of the contextual nuances of language use. Accordingly, it is likely that the prevalence of homophobic language is overstated.

I focus on the United States and Britain, but it should be noted that less research on these issues occurs in Australia and Canada. Michael Kehler (2007, 2009) suggests that similar changes are occurring in Canada, although these are perhaps less pronounced than in the United Kingdom. And although Lingard, Martino, and Mills (2008) offer a fairly pessimistic view of masculinity politics in Australia, their work examines a different issue (and a different age group) than my research. Accordingly, I limit direct comparisons to these countries. Yet a dearth of research is not an excuse to assume homophobia. Rather than arguing that my findings simply do not apply, I urge scholars in Australia and Canada to look for changed and changing attitudes toward homosexuality, and to examine what this means for LGBT youth. Furthermore, scholars and activists can look to the UK situation to predict, anticipate, and understand the changes happening within their own context.

Finally, it is a sad fact that many other parts of the world have extremely homophobic attitudes. In many countries, homosexuality is illegal, and in some it is even punishable by death. This is even the case in certain countries under Western influence; for example, gay Iraqis continue to be executed because of their sexuality, even after the overthrow of Saddam Hussein. Muslim theocracies also have draconian laws against homosexuality. From a global perspective, the continued prevalence of homophobia is a sobering thought. This realization highlights the need for the recognition of gay rights as human rights, and it also shows that gay-friendly high schools are a Western phenomenon.

CHALLENGING A VICTIMIZATION FRAMEWORK OF GAY YOUTH

When considering the prevalence of gay-friendly high schools across English-speaking countries, it is important to recognize that gay youth are often discussed through a framework of victimization (see Savin-Williams, 2005). That is, young gay men and women are automatically positioned as victims of homophobia who have had troubled childhoods and school lives. This is problematic because viewing gay youth through this lens often leads to a form of confirmation bias.

Confirmation bias refers to the tendency that people have to accept evidence that supports their own viewpoint and discount that which does not. Scholars who use a victimization framework for gay youth will likely discount much of the evidence provided in this book, suggesting that it is unique to these schools or the South of England, or maybe arguing that my being openly gay biased the data. The point is that because this work does not position gay youth as victims, it will be discounted. This rejection of contradictory evidence is problematic, but it is not as pervasive as the ready acceptance of evidence that supports one's own position.

The most frequent form of confirmation bias in this regard is with respect to individual homophobic events. The Matthew Shepard case is perhaps emblematic here, but there are many other examples, including the recent story of Tyler Clementi, a Rutgers University student who committed suicide after two other students secretly filmed him having sex with another man and posted the video on the Internet. A spate of these individual horror stories reached the national press in the fall of 2010, causing some social commentators to argue that homophobia is on the rise in America—that a backlash was occurring. However, although these kinds of stories are desperately sad and speak to the evil of oppression, they are not evidence of increasing homophobia.

The media story is that increased numbers of suicides of gay youth are evidence of an epidemic of homophobia. Yet it is questionable whether there actually is an increase in these incidents. It seems highly likely that what is actually occurring is an increase in *reports* of these incidents at a national and international level. It is quite likely that suicides happened more frequently in the past but were not reported to the police or were not picked up by the media. It is also possible that the stigma associated with same-sex desire in the 1980s and 1990s meant that many individuals did not mention their sexuality as a reason for their suicide during that time, or that their parents might have not told people beyond their family. It is also interesting to note that there were no gay suicides reported on major news channels in the winter of 2010; either they stopped occurring or the media stopped covering them. Rather than focus on the (extremely questionable) increase in suicides, scholars should look at the changing media and political response to these events. This is better evidence of how homophobia is viewed by society. Yet those working within the framework of victimization opt for the "easier" way of interpreting these issues.

One recent example of this is the homophobic article written by Australian footballer Jason Akermis. In an interview for a magazine, Akermis warned gay players to stay in the closet. It was a troubling article, and I have observed many academics and activists argue that this is evidence of continued homophobia in sports (and in Australia more generally). However, this conclusion (which fits the victim framework) misses several important points that evidence *decreasing* homophobia. First, Akermis couched his argument in support of gay players. Although he was offering a conservative, homophobic solution, there was no suggestion that he thought homosexuality was sinful, sick, or wrong. Second, and more important, there was great media uproar in response to this article. In short, Akermis was condemned for maintaining his view, and a counter-discourse of supporting openly gay players was present, too (see Kian & Anderson, 2009). I suggest that this simply would not have happened ten years ago in Australia and that viewing it as evidence of homophobia more generally misses the broader cultural change.

It is perhaps easier for adults to view gay youth through the victimization framework. After all, it was the reality for many gay adults during their youth. There is also the reality that it is easier to receive grants from funding bodies if gay youth are in a state of crisis. Yet perpetuating this framework has serious consequences. First, it means that gay youth are more likely to grow up in fear of homophobia, even when it is not there. And although high levels of homophobia might loosen the purse strings of funding bodies, they also scare teachers and administrators away from dealing with sexuality in a holistic manner. As tempting as it is to view gay youth as victims, it is something we must do only when we have clear evidence that it is the case.

THE CONSOLIDATION OF HETEROSEXUALITY AND THE RECOGNITION OF SEXUAL IDENTITY

It is an intriguing finding that even with a decrease in homophobia and the corresponding expansion of acceptable gendered behaviors, heterosexuality is actually *more* consolidated in the high schools discussed in this book. Elaborating on this, scholars researching settings with high homophobia explicate the fragmented and precarious nature of heterosexual identity construction and maintenance, suggesting that even one gender transgression can homosexualize a boy (Anderson, 2008a; Pascoe, 2007). Yet at all three high schools I visited, boys are socially perceived as gay only if they publicly identify as such. Here, decreased homophobia strengthens the boundaries of heterosexual identity while simultaneously permitting individuals to move outside of them. I believe that the shift to accepting a boy's self-identification of sexuality is important, and I suggest that it is the result of decreasing homohysteria.

There are shifts occurring regarding the recognition of sexual identity among both heterosexual and LGBT youth. Savin-Williams (2005) argues that sexual-minority youth are entering a "postidentity" phase in which they no longer find solace or resonance with sexual-identity categories. Cohler and Hammack (2009) disagree, suggesting that rather than identity ceasing to be of importance, it becomes important in different ways. They say that "shifting master narratives of queer identity in the twenty-first century . . . [necessitate] adequate sensitivity to and appreciation for the contextual basis of human development" (p. 456). I argue that this shift is the result of decreasing homohysteria, and whereas Cohler, Hammack, and Savin-Williams were discussing gay identities, it is most apparent in my research when examining heterosexual students. In this instance, a substantive shift has occurred in how straight young men implicitly understand and define their sexual identities.

In the homohysteric 1980s and 1990s, there were two incredibly simplistic ways of determining sexuality for men—one for if you were gay and one for if you were straight. If you said that you were gay, this was accepted at once without any interrogation. The stigma attached to homosexuality meant that you could sleep with women and desire few men, yet still be socially perceived as—unquestionably—gay, just through the proclamation of this stigmatized same-sex desire or identity. Sexuality was determined through self-identification.

The other way of determining sexuality was for heterosexuals. If you claimed that you were straight (which you would often do implicitly, because it was assumed that everyone was), that was only the beginning. Boys and men were then examined for any potential same-sex desire, or any behavior that could be coded as gay. Through a process that Anderson (2008a) calls "the one time rule of homosexuality," straight men who said they were heterosexual were socially perceived as gay if they acted in a nonmasculine way. Their claim to an identity was unimportant because sexuality was determined by their actions.

This polarized binary of how to interpret sexuality set up a nasty and pernicious examination of sexuality. Claiming a gay identity effectively disqualified you from this test—your gay identification went unchallenged, but you were socially ostracized and marginalized according to a whole host of legal, cultural, and moral rules (Flowers & Buston, 2001; Rubin, 1984). If you claimed a heterosexual identity, however, you were then part of a vicious game of proving your sexuality through your behaviors. In this situation, boys and men were hierarchically stratified according to a whole host of gendered variables, and how you acted (that is, your behaviors) was of primary importance. This gulf between straight identity and behavior became a chasm into which the vast majority of men fell.

However, this chasm has been bridged at these gay-friendly high schools. In this research, gay students are still believed to be gay when they say that they are, but there is an important difference. Their identifications are not believed because of the stigma associated with homosexuality as used to be the case, and they are not socially marginalized, either. Instead, their proclamations are treated with respect and sincerity. Furthermore, there has been an important change among heterosexual students. Now, quite simply, how you self-identify is accepted by your peers. This is evidenced by the discussion of Richard in Chapter 7, in which students ponder whether he is gay but decide he is straight because he would have said if he were not. Here, sexual self-identification is consolidated as the main way to understand a person's sexuality. It is increasingly accepted that it is a sign of respect to accept a peer's self-identification of their own sexuality. And, as found in other research (Adams & Anderson, 2010), heterosexual students are more able to ask questions about their sexual identity in open and exploratory ways.

This shift to sexual identity questions some of the more dramatic claims Savin-Williams (2005) makes about sexual minority youth becoming "post-gay." Although some students are undoubtedly eschewing category labels and exploring their sexual desires more freely (phenomena Savin-Williams discusses expertly), my findings among students who strongly identify as LGBT show that sexual identity is still very important for many youth (Cohler & Hammack, 2007). For these young people, identifications have ceased being a battleground—they are now socially perceived as a true statement of sexuality.

This shift also has implications for queer theory (Butler, 1990; Jagose, 1996). The consolidation of heterosexual identities in these settings means that decreased homophobia does not necessarily result in a dissipation of sexual identities. This would suggest that collective identity-movement politics is the most effective platform for social change, and that deconstruction has its emancipatory limits (Anderson, 2009; Kirsch, 2000; Weeks, 2007).

SHIFTING OUR FOCUS

The new forms of heterosexual boundary maintenance at gay-friendly high schools, alongside the consolidation of a heterosexual identity, warrant a shift in analysis from studying overt homophobia to investigating heteronormativity and implicit homophobia in school settings (Ferfolja, 2005; Russell, 2005). Limited scholarship exists on heteronormativity in educational settings (Atkinson & DePalma, 2009; Ferfolja, 2007), and this tends to focus on the exclusion of gay students in schools (Wilkinson & Pearson, 2009). Yet it is necessary to examine how heteronormativity affects heterosexual students as well. As Jackson (2006, p. 117) writes, "[H]eteronormative assumptions interconnect with the institutionalization of heterosexuality and also shape the doing of heterosexuality and being and becoming heterosexual." For example, recent scholarship by Gerulf Rieger and Ritch Savin-Williams (2011) suggests that gender nonconformity may be more relevant for psychological health than a same-sex orientation, which demands further (and in particular, qualitative) study in schools. Scholars need to examine how heteronormativity regulates both gay and heterosexual students in order to fully understand its power.

The new equalities legislation in the United Kingdom compels schools to promote inclusion and diversity with respect to sexual orientation. This should be used as a vehicle to transform discussions of sexuality within schools. As it currently stands, sex education is concerned with "plumbing and prevention"

(Lenskyj, 1990). The equalities agenda provides the perfect opportunity to engage students about sexuality in ways that will enable them to learn about the complexity and pleasure of sexual desire, orientation, and identity. I am currently developing a sex education handbook with Professor Debbie Epstein in order to enable teachers to do precisely this, and academics, activists, and teachers need to be proactive in bringing about this change.

Of course, heteronormativity in schools extends beyond sex education classes. It includes the presumption of heterosexuality, the absence of openly gay teachers, and the erasure of gay history from the broader curriculum. Traditionally, it has been argued that young people are not yet ready to discuss these issues. My research disproves that argument. As well as continuing to investigate heteronormativity in high schools, we must argue for policies and directives to counter these barriers to equality of sexuality.

Another important implication that I want to draw out from this book is a focus on combating covert and implicit forms of homophobia. Here, the distinction between heteronormativity/heterosexism, implicit homophobia, and overt homophobia is important. Overt homophobia is the form that was dominant in the 1980s, when gay bashings occurred, homophobic pejoratives were used frequently, and legal discrimination against gay men and women was explicit. It is not present in any form at gay-friendly high schools.

Implicit homophobia is the intentional yet covert stigmatization of gay men and women. Plummer (1999) defines this as when "antihomosexual connotations are not articulated, but their connotations are understood" (p. 134)—there is malicious intent behind the language used or the action performed. Whereas these connotations would have no cultural traction in gay-friendly high schools, it is possible for broader societal discourses that are implicitly homophobic to impact the discourses within these settings. Finally, I define heteronormativity and heterosexism as the institutional or implicit privileging of heterosexuality. As with the phrase "that's so gay," the privileging of heterosexuality can be unintended, but it nonetheless results in unequal relations between heterosexuals and LGBT people.

I argue that though we must continue to challenge explicit homophobia, this must not be all we do. We must combat heteronormativity, but not at the expense of implicit homophobia. For example, challenging the heteronormative phrase "that's so gay" and calling it homophobic misses the point and focuses on a challenge that is both more difficult and less important to win. In the United Kingdom, homophobes are no longer in the media saying that homosexuality is an abomination, that it should be illegal and that the thought of gay sex makes them sick. I remember Conservative cabinet members in the 1990s (such as Peter Lilley) making such statements, but it simply is not acceptable today. So, rather than exhaustively searching out any word that could be considered anti-gay and silencing its usage, progressive campaigners should contest and challenge forms of implicit homophobia. This would include arguments that equality laws are a challenge to morality (as Roman Catholics believe), that gay people can only give blood after a year of abstinence (as the National Health Service states), that gay people should not adopt (the Roman Catholics again), or that gay people should have civil partnerships rather than marriage (Stonewall, the UK gay rights group, find themselves perilously close to the wrong side of the argument in arguing that heterosexual couples should not have the right to civil partnerships). There is plenty of work for us to do in this regard, and I suggest that trying to ban the phrase "that's so gay" is a waste of time. Instead, we should focus our energies on the real issues of implicit homophobia that damage LGBT youth.

INCLUSIVE MASCULINITY THEORY

In terms of understanding the impact of my findings on how masculinities are theorized, it is first important to note that hegemonic masculinity theory has maintained great utility in furthering understanding of homohysteric cultures, and, because of this, it has received wide take-up in the masculinities literature (Connell & Messerschmidt, 2005). However, as I argue in Chapter 4, hegemonic masculinity theory maintains utility only in some cultures—namely, homohysteric ones. Related to this issue, scholars have argued that there is an over-reliance on Connell's theorizing (Pringle, 2005; Rowe, 1998; Sparkes, 1992), amounting to hegemony concerning the use of hegemonic masculinity theory (Anderson, 2009).

Many scholars fall into the trap of examining *for* the processes of hegemonic masculinity rather than evaluating what theoretical model provides the most heuristic utility (Moller, 2007). When they do this, they seem to find hegemonic masculinity theory useful despite their findings. This is possible because the definitions that Connell provides are broad and extremely vague. For example, if complicit masculinities are those that gain from patriarchy, it is hard to locate masculinities that are not, to some extent, complicit. Furthermore, Connell describes the process of hegemonic masculinity as occurring through the mechanisms of domination and marginalization. Although this accurately captures the social dynamics of a homohysteric zeitgeist, these social processes can be found to some extent in most social situations. The problem is that evidence of limited domination and marginalization is not sufficient evidence of hegemonic masculinity—of a *gendered* form of hierarchical stratification. Even so, the way in which hegemonic masculinity theory is presented means that scholars looking for these processes will most likely find evidence for their existence at some level.

In Chapter 4, I explicate the theoretical differences between hegemony and hegemonic masculinity theory. I argue, following Howson (2006, 2008) and others (Beasley, 2008; Hearn, 2004), that the conceptualization of hegemony that Connell employs is rather narrow and does not allow for the development of benevolent forms of hegemony. This means that although it is possible for less homophobic attitudes to develop within hegemonic masculinity theory, this would not alter the fundamental dynamics of the relations between men. As Connell and Messerschmidt (2005, p. 846) continue to argue, "the concept of hegemonic masculinity presumes the subordination of nonhegemonic masculinities."

Put simply, in Connell's framework, even if homosexuality is esteemed in a setting, other stigmatized forms of masculinity will nonetheless continue to exist. This is clearly different from the patterns of masculinity that are found in the high schools in this book. Accordingly, hegemonic masculinity cannot explain the findings of this research.

Hegemony theory can, however, provide a way of understanding the attitudes toward homosexuality exhibited at these three schools. Raymond Williams (1977) explicated a framework for understanding the stratification of ideas and people within a hegemonic system. He described the dominant as that which maintains hegemonic power; the residual as that which once maintained cultural power and is now deemed archaic, but which still has influence on the culture; and the emergent as those nascent ways of thinking or being that come forward at the particular cultural moment. Picking up on the latter theme, in 1998, Epstein and Johnson argued that equality for lesbians and gay men was an emergent aspect of the society of the time, recognizing that this notion was "being accepted by more and more people" (Epstein & Johnson, 1998, p. 192). My research, alongside other work documenting positive attitudes toward LGBT rights (Anderson, 2009; McNair, 2002; Weeks, 2007), would suggest that the notion of gay equality has become a dominant aspect of British society today. Although there are residual claims for "family values" alongside other homophobic views, the stigma now attached to homophobia indicates that the concept of gay equality has become dominant itself (even if this has yet to be fully realized).

Although the concept of hegemony is of use in understanding the change in attitudes toward homosexuality, it maintains less heuristic utility for understanding the complex intragender relations of the masculine peer group. Whether it is with respect to how boys deploy heterosexual recuperation, how they use gay discourse, or the social stratification of their friendship groups, hegemony theory does little explanatory work regarding these social dynamics, particularly in the wider context of the existing literature that discusses these topics (see Francis, Skelton, & Read, 2010; C. Jackson, 2006; Pascoe, 2007).

There is a further reason why I reject both hegemony theory and hegemonic masculinity theory as an overarching theoretical framework for understanding my results: the social stratification of boys that I describe at Standard High cannot be explained by either of these theories.

First, hegemonic masculinity theory cannot account for the variety of masculine archetypes that are equally esteemed in this setting—Connell (2005) allows for only *one* archetype of masculinity to maintain hegemonic standing in a setting. Indeed, Anderson developed inclusive masculinity theory because he found two competing forms of masculinity that both maintained equal validation (Anderson, 2005b, 2009). Furthermore, although hegemonic masculinity theory is very useful in understanding homohysteric cultures, it provides little heuristic utility when it comes to understanding settings with decreased homophobia. The processes of domination and marginalization that Connell (1995, 2005) describes as fundamental to hegemonic masculinity are not present at these high schools. This might be attributable to the age of hegemonic masculinity theory, developed in the highly homohysteric 1980s (Anderson, 2009; Connell, 1987, 1995). In any case, hegemonic masculinity theory does not capture the social dynamics of these settings.

Second, hegemony theory also does not capture the social dynamics of Standard High. This is because the students there are cognizant of what makes a boy popular, and many participants proclaim that they do not desire to be like the more popular boys. Hegemony requires that people always try to improve their position in the hierarchy (Anderson, 2005a; Bocock, 1986), yet many of these students do not desire to be more popular. Accordingly, hegemony theory offers little heuristic utility in this instance.

The findings in this book are instead best explained by Anderson's (2009) inclusive masculinity theory. Inclusive masculinity theory posits that in a culture of decreased homohysteria, physical affection and emotional intimacy between heterosexual male students are both common and esteemed. And, as Anderson predicts, multiple archetypes of masculinity are esteemed in these settings. Finally, the positive experiences of openly gay students confounds Connell's (1987, 1995, 2005) theorizing, which has always placed gay men at the bottom of a masculine hierarchy.

The central contribution of inclusive masculinity theory is that it enables an examination of the construction of masculinities in settings that are not homohysteric, where homophobia no longer regulates masculine identities. Anderson's theory explicitly takes account of the cultural changes regarding homosexuality and homophobia that have occurred in the past 20 years (Anderson, 2009; McNair, 2002; Savin-Williams, 2005; Weeks, 2007) and provides a framework for understanding how broad cultural changes impact the youthful subjectivities of young men.

In addition to offering the empirical finding that inclusive masculinities exist and are esteemed in these settings, my research contributes conceptually to inclusive masculinity theory. By showing that emotional support and social fluidity are attributes that increase a boy's popularity, I show that the stratification of boys at Standard High is less hierarchical than in homohysteric cultures (C. Jackson, 2006; Stoudt, 2006). Although popularity is also dependent on charisma and authenticity (something that has also been found in more homohysteric cultures), I show that the way these characteristics are enacted is less aggressive and does not maintain the negative social effect that they once did (Salisbury & Jackson, 1996).

METHODOLOGICAL IMPLICATIONS

There are also important methodological implications from this research. One concerns how accurately quantitative methods can capture the meanings of homosexually themed language. In Chapter 7, I discuss how boys at Standard High have begun to redefine homophobia so that it includes aspects of what scholars would call heterosexism or heteronormativity. These issues include the lack of openly gay teachers, the erasure of LGBT history from school curricula, and the different ways in which openly gay people are discussed in the media. This is clearly very different from the type of homophobia discussed years ago (cf. Epstein, 1994; Rivers, 2001; Warwick, Aggleton, & Douglas, 2001). Accordingly, quantitative research about the levels of homophobia in schools might have very little internal validity, particularly if it compares findings with older research (Ellis & High, 2004; Goetz & LeCompte, 1984). That is, students' understanding of what constitutes homophobia today is markedly different from and encompasses a great deal more than students' conceptualizations of homophobia a decade ago. This might be one reason why the GLSEN study (Kosciw et al, 2009), as well as the methodologically and analytically flawed work from Stonewall, finds elevated rates of homophobia in schools today (Guasp, 2008; Hunt & Jensen, 2007)—they are simply not comparing like with like. In this regard, my research raises significant questions regarding the validity of research using quantitative measures of homophobia.

Another important methodological issue in this research is the importance of the sexuality of the researcher when collecting data. First, it is important to recognize that I reflect throughout the results chapters on the potential impact that my sexuality had on the behaviors and espoused attitudes of students in the schools. I have provided several pieces of evidence to support the notion that researcher effect played little part in the levels of homophobia documented throughout this book; this includes inter-rater reliability, reflexivity, examining any changes in levels of homophobic language after my coming out, and corroborating findings with key informants and members of staff.

However, it is also important to highlight a problematic association with a focus on reflexivity with openly gay researchers. The argument for focusing on gay researchers' subjectivities is that knowledge about gay identity might cause participants to hide their homophobia, bringing the validity of findings about levels of homophobic language into question. However, if this is to be accepted, then it is also necessary to investigate the impact of heterosexual researchers' subjectivities regarding attitudes toward homosexuality, and I argue that this is not done in the same way.

The seminal literature on masculinities in schools was written in highly homohysteric cultures. In such settings, a pervasive form of heterosexual presumption (Epstein & Johnson, 1994) meant that if researchers did not discuss their sexual identity, it would likely be presumed that they were straight. Given the pervading homophobia of both students and teachers (Epstein & Johnson, 1998; Mac an Ghaill, 1994; Salisbury & Jackson, 1996), it is possible that participants *exaggerated* the levels of homophobia, thinking this would increase their social capital with the (presumed) heterosexual researchers, and particularly with male researchers. This is something not considered in much of the seminal literature (Mac an Ghaill, 1994; Redman & Mac an Ghaill, 1997; Salisbury & Jackson, 1996). The point is that, regardless of whether this hypothesis is valid, the same level of reflexivity should be applied to researchers, regardless of their sexual identity. Although it is imperative for researchers to be critically reflective, it is also important that reflexivity is not used as a form of confirmation bias against new findings, because to do this would be to support an implicit form of homophobia.

A FINAL NOTE ON GENERALIZABILITY

Despite my discussion above of the applicability of my findings, the issue of generalizability is a troubling one about which academics hold many different views. Having discussed the issue of confirmation bias, it is worth noting the personal element involved in generalizability. In reading the literature, attending conferences, and talking with colleagues, I have noticed that research documenting high levels of homophobia seems to be generalized to the population more readily than studies that find decreased levels of homophobia, which are examined for the uniqueness of their setting. Accordingly, I suggest that the generalizability of my findings will be largely dependent on you, the reader. In other words, if you are looking for evidence that homophobia is still prevalent, you will find reasons to question my findings—you might highlight that I do not examine for race, or that I do not examine for homophobia in private schools, primary schools, or single-sex schools. You might maintain that this part of England is unique for some reason. You might even discuss a single episode that occurred recently in your life that you feel contradicts what I discuss here. Whatever the reason, you will conclude that the findings will be limited to these three institutions.

Conversely, if you believe that homophobia is on the decline, you will look at the research that documents the decreasing significance of homophobia in a number of social settings (Adams, Anderson, & McCormack, 2010; Anderson, 2011b; Anderson & McGuire, 2010; McNair, 2002; Swain, 2006b; Taulke-Johnson, 2008; Weeks, 2007) and argue that my research contributes to the literature documenting this changing social zeitgeist (see Anderson, 2009; Savin-Williams, 2005). Ultimately, although I believe there is a strong argument that my research documents a changing social zeitgeist, I realize that your own views will influence how you resolve the question of generalizability.

REFERENCES

Acker, J. (1990). Hierarchies, jobs, bodies: A theory of gendered organizations. *Gender & Society, 4*(2), 139–158.

Acker, J. (1992). Gendered institutions: From sex roles to gendered institutions. *Contemporary Sociology, 21,* 565–569.

Adam, B. (1998). Theorising homophobia. *Sexualities, 1*(4), 387–404.

Adam, B., Duyvendak, J. W., & Krouwel, A. (1999). *The global emergence of gay and lesbian politics: National imprints of a worldwide movement.* Philadelphia, PA: Temple University Press.

Adams, A. (2011). "Josh wears pink cleats": Inclusive masculinity on the Soccer field. *Journal of Homosexuality, 58*(5), 579–596.

Adams, A., & Anderson, E. (2010). "Aren't we all a little bisexual?": The recognition of bisexuality in an unlikely place. *Journal of Bisexuality, 11*(1), 3–22.

Adams, A., & Anderson, E. (2011). Homosexuality and sport: Exploring theinfluence of coming out to the teammates of a small, Midwestern Catholic college soccer team. *Sport, Education and Society.* DOI:10.1080/13573322.2011.608938

Adams, A., Anderson, E., & McCormack, M. (2010). Establishing and challenging masculinity: The influence of gendered discourses in organized sport. *Journal of Language and Social Psychology, 29*(3), 278–300.

Adler, P. A., & Adler, P. A. (1987). *Membership roles in field research.* Newbury Park, CA: Sage

Adler, P. A., & Adler, P. A. (1995). Dynamics of inclusion and exclusion in preadolescent cliques. *Social Psychology Quarterly, 58*(3), 145–162.

Adler, P. A., & Adler, P. A. (1998). *Peer preadolescent culture and identity.* Piscataway, NJ: Rutgers University Press.

Agar, M. H. (1980). *The professional stranger: An informal introduction to ethnography.* London: Academic Press.

Aggleton, P. (1987). *Rebels without a cause? Middle-class youth and the transition from school to work.* London: Taylor and Francis.

Allen, L. (2007a). Denying the sexual subject: Schools' regulation of student sexuality. *British Educational Research Journal, 33*(2), 221–234.

Allen, L. (2007b). Doing 'it' differently: Relinquishing the disease and pregnancy prevention focus in sexuality education. *British Journal of Sociology of Education, 28*(5), 575–588.

Altman, D. (1973). *Homosexual liberation and oppression.* New York: Avon.

Altmeyer, B. (2001). Changes in attitudes toward homosexuality. *Journal of Homosexuality, 42*, 63–75.

Anderson, E. (2000). *Trailblazing: America's first openly gay track coach*. Los Angeles: Alyson Press.

Anderson, E. (2002). Openly gay athletes: Contesting hegemonic masculinity in a homophobic environment. *Gender & Society, 16*(6), 860–877.

Anderson, E. (2005a). *In the game: Gay athletes and the cult of masculinity*. New York: State University of New York Press.

Anderson, E. (2005b). Orthodox and inclusive masculinity: Competing masculinities among heterosexual men in a feminized terrain. *Sociological Perspectives, 48*(3), 337–355.

Anderson, E. (2008a). "Being masculine is not about who you sleep with...": Heterosexual athletes contesting masculinity and the one-time rule of homosexuality. *Sex Roles, 58*, 104–115.

Anderson, E. (2008b). "I used to think women were weak": Orthodox masculinity, gender segregation and sport. *Sociological Forum, 23*(2), 257–280.

Anderson, E. (2008c). Inclusive masculinity in a fraternal setting. *Men and Masculinities, 10*(5), 604–620.

Anderson, E. (2009). *Inclusive masculinity: The changing nature of masculinities*. London: Routledge.

Anderson, E. (2010). *Sport, theory and social problems: A critical introduction*. London: Routledge.

Anderson, E. (2011a). *The monogamy gap: Men, love and the reality of cheating*. New York: Oxford University Press.

Anderson, E. (2011b). Updating the outcome: Gay athletes, straight teams, and coming out in educationally based sport teams. *Gender & Society, 25*(2), 250–268.

Anderson, E. (2011c). Inclusive masculinity and soccer at a Catholic university in the American Midwest. *Gender and Education*.iFirst, 1–18.

Anderson, E., Adams, A., & Rivers, I. (2010). "I kiss them because I love them": The emergence of heterosexual men kissing in British institutes of education. *Archives of Sexual Behaviors*. Advance online publication. doi: 10.1007/s10508-010-9678-0.

Anderson, E., & McCormack, M. (2010a). Intersectionality, critical race theory and American sporting oppression: Examining black and gay male athletes. *Journal of Homosexuality, 57*, 949–967.

Anderson, E., & McCormack, M. (2010b). Comparing the black and gay male athlete: Patterns in American oppression. *The Journal of Men's Studies, 18*(2), 145–158.

Anderson, E., & McGuire, R. (2010). Inclusive masculinity theory and the politics of men's rugby. *Journal of Gender Studies, 19*(3), 249–262.

Archer, L., & Yamashita, H. (2003). Theorising inner-city masculinities: "Race," class, gender and education. *Gender & Education, 15*(2), 115–132.

Arendt, H. (1971). *The life of the mind*. New York: Harcourt Brace.

Armstrong, J. D. (1997). Homophobic slang as coercive discourse among college students. In A. Livia and K. Hall (Eds.), *Queerly phrased: Language, gender and sexuality* (pp. 326–334). New York: Oxford University Press.

Arnett, J. J. (2000). Emerging adulthood: A theory of development from the late teens to the late twenties. *American Psychologist, 55*, 469–480.

Arnett, J. J. (2004). *Emerging adulthood: The winding road from the late teens through the twenties*. New York: Oxford University Press.

Atkinson, E. & DePalma, R. (2008). *Invisible boundaries: addressing sexualities equality in children's worlds*. Stoke-on-Trent, England: Trentham Books.

Atkinson, E., & DePalma, R. (2009). *Interrogating heteronormativity in primary schools*. Stoke-on-Trent, England: Trentham Books.

Barnard, H. R. (2002). *Research methods in anthropology: Qualitative and quantitative methods*. Walnut Creek, CA: Altamira.

Barrett, F. J. (1996). The organizational construction of hegemonic masculinity: The case of the U.S. *Navy. Gender, Work and Organization, 3*(3), 129–142.

Beasley, C. (2008). Rethinking hegemonic masculinity in a globalizing world. *Men and Masculinities, 11*(1), 86–103.

Becker, G. (1964). *Human capital*. Chicago: University of Chicago Press.

Beckett, L., Tweed, M., & Fisher, S. (1999). 'No fear' in our school. In D. Epstein & J. T. Sears (Eds.), *A Dangerous Knowing* (pp. 257–269). London: Cassell.

Bem, S. L. (1993). *The lenses of gender: Transforming the debate on sexual inequality*. London: Yale University Press.

Benhabib, S. (1995). Feminism and postmodernism: An uneasy alliance. In S. Benhabib, J. Butler, D. Cornell, and N. Fraser (Eds.), *Feminist contentions: A philosophical exchange* (pp. 17–34). New York: Routledge.

Bernstein, M. (1997). Celebration and suppression: The strategic uses of identity by the lesbian and gay movement. *The American Journal of Sociology, 103*(3), 531–565.

Bernstein, M. (2005). Identity politics. *Annual Review of Sociology, 31,* 47–74.

Blackman, S. J. (2007). "Hidden ethnography": Crossing emotional borders in qualitative accounts of young people's lives. *Sociology, 41*(4), 699–716.

Blasius, M. (1998). Contemporary lesbian, gay, bisexual, transgender, queer theories and their politics. *Journal of the History of Sexuality, 8*(4), 642–674.

Bocock, R. (1986). *Hegemony*. London: Tavistock.

Bogle, K. (2008). *Hooking up: Sex, dating and relationships on campus*. New York: New York University Press.

Bolding, G., Davis, M., Hart, G., Sherr, L., & Elford, J. (2007). Where young MSM meet their first sexual partner: The role of the internet. *AIDS and Behavior, 11,* 522–526.

Bortolin, S. (2010). "I don't want him hitting on me": The role of masculinities in creating a chilly high school climate. *Journal of LGBT Youth, 7*(3), 200–223.

Brannon, D. (1976). The male sex role and what it's done for us lately. In R. Brannon & D. David (Eds.), *The forty-nine percent majority* (pp. 1–40). Reading, MA: Addison-Wesley.

Brickell, C. (2006). The sociological construction of gender and sexuality. *The Sociological Review, 54*(1), 87–113.

Britton, D. M. (2000). The epistemology of the gendered organization. *Gender & Society, 14*(3), 418–434.

Brown, J. R. (2011). No homo. *Journal of Homosexuality, 58*(3), 299–314.

Burawoy, M. (2004). Introduction. Public sociologies: A symposium from Boston High, edited by W. Gamson, C. Ryan, S. Pfol, D. Vaughn, C. Derber, and J. Schor. *Social Problems, 51*(1), 103–130.

Burawoy, M. (2005). For public sociology. *American Sociological Review, 70*(1), 4–28.

Burgess, I., Edwards, A., & Skinner, J. (2003). Football culture in an Australian school setting: The construction of masculine identity. *Sport, Education and Society, 8*(2), 199–212.

Bush, A., Anderson, E. & Carr, S. (in press). The declining existence of men's homophobia in British sport. *Journal for the Study of Sports and Athletes in Education*

Butler, J. (1990). *Gender trouble: Feminism and the subversion of identity*. London: Routledge.

Butler, J. (1991). Imitation and gender insubordination. In D. Fuss (Ed.), *Inside/Out: Lesbian theories, gay theories* (pp. 13–31). London: Routledge.

Butler, J. (2006). Response. *British Journal of Sociology of Education, 27*(4), 529–534.

Cameron, D. (1985). *Feminism and linguistic theory*. London: MacMillan.

Cameron, D., & Kulick, D. (2003). *Language and sexuality*. Cambridge: Cambridge University Press.

Cancian, F. M. (1987). *Love in America: Gender and self-development*. Cambridge: Cambridge University Press.

Carrigan, T., Connell, R. W., & Lee, J. (1985). Toward a new sociology of masculinity. *Theory and Society, 14,* 551–604.

Carspecken, P. F. (1996). *Critical ethnography in educational research*. London: Routledge.

Chambers, D., Tincknell, E., & Van Loon, J. (2004). Peer regulation of teenage sexual identities. *Gender and Education, 16*(3), 397–415.

Chang, Y. K. (2005). Through queers' eyes: Critical educational ethnography in queer studies. *The Review of Education, Pedagogy, and Cultural Studies, 27,* 171–208.

Chodorow, N. (1978). *The reproduction of mothering*. Berkeley: University of California Press.

Cillessen, A. H. N., & Rose, A. J. (2005). Understanding popularity in the peer system. *Current Directions in Psychological Science, 14*(2), 102–105.

Coad, D. (2008). *The metrosexual: Gender, sexuality and sport*. Albany: State University of New York Press.

Coffey, A. (1999). *The ethnographic self: Fieldwork and the representation of identity*. London: Sage.

Cohler, B. J., & Hammack, P. L. (2007). The psychological world of the gay teenager: Social change, narrative, and "normality." *Journal of Youth and Adolescence, 36,* 47–59.

Cohler, B. J., & Hammack, P. L. (2009). Lives, times, and narrative engagement: Multiplicity and meaning in sexual lives. In P. L. Hammack & B. J. Cohler (Eds.), *The story of sexual identity* (pp. 453–466). New York: Oxford University Press.

Collier, R. (1998). *Masculinities, crime and criminology: Men, heterosexuality and the criminal(ised) other*. London: Sage.

Collins, P. H. (2000). *Black feminist thought: Knowledge, consciousness, and the politics of empowerment* (2nd ed.). London: Routledge.

Connell, R. W. (1987). *Gender and power*. Stanford, CA: Stanford University Press.

Connell, R. W. (1989). Cool guys, swots and wimps: The interplay of masculinity and education. *Oxford Review of Education, 15*(2), 291–303.

Connell, R. W. (1992). A very straight gay: Masculinity, homosexual experience, and the dynamics of gender. *American Sociological Review, 57,* 735–751.

Connell, R. W. (1995). *Masculinities*. Berkley: University of California Press.

Connell, R. W. (2005). *Masculinities* (2nd ed.). Berkley: University of California Press.

Connell, R. W. (2008a). A thousand miles from kind: Men, masculinities and modern institutions. *The Journal of Men's Studies, 16*(3), 237–252.

Connell, R. W. (2008b). Masculinity construction and sport in boys' education: A framework for thinking about the issue. *Sport, Education and Society, 13*(2), 131–145.

Connell, R. W., Hearn, J., & Kimmell, M. S. (2005). Introduction. In M. S. Kimmel, J. Hearn, and R. W. Connell (Eds.), *Handbook of studies on men and masculinities* (pp. 1–12). London: Sage.

Connell, R. W., & Messerschmidt, J. (2005). Hegemonic masculinity: Rethinking the concept. *Gender & Society, 19*(6), 829–859.

Crawley, S. L., Foley, L. J., & Shehan, C. L. (2007). *Gendering bodies.* New York: Rowman & Littlefield.

Crenshaw, K. (1991). Mapping the margins: Intersectionality, identity politics, and violence against women of color. *Stanford Law Review, 43*, 1241–1299.

Cretney, S. (2006). *Same-sex relationships: From 'odious crime' to 'gay marriage'.* London: Oxford University Press.

Csikszentmihalyi, M., & Larson, R. (1984). *Being adolescent: Conflict and growth in the teenage years.* New York: Basic books.

Daniels, A. (1975). Feminist perspectives in sociological research. In M. Millman and R. M. Kanter (Eds.), *Another voice: Feminist perspectives on social life and social science* (pp. 340–380). New York: Anchor Books.

D'Augelli, A. R., & Hershberger, S. L. (1993). Lesbian, gay and bisexual youth in community settings: Personal challenges and mental health problems. *American Journal of Community Psychology, 21*, 421–448.

D'Augelli, A., Hershberger, S. L., & Pilkington, N. W. (2001). Suicidality patterns and sexual orientation-related factors among lesbian, gay, and bisexual youths. *Suicide and Life-Threatening Behavior, 31*(3), 250–264.

David, D., & Brannon, R. (1976). *The forty-nine per-cent majority.* Reading, MA: Addison-Wesley.

Davies, B. (1993). *Shards of glass: Children reading and writing beyond gendered identities.* New York: Hampton Press.

Davies, C. A. (1999). *Reflexive ethnography: A guide to researching selves and others.* London: Routledge.

Davis, L. R. (1990). Male cheerleaders and the naturalisation of gender. In M. A. Messner & D. Sabo (Eds.), *Sport, men and the gender order* (pp. 101–113). London: Human Kinetics.

Delamont, S. (2002). *Fieldwork in educational settings: Methods, pitfalls and perspectives* (2nd ed.). London: Routledge.

Delamont, S. (2004). Ethnography and participant observation. In C. Seale, G. Gobo, J. Gubrium, & D. Silverman (Eds.), *Qualitative research practice* (pp. 217–229). London: Sage.

Demetriou, D. Z. (2001). Connell's concept of hegemonic masculinity: A critique. *Theory and Society, 30*(3), 337–361.

Denzin, N. K., & Lincoln, Y. S. (2005). Introduction. In N. K. Denzin and Y. S. Lincoln (Eds.), *The Sage handbook of qualitative research* (3rd ed., pp. 1–32). London: Sage.

DePalma, R., & Jennett, M. (2010). Homophobia, transphobia and culture: Deconstructing heteronormativity in English Primary schools. *Intercultural Education, 21*(1), 15–26.

Derlega, V. J., Lewis, R. J., Harrison, S., Winstead, R. A. & Costanza, R. (1989). Gender differences in the initiation and attribution of tactile intimacy. *Journal of Nonverbal Behavior, 13*(2), 83–96.

Dollimore, J. (1994). *Sexual dissidence: Augustine to Wilde, Freud to Foucault*. Oxford, England: Clarendon Press.

Douglas, N., Warwick, I., Kemp, S., Whitty, G., & Aggleton, P. (1999). Homophobic bullying in secondary schools in England and Wales—teachers' experiences. *Health Education, 99*(2), 53–60.

Drummond, M. (2007). The meaning of difference: Young gay male's experiences at school in Australia. *Thymos: Journal of Boyhood Studies, 1*(1), 95–110.

Dyer, R. (1997). *White*. London: Routledge.

Edley, N., & Wetherell, M. (1995). *Men in perspective: Practice, power and identity*. London: Prentice Hall/Harvester Wheatsheaf.

Elliot, A., & Lemert, C. (2006). *The new individualism: The emotional costs of globalization*. London: Routledge.

Ellis, V., & High, S. (2004). Something more to tell you: Gay, lesbian or bisexual young people's experience of secondary schooling. *British Educational Research Journal, 30*(2), 213–225.

Emerson, R. M., Fretz, R. I., & Shaw, L. L. (1995). *Writing ethnographic field notes*. Chicago: University of Chicago Press.

Epstein, D. (1993). Practicing heterosexuality. *Curriculum Studies, 1*(2), 275–286.

Epstein, D. (1994). Introduction. In D. Epstein (Ed.), *Challenging gay and lesbian inequalities in education* (pp. 1–17). Buckingham, England: Open University Press.

Epstein, D. (1996). Keeping them in their place: Hetero/sexist harassment, gender and the enforcement of heterosexuality. In J. Holland & L. Adkins (Eds.), *Sex, sensibility and the gendered body* (pp. 86–99). London: Macmillan.

Epstein, D. (1997). Boyz' own stories: Masculinities and sexualities in schools. *Gender and Education, 9*(1), 105–115.

Epstein, D., Elwood, J., Hey, V., & Maw, J. (1998). *Failing boys: Issues in gender and achievement*. Basingstoke, England: Open University Press.

Epstein, D., & Johnson, R. (1994). On the straight and narrow: The heterosexual presumption, homophobias and schools. In D. Epstein (Ed.), *Challenging gay and lesbian inequalities in education* (pp. 197–230). Buckingham, England: Open University Press.

Epstein, D., & Johnson, R. (1998). *Schooling sexualities*. Buckingham, England: Open University Press.

Epstein, D., O'Flynn, S., & Telford, D. (2003). *Silenced sexualities in schools and universities*. Stoke-on-Trent, England: Trentham Press.

Farley, R. (1997). Racial trends and differences in the United States 30 years after the Civil Rights decade. *Social Science Research, 26*, 235–262.

Fausto-Sterling, A. (1992). *Myths of gender: Biological theories about men and women*. New York: Basic Books.

Fausto-Sterling, A. (2000). *Sexing the body: Gender politics and the construction of sexuality*. New York: Basic Books.

Fausto-Sterling, A. (2005). The bare bones of sex: Part 1—sex and gender. *Signs: Journal of Women in Culture and Society, 30*(2), 1491–1528.

Femia, J. (1981). *Gramsci's political thought: Hegemony, consciousness, and the revolutionary process*. Oxford, England: Clarendon Press.

Fenstermaker, S., & West, C. (2002). *Doing gender, doing difference: Inequality, power, and institutional change*. New York: Routledge.

Ferfolja, T. (2005). Institutional silence: Experiences of Australian lesbian teachers working in Catholic high schools. *Journal of Gay and Lesbian Issues in Education, 2*(3), 51–66.

Ferfolja, T. (2007). Schooling cultures: Institutionalising heteronormativity and heterosexism. *International Journal of Inclusive Education, 11*(2), 147–162.

Ferguson, A. A. (2000). *Bad boys: Public schools in the making of black masculinity.* Ann Arbor: The University of Michigan Press.

Field, T. (1999). American adolescents touch each other less and are more aggressive toward their peers as compared with French adolescents. *Adolescence, 34*(4), 22–34.

Filiault, S., & Drummond, M. (2009). All the right labels: Gay male athletes and their perceptions of clothing. *Culture, Society and Masculinities, 1*(2), 177–196.

Firestein, B. A. (Ed.). (1996). *Bisexuality: The psychology and politics of an invisible minority.* Thousand Oaks, CA: Sage.

Flood, M. (2002). Between men and masculinity: An assessment of the term "masculinity" in recent scholarship on men. In S. Pearce & V. Muller (Eds.), *Manning the next millennium: Studies in masculinities* (pp. 66–83). Perth, Australia: Black Swan.

Flowers, P., & Buston, K. (2001). "I was terrified of being different": Exploring gay men's accounts of growing-up in a heterosexist society. *Journal of Adolescence, 24,* 51–65.

Floyd, K. (2000). Affectionate same-sex touch: The influence of homophobia on observers' perceptions. *The Journal of Social Psychology, 140*(6), 774–788.

Flyvbjerg, B. (2006). Five misunderstandings about case-study research. *Qualitative Inquiry, 12*(2), 219–245.

Forman, R. (2011). Gay high schooler becomes prom king. *Windy City Times,* 22nd June.

Foster, V., Kimmel, M., & Skelton, C. (2001). 'What about the boys?' An overview of the debates. In W. Martino and B. Meyenn (Eds.), *What about the boys? Issues of masculinity in schools* (pp. 1–23). Buckingham, England: Open University Press.

Foucault, M. (1984). *The history of sexuality, Volume 1: An introduction* (F. Hurley, Trans.). New York: Vintage.

France, A. (2007). *Understanding youth in late modernity.* Buckingham, England: Open University Press.

Francis, B. (1999). Lads, lasses, and (new) labour. *British Journal of Sociology of Education, 20*(3), 355–371.

Francis, B., Skelton, C., & Read, B. (2010). The simultaneous production of educational achievement and popularity: How do some pupils accomplish it? *British Educational Research Journal, 36,* 317–340.

Freud, S. (1905). Three essays on the theory of sexuality. *Complete psychological works* (Vol. 7). (pp. 215–282). London: Hogarth.

Frosh, S., Phoenix, A., & Pattman, R. (2002). *Young masculinities: Understanding boys in contemporary society.* Basingstoke, England: Palgrave.

Froyum, C. M. (2007). "At least I'm not gay": Heterosexual identity making among poor black teens. *Sexualities, 10*(5), 603–622.

Gamson, J. (2000). Sexualities, queer theory, and qualitative research. In N. Denzin and Y. Lincoln (Eds.), *Handbook of Qualitative Methods.* London: Routledge.

Gard, M. (2001). 'I like smashing people and I like getting smashed myself': Addressing issues of masculinity in physical education and sport. In W. Martino & B. Meyenn (Eds.), *What about the boys?* Buckingham, England: Open University Press.

Geertz, C. (1973). *The interpretation of cultures: Selected essays.* New York: Basic books.

Goetz, J. P., & LeCompte, M. D. (1981). Ethnographic research and the problem of data reduction. *Anthropology & Education Quarterly, 12*(1), 51–70.

Goetz, J. P., & LeCompte, M. D. (1984). *Ethnography and qualitative design in educational research.* Orlando, FL: Academic Press.

Goffman, E. (1961). *Asylums: Essays on the social situation of mental patients and other inmates.* New York: Double Day.

Goffman, E. (1963). *Stigma: Notes on the management of spoiled identity.* New York: Simon & Schuster.

Gramsci, A. (1957). *The Modern Prince and other writings.* New York: International.

Gramsci, A. (1971). *Selections from prison notebooks.* London: New Left Books.

Gramsci, A. (1975). *History, philosophy and culture in the young Gramsci.* Saint Louis, MO: Telos Press.

Gramsci, A. (1985). *Selections from cultural writings.* Cambridge, MA: Harvard University Press.

Gray, M. L. (2009). *Out in the country: Youth, media, and queer visibility in rural America.* New York: New York University Press.

Green, A. I. (2007). Queer theory and sociology: Locating the subject and the self in sexuality studies. *Sociological Theory, 25*(1), 26–45.

Griffin, P. (1998). *Strong women, deep closets: Lesbians and homophobia in sport.* Champaign, IL: Human Kinetics.

Griffin, P. (2009, November). No homo! No dumbo. *Pat Griffin's LGBT Sport Blog.* Retrieved from http://ittakesateam.blogspot.com/2009/11/no-homo-no-dumbo.html

Grossman, A., & D'Augelli, A. R. (2006). Transgender youth: invisible and vulnerable. *Journal of Homosexuality, 51*(1), 111–128.

Guasp, A. (2008). *The teacher's report: Homophobic bullying in Britain's schools.* London: Stonewall.

Halkitis, P. N. (1999). Redefining masculinity in the age of AIDS: Seropositive gay men and the "buff agenda." In P. Nardi (Ed.), *Gay masculinities* (pp. 130–151). Newbury Park, CA: Sage.

Hammack, P. L., & Cohler, B. J. (2009). *The story of sexual identity: Narrative perspectives on the gay and lesbian life course.* New York: Oxford University Press.

Harper, G. W., Bruce, D., Serrano, P., & Jamil, O. B. (2009). The role of the Internet in the sexual identity development of gay and bisexual male adolescents. In P. L. Hammack & B. J. Cohler (Eds.), *The story of sexual identity: Narrative perspectives on the gay and lesbian life course* (pp. 297–326). New York: Oxford University Press.

Harris, F. (2010). College men's meanings of masculinities and contextual influences: Toward a conceptual model. *Journal of College Student Development, 51*(3), 297–318.

Harris, J., & Clayton, B. (2007). The first metrosexual rugby star: Rugby union, masculinity, and celebrity in contemporary Wales. *Sociology of Sport Journal, 24*, 145–164.

Harry, J. (1992). Conceptualising anti-gay violence. In G. M. Herek & K. T. Berrill (Eds.), *Hate crimes: Confronting violence against lesbians and gay men* (pp. 113–122). London: Sage.

Hartmann, H. (1976). Capitalism, patriarchy and job segregation. *Signs: Journal of Women in Culture and Society, 1*(3), 137–169.

Hearn, J. (2004). From hegemonic masculinity to the hegemony of men. *Feminist Theory, 5*(1), 49–72.

Hey, V. (1993). *The company she keeps.* London: Routledge.

Hey, V. (2006). The politics of performative resignification: Translating Judith Butler's theoretical discourse and its potential for a sociology of education. *British Journal of Sociology of Education, 27*(4), 439–457.

Hickey, C. (2008). Physical education, sport and hyper-masculinity in schools. *Sport, Education and Society, 13*(2), 147–161.

Hillier, L., & Harrison, L. (2004). Homophobia and the production of shame: Young people and same-sex attraction. *Culture, Health & Sexuality, 6*(1), 79–94.

Hillier, L., & Harrison, L. (2007). Building realities less limited than their own: Young people practicing same-sex attraction on the internet. *Sexualities, 10*(1), 82–100.

Hite, S. (1976). *The Hite report: A nationwide study of female sexuality.* New York: Tamlyn Franklin.

Hodkinson, P. (2005). "Insider research" in the study of youth cultures. *Journal of Youth Studies, 8*(2), 131–149.

Hoffman, E. A. (2007). Open-ended interviews, power, and emotional labour. *Journal of Contemporary Ethnography, 26*(3), 318–346.

Holmlund, M., & Youngberg, G. (2003). *Inspiring women: A celebration of herstory.* Regina, SK, Canada: Coteau Books.

Holt, N. L., & Sparkes, A. C. (2001). An ethnographic study of cohesiveness in a college soccer team over a season. *The Sport Psychologist, 15,* 237–259.

Hooks, B. (1992). *Black looks: Race and representation.* Boston: South End Press.

Howson, R. (2006). *Challenging hegemonic masculinity.* London: Routledge.

Howson, R. (2008). Hegemonic masculinity in the theory of hegemony: A brief response to Christine Beasley's "Rethinking hegemonic masculinity in a globalizing world." *Men and Masculinities, 11*(1), 109–113.

Hunt, R., & Jensen, J. (2007). *The school report: The experiences of young gay people in Britain's schools.* London: Stonewall.

Hunter, J. D. (1991). *Culture wars: The struggle to define America.* New York: Basic Books.

Huuki, T., Manninen, S., & Sunnari, V. (2010). Humour as a resource and strategy for boys to gain status in the field of informal school. *Gender and Education, 22,* 369–383.

Ibson, J. (2002). *Picturing men: A century of male relationships in everyday life.* Washington, DC: Smithsonian Books.

Jackson, C. (2006). *Lads and ladettes in school.* Buckingham, England: Open University Press.

Jackson, C., & Dempster S. (2009). "I sat back on my computer . . . with a bottle of whisky next to me": Constructing "cool" masculinity through "effortless" achievement in secondary and higher education. *Journal of Gender Studies, 18*(4), 341–356.

Jackson, P. W. (1966). The student's world. *The Elementary School Journal, 66*(7), 345–357.

Jackson, S. (2006). Gender, sexuality and heterosexuality. *Feminist theory, 7*(1), 105–121.

Jackson, S., & Scott, S. (2010). Rehabilitating interactionism for a feminist sociology of sexuality. *Sociology, 44*(5), 811–826.

Jagose, A. (1996). *Queer theory: An introduction.* New York: New York University Press.

Jones, R., & Clarke, G. (2007). The school experiences of same-sex attracted students in the 14- to 19-year-old secondary sector in England: Within and beyond the safety and tolerance framework. *Journal of Gay & Lesbian Social Services, 19*(3/4), 119–138.

Kaplan, D. (2005). Public intimacy: Dynamics of seduction in male homosocial interactions. *Symbolic interaction, 28*(4), 571–595.

Kehily, M. J., & Pattman, R. (2006). Middle-class struggle? *British Journal of Sociology of Education, 27*(1), 37–52.

Kehler, M. (2007). Hallway fears and high school friendships: The complications of young men (re)negotiating heterosexualized identities. *Discourse: Studies in the Cultural Politics of Education, 28*(2), 259–277.

Kehler, M. (2009). Boys, friendships and knowing "it wouldn't be unreasonable to assume I am gay." In W. Martino, M. D. Kehler, & M. B. Weaver-Hightower (Eds.), *The problem with boys' education: Beyond the backlash.* (pp. 198–223). London: Routledge.

Kenway, J., & Kraack, A. (2004). Reordering work and destabilizing masculinity. In N. Dolby & G. Dimitriadis (Eds.), *Learning to labor in new times* (pp. 95–110). New York: Routledge Falmer.

Kessler, S. J., & McKenna, W. (1978). *Gender: An ethnomethodological approach.* Chicago: The University of Chicago Press.

Kian, T., & Anderson, E. (2009). Max Amaechi: Changing the way sport reporters examine gay athletes. *Journal of Homosexuality, 56*, 799–818.

Kiesling, S. F. (2007). Men, masculinities, and language. *Language and Linguistics Compass, 1*(6), 653–673.

Kimmel, M. S. (1994). Masculinity as homophobia: Fear, shame, and silence in the construction of gender identity. In H. Brod & M. Kaufman (Eds.), *Theorising masculinities.* London: Sage.

Kimmel, M. S. (2004). *The gendered society* (2nd ed.). New York: Oxford University Press.

Kimmel, M. S. (2005). *The gender of desire: Essays on male sexuality.* New York: State University of New York Press.

Kimmel, M. S. (2008). *Guyland: The perilous world where boys become men.* New York: Harper Collins.

Kimmel, M. S. (2009, November). From "that's so gay" to "no homo": A small sign of progress. *The Huffington Post.* Retrieved from http://www.huffingtonpost.com/michael-kimmel/from-thats-so-gay-to-no-h_b_345390.html

Kimmel, M. S., & Messner, M. (2007). Introduction. In M. S. Kimmel and M. Messner (Eds.), *Men's lives* (7th ed., pp. xv–xxiii). London: Allyn and Bacon.

Kimmel, S. B., & Mahalik, J. R. (2005). Body image concerns of gay men: The roles of minority stress and conformity to masculine norms. *Journal of Consulting and Clinical Psychology, 73*(6), 1185–1190.

Kirsch, M. H. (2000). *Queer theory and social change.* London: Routledge.

Kong, T. S., Mahoney, D., & Plummer, K. (2002). Queering the interview. In J. F. Gubrium and J. A. Holstein (Eds.), *Handbook of interview research* (pp. 239–258). London: Sage.

Kosicw, J. G., Greytak, E. A., Diaz, E. M., & Bartkiewicz, M. J. (2009). *The 2009 national school climate survey: The experiences of lesbian, gay, bisexual and transgender youth in our nation's schools.* New York: GLSEN.

Kozloski, M. (2010). Homosexual moral acceptance and social tolerance: Are the effects of education changing? *Journal of Homosexuality, 57*(10), 1370–181.

Kreager, D. (2007). Unnecessary roughness? School sports, peer networks, and male adolescent violence. *American Sociological Review, 72*, 705–724.

Laclau, E., and Mouffe, C. (1985). *Hegemony and socialist strategy: Towards a radical democratic politics.* London: Verso.

Lalor, T., & Rendle-Short, J. (2007). 'That's so gay': A contemporary use of *gay* in Australian English. *Australian Journal of Linguistics, 27*(2), 147–173.

LeCompte, M. D., & Goetz, J. P. (1982). Problems of reliability and validity in ethnographic research. *Review of Educational Research, 52*(1), 31–60.

Lees, S. (1993). *Sugar and spice: Sexuality and adolescent girls.* London: Penguin.

Lenskyj, H. (1990). Beyond plumbing and prevention: feminist approaches to sex education. *Gender and Education,* 2(2), 217–230.

LeVay, S. (1996). *Queer science: The use and abuse of research on homosexuality.* Cambridge, MA: MIT Press.

LeVay, S. (2010). *Gay, straight and the reason why: The science of sexual orientation.* New York: Oxford University Press.

Light, R., & Kirk, D. (2000). High school rugby, the body and the reproduction of hegemonic masculinity. *Sport, Education and Society, 5*(2), 163–176.

Lingard, K., Martino, B., & Mills, M. (2008). *Boys and schooling: Beyond educational reform.* Hampshire, England: Palgrave Macmillan.

Loftus, J. (2001). America's liberalization in attitudes towards homosexuality, 1973–1998. *American Sociological Review, 66,* 762–782.

Lorber, J. (1994). *Paradoxes of gender.* New Haven, CT: Yale University Press.

Lorde, A. (1984). *Sister outsider.* Langhorne, PA: Crossing Press.

Lyng, S. T. (2009). Is there more to "antischoolishness" than masculinity? On multiple student styles, gender, and educational self-exclusion in secondary school. *Men and Masculinities, 11*(4), 462–487.

Mac an Ghaill, M. (1994). *The making of men: Masculinities, sexualities and schooling.* Buckingham, England: Open University Press.

Mac an Ghaill, M., & Haywood, C. (2007). *Gender, culture and society: Contemporary femininities and masculinities.* London: Palgrave Macmillan.

MacKinnon, C. A. (1999). Points against postmodernism. *Chicago-Kent Law Review, 75,* 687–702.

Malinowski, B. (1922). *Argonauts of the Western Pacific: An account of native enterprise and adventure in the archipelagos of Melanesian New Guinea.* Prospect Heights, IL: Waveland Press.

Markula, P., & Pringle, R. (2005). No pain is sane after all: A Foucauldian analysis of masculinities and men's experiences in rugby. *Sociology of Sport Journal, 22*(4), 472–489.

Martin, P. Y. (1998). Why can't a man be more like a woman: Reflections on Connell's *Masculinities. Gender & Society, 12*(4), 472–474.

Martino, W. (1995). Boys and literacy: Exploring the construction of hegemonic masculinities and the formation of literate capacities for boys in the English classroom. *English in Australia, 112,* 11–24.

Martino, W., Kehler, M., & Weaver-Hightower, M. (Eds.). (2009). *The problem with boys' education: beyond the backlash.* New York: Routledge.

Martino, W., & Pallotta-Chiarolli, M. (2003). *So what's a boy: Addressing issues of masculinity and schooling.* Buckingham, England: Open University Press.

Mauthner, N. S., & Doucet, A. (2003). Reflexive accounts and accounts of reflexivity in qualitative data analysis. *Sociology, 37*(3), 413–431.

May, R. A. B., & Pattillo-McCoy, M. (2000). Do you see what I see? Examining a collaborative ethnography. *Qualitative Inquiry, 6*(1), 65–87.

McCall, L. (2005). The complexity of intersectionality. *Signs: Journal of Women in Culture and Society, 30,* 1771–1800.

McCormack, M. (2011). Queer masculinities and gender conformity in the secondary school. In N. Rodriguez & J. Landreau (Eds.), *Queer masculinities: A critical reader in education* (pp. 23–38). New York: Springer.

McCormack, M., & Anderson, E. (2010). The re-production of homosexually-themed discourse in educationally-based organised sport. *Culture, Health & Sexuality, 12*(8), 913–927.

McDowell, L. (1991). Life without Father and Ford: The new gender order of postFordism. *Transactions of the Institute of British Geographers, 16*, 400–419.

McDowell, L. (2003). *Redundant masculinities: Employment change and white working class youth.* Oxford, England: Blackwell.

McGuffey, C. S., & Rich, B. L. (1999). Playing in the gender transgression zone: Race, class and hegemonic masculinity in middle childhood. *Gender & Society, 13*(5), 608–627.

McNair, B. (2002). *Striptease culture: The democratisation of desire.* London: Routledge.

McRobbie, A. (1989). *Feminism and youth culture: From Jackie to just seventeen.* Boston: Unwin Hyman.

Messerschmidt, J. (2008). And now, the rest of the story . . .: A commentary on Christine Beasley's "Rethinking hegemonic masculinity in a globalizing world." *Men and Masculinities, 11*(1), 104–108.

Messner, M. (1992). *Power at play: Sports and the problem of masculinity.* Boston: Beacon Press.

Messner, M. (1997). *Politics of masculinities: Men in movements.* Oxford, England: AltaMira Press.

Messner, M. (2009). *It's all for the kids: Gender, families and youth sports.* Albany, NY: State University of New York Press.

Miceli, M. (2005). *Standing out, standing together: The social and political impact of gay-straight alliances.* London: Routledge.

Miller, N. (1995). *Out of the past: Gay and lesbian history from 1869 to the present.* New York: Vintage.

Mizen, P. (2004). *The changing state of youth.* London: Palgrave MacMillan.

Moller, M. (2007). Exploiting patterns: A critique of hegemonic masculinity. *Journal of Gender Studies, 16*(3), 263–276.

Morrison, L. L., & L'Heureux, J. (2001). Suicide and gay/lesbian/bisexual youth: Implications for clinicians. *Journal of Adolescence, 24*, 39–49.

Mouffe, C. (1979). *Gramsci and Marxist theory.* London: Routledge and Kegan Paul.

Mustanski, B. S., Garofalo, R., & Emerson, E. M. (2010). Mental health disorders, psychological distress, and suicidality in a diverse sample of lesbian, gay, bisexual, and transgender youths. *American Journal of Public Health, 100*(12), 2426–2432.

Nagel, J. (2003). *Race, ethnicity and sexuality: Intimate intersections, forbidden frontiers.* Oxford, England: Oxford University Press. Producing contradictory masculine subject positions: Producing narratives of threat, homophobia and bullying in 11–14 year old boys.

Netzley, S. B. (2010). Visibility that demystifies: Gays, gender, and sex on television. *Journal of Homosexuality, 57*(8), 949–967.

Nixon, D. (2010). Discrimination, performance and recuperation: How teachers and pupils challenge and recover discourses of sexualities in schools. *Teaching and Teacher Education, 26*(2), 145–151.

Nixon, D., & Givens, D. (2007). An epitaph to Section 28? Telling tales out of school about changes and challenges to discourses of sexuality. *International Journal of Qualitative Studies in Education, 20*(4), 449–471.

Nixon, D. B. (2009). "I can't put a smiley face on": Working-class masculinity, emotional labour and service work in the new economy. *Gender, Work and Organization, 16*(3), 300–322.

Norton, R. (1992). *Mother clap's molly house: The gay subculture in England, 1700–1830*. London: GMP Publishers.

Nussbaum, M. (1995). Objectification. *Philosophy and Public Affairs, 24*(4), 279–283.

Nussbaum, M. (1999a, February 22). The professor of parody. The *New Republic Online*. Retrieved April 12, 2010, from http://www.akad.se/Nussbaum.pdf

Nussbaum, M. (1999b). *Sex and social justice*. Oxford, England: Oxford University Press.

O'Connell Davidson, J. (2005). *Children in the global sex trade*. Cambridge, England: Polity Press.

O'Donnell, M., & Sharpe, S. (2000). *Uncertain masculinities; youth, ethnicity and class in contemporary Britain*. London: Routledge.

Ogburn, W. F. (1950). *On culture and social change*. Chicago: Chicago University Press.

Page, B. I., & Shapiro, R. Y. (1992). *The rational public: Fifty years of trends in Americans' policy preferences*. Chicago: University of Chicago Press.

Parsons, T., & Bales, R. (1955). *Family: Socialization and interaction process*. Glencoe, IL: Free Press.

Pascoe, C. J. (2003). Multiple masculinities: Teenage boys talk about jocks and gender. *American Behavioural Scientist, 46*(10), 1423–1438.

Pascoe, C. J. (2005). "Dude, you're a fag": Adolescent masculinity and the fag discourse. *Sexualities, 8*, 329–346.

Pascoe, C. J. (2007). *Dude, you're a fag*. London: University of California Press.

Patai, D. (1994). When method becomes power. In A. Gitlin (Ed.), *Power and method* (pp. 61–76). London: Routledge.

Peterson, G.T. (2011). Clubbing masculinities: Gender shifts in gay men's dance floor choreographies. *Journal of Homosexuality, 58*(5), 608—625.

Pharr, S. (1997) *Homophobia: A weapon of sexism*. Berkeley, CA: Chardon Press.

Phoenix, A., Frosh, S., & Pattman, R. (2003). Producing contradictory masculine subject positions: Narratives of threat, homophobia and bullying in 11–14 year old boys. *Journal of Social Issues, 59*(1), 179–195.

Pleck, J. (1981). *The myth of masculinities*. Cambridge, MA: MIT Press.

Plummer, D. (1999). *One of the boys: Masculinity, homophobia and modern manhood*. New York: Harrington Park Press.

Plummer, D. (2001). Policing manhood: New theories about the social significance of homophobia. In C. Wood (Ed.), *Sexual Positions: An Australian View* (pp. 38–51). Melbourne, Australia: Hill of Content/Collins.

Plummer, K. (2003). *Intimate citizenship: Private decisions and public dialogues*. Seattle: University of Washington Press.

Plummer, K. (2006). Rights work: Constructing lesbian, gay and sexual rights in late modern times. In L. Morris (Ed.), *Rights* (pp. 152–167). London: Routledge.

Pollack, W. (1998). *Real boys*. New York: Random House.

Poteat, V. P., Espelage, D., & Green, H. (2007). The socialization of dominance: Peer group contextual effects on homophobic and dominance attitudes. *Journal of Personality and Social Psychology, 92*(6), 1040–1050.

Poteat, V. P., Espelage, D., & Koenig, B. W. (2009). Willingness to remain friends and attend school with lesbian and gay peers: Relational expressions of prejudice among heterosexual youth. *Journal of Youth and Adolescence, 38*, 952–962.

Price, M., & Parker, A. (2003). Sport, sexuality, and the gender order: Amateur rugby union, gay men and social exclusion. *Sociology of Sport Journal, 20*, 108–126.

Pringle, R. (2005). Masculinities, sport and power. *Journal of Sport and Social Issues, 29*, 256–278.

Pronger, B. (1990). *The arena of masculinity: Sports, homosexuality, and the meaning of sex*. New York: St. Martin's Press.

Ransome, P. (1992). *Antonio Gramsci: A new introduction*. London: Harvester Wheatsheaf.

Rasmsussen, M. L. (2004). "That's so gay!": A study of the deployment of signifiers of sexual and gender identity in secondary school settings in Australia and the United States. *Social Semiotics, 14*(3), 289–308.

Rasmussen, M. L. (2006). *Becoming subjects: Sexualities and secondary schooling*. London: Routledge.

Redman, P., & Mac an Ghaill, M. (1997). Educating Peter: The making of a history man. In D. L. Steinberg, D. Epstein, & R. Johnson (Eds.), *Border patrols: Policing the boundaries of heterosexuality* (pp. 162–182). London: Cassell.

Remafedi, G. (1994). *Death by denial: Studies of suicide in gay and lesbian teenagers* (ed.). Los Angeles: Alyson Press.

Renold, E. (2004). "Other" boys: Negotiating non-hegemonic masculinities in the primary school. *Gender and Education, 16*(2), 247–266.

Renold, E. (2005). *Girls, boys and junior sexualities*. London: Routledge.

Rich, A. (1980). Compulsory heterosexuality and lesbian existence. *Signs: Journal of Women in Culture and Society, 5*(4), 631–660.

Richardson, D. (Ed.). (1996). *Theorising heterosexuality: Telling it straight*. Maidenhead, England: Open University Press.

Richardson, D. (2010). Youth masculinities: Compelling male heterosexuality. *British Journal of Sociology, 61*(4), 737–756.

Rieger, G. & Savin-Williams, R.C. (2011). Gender nonconformity, sexual orientation, and psychological well-being. *Archives of Sexual Behavior*, online first: DOI: 10.1007/s10508-011-9738-0.

Rivers, I. (1995). The victimization of gay teenagers in schools: Homophobia in education. *Pastoral Care, March*, 35–41.

Rivers, I. (1996). Protecting the gay adolescent at school. *Medicine, Mind and Adolescence, 11*(2), 15–24.

Rivers, I. (2001). The bullying of sexual minorities at school. *Educational and Child Psychology, 18*(1), 32–46.

Rivers, I. (2011). *Homophobic bullying: Research and theoretical perspectives*. New York: Oxford University Press.

Rivers, I., & Cowie, H. (2006). Bullying and homophobia in UK schools: A perspective on factors affecting resilience and recovery. *Journal of Gay & Lesbian Issues in Education, 3*(4), 11–43.

Rivers, I., Duncan, N., & Besag, V. E. (2007). *Bullying: A handbook for educators and parents*. Plymouth, England: Rowman and Littlefield.

Robards, B. (2010). Randoms in my bedroom: Negotiating privacy and unsolicited contact on social network sites. *PRism, 7*(3), 1–17.

Roberts, J. M., & Sanders, T. (2005). Before, during and after: Realism, reflexivity and ethnography. *The Sociological Review, 53*(2), 294–313.

Robertson, J. (2002). Reflexivity redux: A pithy polemic on "positionality." *Anthropological Quarterly, 75*(4), 785–792.

Robinson, K. H. (2005). Reinforcing hegemonic masculinities through sexual harassment: Issues of identity, power and popularity in secondary schools. *Gender and Education, 17*(1), 19–37.

Rose, S., Kamin, L. J., & Lewontin, R. C. (1984). *Not in our genes: Biology, ideology and human nature*. Harmondsworth, England: Pelican Books.

Rowe, D. (1998). Play up: Rethinking power and resistance. *Journal of Sport and Social Issues, 22*(2), 241–251.

Rubin, G. (1984). Thinking sex: Notes for a radical theory of the politics of sexuality. In C. Vance (Ed.), *Pleasure and danger: Exploring female sexuality* (pp. 143–179). Boston: Routledge.

Rubin, G. (1993a). Misguided, dangerous and wrong: An analysis of anti-pornography politics. In A. Assiter & A. Carol (Eds.), *Bad girls and dirty pictures: The challenge to reclaim feminism* (pp. 1–17). London: Pluto Press.

Rubin, G. (1993b). Thinking sex: Notes for a radical theory of the politics of sexuality. In L.S. Kauffman (Ed.), *American feminist thought at Century's end: A reader* (pp. 3–64). Oxford, England: Blackwell.

Russell, B. (1938). *Power: A social analysis*. London: Allen & Unwin.

Russell, S.T. (2005). Beyond risk: Resilience in the lives of sexual minority youth. *Journal of Gay & Lesbian Issues in Education, 2*(3), 5–18.

Russell, S. T., Muraco, A., Subramaniam, A., & Laub, C. (2009). Youth empowerment and high school gay-straight alliances. *Journal of Youth and Adolescence, 38*, 891–903.

Ryan, C., & Rivers, I. (2003). Lesbian, gay, bisexual and transgender youth: Victimization and its correlates in the USA and UK. *Culture, Health & Sexuailty, 5*(2), 103–119.

Sabo, D., & Runfola, R. (1980). *Jock: Sports and male identity*. Englewood Cliffs, NJ: Prentice-Hall.

Salisbury, J., & Jackson, D. (1996). *Challenging macho values: Practical ways of working with adolescent boys*. London: Falmer Press.

Sanders, S. (2008). Tackling homophobia, creating safer spaces. In R. dePalma & E. Atkinson (Eds.), *Invisible boundaries: Addressing sexualities equality in children's worlds* (pp. 3–12). Stoke-on-Trent, England: Trentham.

Sargent, P. (2001). *Real men or real teachers?: Contradictions in the lives of men elementary school teachers*. Harriman, TN: Men's Studies Press.

Savin-Williams, R. C. (2001). A critique of research on sexual-minority youths. *Journal of Adolescence, 24*(1), 5–13.

Savin-Williams, R. C. (2005). *The new gay teenager*. London: Harvard University Press.

Sayer, A. (1997). Essentialism, social constructionism and beyond. *The Sociological Review, 45*(3), 453–487.

Schact, S. (1996). Misogyny on and off the "pitch": The gendered world of male rugby players. *Gender & Society, 10*, 550–565.

Sedgwick, E. K. (1990). *Epistemology of the closet*. London: Harvester Wheatsheaf.

Seidman, S. (1996). Introduction. In S. Seidman (Ed.), *Queer theory, sociology* (pp. 1–30). Malden, MA: Wiley-Blackwell.

Sherkat, D.E., Powell-Williams, M., Maddox, G. & de Vries, K.M. (2011). Religion, politics, and support for same-sex marriage in the United States, 1988–2008. *Social Science Research*, 40, 167–180.

Skelton, C. (2001). *Schooling the boys*. Buckingham, England: Open University Press.

Smith, S.J., Axelton, A.M., & Saucier, D.A. (2009). The effects of contact on sexual prejudice: A meta-analysis. *Sex Roles*, *61*(3–4), 178–191.

Southall, R. M., Nagel, M. S., Anderson, E., Polite, F. G., & Southall, C. (2009). An investigation of male college athletes' attitudes toward sexual orientation. *Journal of Issues in Intercollegiate Athletics*, 62–77.

Sparkes, A. C. (1992). The paradigms debate: An extended review and celebration of difference. In A. C. Sparkes (Ed.), *Research in physical education and sport: Exploring alternative visions* (pp. 15–46). London: Routledge.

Spencer, C. (1995). *Homosexuality in history*. Boston, MA: Harcourt Brace.

Spradley, J. P. (1970). *You owe yourself a drunk*. Boston: Little, Brown.

Sprague, J. (2008). Sociology: The good, the bad, and the public. *Gender & Society, 22*(6), 697–704.

Stacey, J., & Thorne, B. (1985). The missing feminist revolution in sociology. *Social Problems, 32*(4), 301–316.

Stein, A., & Plummer, K. (1996). "I can't even think straight": "Queer" theory and the missing sexual revolution in sociology. In S. Seidman (Ed.), *Queer theory, sociology* (pp. 129–144). Cambridge, MA: Blackwell.

Steinberg, D., Epstein, D., & Johnson, R. (1997). *Border patrols: Policing the boundaries of heterosexuality*. London: Cassell.

Stoudt, B. G. (2006). "You're either in or you're out": School violence, peer discipline, and the (re)production of hegemonic masculinity. *Men and Masculinities, 8*(3), 273–287.

Swain, J. (2006a). An ethnographic approach to researching children in junior school. *International Journal of Social Research Methodology, 9*(3), 199–213.

Swain, J. (2006b). Reflections on patterns of masculinity in school settings. *Men and Masculinities, 8*(3), 331–349.

Taulke-Johnson, R. (2008). Moving beyond homophobia, harassment and intolerance: Gay male university students' alternative narratives. *Discourse: Studies in the Cultural Politics of Education, 29*(1), 121–133.

Taylor, C. (1989). *Sources of the self: The making of the modern identity*. Cambridge, MA: Harvard University Press.

Taylor, Y. (2007). Brushed behind the bikeshed: Working-class lesbians' experiences of school. *British Journal of Sociology of Education, 28*(3), 349–362.

Thorne, B. (1993). *Gender play: Girls and boys in school*. New Brunswick, NJ: Rutgers University Press.

Thorne, B., & Luria, Z. (1986). Sexuality and gender in children's daily worlds. *Social Problems, 33*(3), 176–190.

Thurlow, C. (2001). Naming the "outsider within": Homophobic pejoratives and the verbal abuse of LGB high-school pupils. *Journal of Adolescence, 24*, 25–38.

Vaillancourt, T., Hymel, S., & McDougall, P. (2003). Bullying is power: Implications for school-based intervention strategies. In M. J. Elias & J. E. Zins (Eds.), *Bullying, peer harassment, and victimization in schools: The next generation of prevention* (pp. 157–176). New York: Haworth Press.

Valkenburg, P. M., & Peter, J. (2008). Adolescents' identity experiments on the Internet: Consequences for social competence and self-concept unity. *Communication Research, 35*(2), 208–231.

Vicars, M. (2006). Who are you calling queer? Sticks and stones may break my bones but names will always hurt me. *British Educational Research Journal, 32*(3), 347–361.

Walls, N. E., Kane, S. B., & Wisneski, H. (2010). Gay-straight alliances and school experiences of sexual minority youth. *Youth & Society, 41*(3), 307–332.

Walters, S. D. (1996). From here to queer: Radical feminism, postmodernism, and the lesbian menace (or, why can't a woman be more like a fag?). *Signs, 21*(4), 830–869.

Walters, S. D. (2001). *All the rage: The story of gay visibility in America*. Chicago: The University of Chicago Press.

Warrington, M., & Younger, M. (2011). "Life is a tightrope": Reflections on peer group inclusion and exclusion amongst adolescent girls and boys. *Gender and Education, 23*(2), 153–168.

Warwick, I., Aggleton, P., & Douglas, N. (2001). Playing it safe: addressing the emotional and physical health of lesbian and gay pupils in the U.K. *Journal of Adolescence, 24*, 129–140.

Wax, R. H. (1971). *Doing fieldwork: Warnings and advice*. London: University of Chicago Press.

Way, N. (2011). *Deep secrets: Boys secrets and the crisis of connection*. New York: Harvard University Press.

Weeks, J. (1985). *Sexuality and its discontents*. London: Routledge & Kegan Paul.

Weeks, J. (1990). *Coming out: Homosexual politics in Britain from the nineteenth century to the present*. London: Quartet.

Weeks, J. (2007). *The world we have won*. London: Routledge.

Wellard, I. (2006). Able bodies and sport participation: Social constructions of physical ability for gendered and sexually identified bodies. *Sport, Education, and Society, 11*(2), 105–119.

West, C. (1993). *Race matters*. Boston: Beacon Press.

West, C., & Zimmerman, D. (1987). Doing gender. *Gender & Society, 1*(2), 125–151.

Wetherell, M., & Edley, N. (1999). Negotiating hegemonic masculinity. *Feminism & Psychology, 9*(3), 335–356.

Whitehead, S. (1999). From paternalism to entrepreneuralism: The experience of men managers in UK postcompulsory education. *Discourse, 20*(1), 15–27.

Whitehead, S. (2001). The invisible gendered subject: Men in education management. *Journal of Gender Studies, 10*(1), 33–45.

Whitehead, S. (2002). *Men and masculinities: Key themes and new directions*. Cambridge, England: Polity.

Wilkinson, L., & Pearson, J. (2009). School culture and the well-being of same-sex-attracted youth. *Gender & Society, 23*(4), 542–568.

Williams, C. (1989). *Gender differences at work*. Berkeley: University of California Press.

Williams, C. (Ed.). (1993). *Doing "women's work": Men in nontraditional occupations*. Newbury Park, CA: Sage.

Williams, R. (1977). *Marxism and literature*. Oxford, England: Oxford University Press.

Willis, P. (1977). *Learning to labour: How working class kids get working class jobs.* Farnborough, England: Saxon House.

Willis, P. (1978). *Profane culture.* London: Routledge and Kegan Paul.

Willis, P., & Trondman, M. (2002). Manifesto for ethnography. *Cultural Studies: Critical Methodologies, 2*(3), 394–402.

Wilson, B. D. M., Harper, G. W., Hidalgo, M. A., Jamil, O. B., Torres, R. S., & Fernandez, M. I. (2010). Negotiating dominant masculinity ideology: Strategies used by gay, bisexual and questioning male adolescents. *American Journal of Community Psychology, 45,* 169–185.

Wilson, E. O. (1975). *Sociobiology.* London: Harvard University Press.

Wilson, G., & Rahman, Q. (2005). *Born gay: The psychobiology of sex orientation.* London: Peter Owen.

Woody, E. L. (2003). Homophobia and heterosexism in public school reform: Constructions of gender and sexuality in California's single gender academies. *Equity & Excellence in Education, 36*(2), 148–160.

Youdell, D. (2004). Wounds and reinscriptions: Schools, sexualities and performative subjects. *Discourse: studies in the cultural politics of education, 25*(4), 477–493.

INDEX